Step-By-Step Guide T

PC GUIDE™
for
DOS

The Easiest Way To Master DOS

Inter Trade Corporation
ITC Publishing Group
Norcross, Georgia 30092

PC GUIDE™ for DOS

Copyright © 1993 by Inter Trade Corporation

Book ISBN 1-881979-04-0

All rights reserved. No part of this product may be reproduced, used, transmitted, or distributed in any form or by any means, or stored in a database or retrieval system, without the written permission of the publisher. Producing any copies of any part of this book, video tape, or tutorial software for any purpose other than the personal use of the original purchaser is a violation of the copyright laws of the United States.

For special quantity orders or other information contact the publisher: Inter Trade Corporation, ITC Publishing Group, 6767-B Peachtree Industrial Blvd., Norcross, Georgia 30092-3665.   Tel: (404) 446-2650   Fax: (404) 446-2685

Produced and Printed in the United States of America.

PC GUIDE™ is a trademark of Inter Trade Corporation.

Inter Trade Corporation is not affiliated with any manufacturers.

Every effort has been made to provide accurate and complete information throughout this product. However, the information and material contained in this product are supplied "as is", without any kind of warranty, either express or implied, including without limitation any warranty regarding the product's accuracy, completeness, quality, performance, or fitness for any particular purpose. Neither Inter Trade Corporation, nor its retailers or distributors shall be responsible to any person or entity, including the original purchaser, for any claims for liability, damage or loss caused or alleged to have been caused by this product, directly or indirectly. In no event shall Inter Trade Corporation be liable for any damages, direct, indirect, incidental, or consequential, caused or alleged to be caused by the use of information and material contained in this product.

Foreword

By: Bill Goodhew
President & CEO
Peachtree Software, Inc.

Owning a personal computer ten years ago was a luxury that most homes and small businesses couldn't afford. But today, thanks to a dramatic decrease in both hardware and software prices, the PC is an important part of our lives, often becoming a necessity to many users.

We use our PCs to shop, to pay our bills, to balance our checkbooks, to run our businesses, to play games, and to communicate with others across the country and across the world.

But while we have seen tremendous strides in development since the PC was first introduced in 1981, we are now at the threshold of what promises to be an immense explosion of technology.

On the horizon are even faster, more powerful PCs and intuitive, easier-to-use software. And beyond that is a future of interactive communications speeding along electronic highways that link communities worldwide and allow PCs to communicate and to interact. As cable operators and telephone companies become part of the PC revolution, we'll use their technology to download programs right from our telephone lines or from our cable channels on television directly to our PCs.

At Peachtree, we've been creating and selling software since the PC was first introduced. In fact, we were one of the first three software programs written for the PC. While we've seen the industry change, we've noted that one thing has remained constant: the importance of knowing how to use your personal computer.

That's why PC GUIDE is so important for PC users. You need to get the most out of your personal computer. If you want to keep pace in the PC revolution, both today and tomorrow, then you must know how to use a computer and how to use it effectively.

Acknowledgments

Special thanks to the following individuals for their participation in the development and production of the PC GUIDE for DOS book, video tape, and software tutorial.

Sol Rezai	Helene Erb	Buddy Booker
Dick Hays	Ron Reynolds	Fred Huff
Mallie Sharafat	Rick Mabeus	Karen Smith

The staff of the reference library at the Georgia Institute of Technology

Trademarks

IBM, IBM PC, IBM XT, IBM AT, OS/2, PS/1, PS/2, Micro Channel are registered trademarks of International Business Machines

Compaq is a registered trademark of Compaq Computer Corporation

Intel is a registered trademark of Intel Corporation

Apple, Macintosh are registered trademarks of Apple Computer, Inc.

HP, HP DeskJet, HP LaserJet are registered trademarks of Hewlett Packard Corporation

MS-DOS, MS Windows, Word for Windows, MS Works, Excel are registered trademarks of Microsoft Corporation

1-2-3, Lotus are registered trademarks of Lotus Development Corporation

DR-DOS is a registered trademark of Digital Research Corporation

PageMaker is a registered trademark of Aldus Corporation

Peachtree Accounting, Peachtree Accounting for Windows are registered trademarks of Peachtree Software, Inc.

Prodigy is a registered trademark of Prodigy Services Company

Postscript is a registered trademark of Adobe Systems, Inc.

Hayes is a registered trademark of Hayes Microcomputer Products, Inc.

Quicken is a registered trademark of Intuit Corporation

PC Tools is a trademark of Central Point Software, Inc.

Desk Top Set is a registered trademark of Okna Corporation

Corel Draw is a registered trademark of Corel Corporation

All other products, product names and services identified throughout this book, video and software are trademarks or registered trademarks of their respective companies. They are used throughout this product for demonstration purposes only. No such demonstrations or uses, including display or use of any trade name in this product is intended to imply any affiliation or endorsement of the product, service, or trade name.

About This Book

Remember how you learned to drive a car or learned to read and write? It wasn't easy, yet it wasn't really that difficult either. You started with a few basics and through practice learned everything else. We're going to do the same thing in this book. You are in good hands with PC GUIDE, so don't worry about all the technical gibberish you may have heard about DOS. Just relax and enjoy learning to use your PC like a pro.

You are going to learn DOS in short, easy steps. Obviously, if you are reading this book, it means that you don't like the dry, technical manuals that you already have. So, take your time when you read this book. It wasn't designed to be read from cover to cover. Each chapter is independent of the others. But there is a logical progression in the way this book is organized.

Chapter 1 begins by simply explaining to you what DOS is supposed to do and how you can use it. This is really DOS 101!

Chapter 2 will try to make you a little more familiar with your PC and various things that work with it. It's safe to assume that if you want to learn DOS, you have to have a fairly good understanding of what your PC is all about.

Chapter 3 explains some of the most frequently used terms that you need to know. Don't panic, its kept as simple as possible. You know that there are certain things you can't avoid. Well, to learn DOS, you have to learn a few new terms and there is no way around it.

Chapter 4 is useful if you have just upgraded to MS-DOS version 6, or you have bought a new PC without MS-DOS 6, put on it. Otherwise, you can skip this chapter.

Chapter 5 shows you some basic things you can do with DOS. These are really simple things like copying a document, organizing your information in directories, moving things around and getting rid of junk, etc.

Chapter 6 gets into more advanced DOS. Right now you'll probably think that you'll never get that far! Well, you can even surprise yourself! Just go with the flow. With every chapter you'll become more knowledgeable and feel more comfortable with everything. By the time you get to this chapter you'll be practicing DOS in your sleep!

Chapter 7 tells you about something that can make using your PC a lot easier. Best of all it comes free with your DOS. That's called the DOS Shell. You'll learn how the Shell makes it easier and more intuitive to use DOS.

Chapter 8 explains all the DOS commands in detail. It's only there as a reference. You don't have to study it. Simply read it to get a feel for some of the other things that DOS can do.

Chapter 9 will tell you about those annoying error messages that may occasionally pop up on your screen. If you haven't used a PC before, you probably don't know what that means. If you have used a PC, then you've probably had a few encounters with those messages. This is a reference chapter, so you don't need to read it now. Just refer to it whenever an error message appears on your screen. The error messages are listed alphabetically and you can easily find the one you are looking for, from the Table of Contents.

Chapter 10 is a complete troubleshooting guide that you can use when you get in trouble. You'll get your money's worth out of this chapter! You can review it briefly if you like, but clearly, it's written to be used as a reference guide.

Chapter 11 is chock full of helpful hints and tips that you can use everyday. You are going to learn some real goodies in this chapter. If you think that your PC is just good for typing letters and calculating payroll, think again.

Chapter 12 will help you understand what is involved in upgrading and maintaining your PC. Unlike an automobile, your PC will grow on you like a puppy! After a while you'll want to teach it new tricks and buy things for it.

Appendix is a reference guide with a variety of helpful information such as an extensive list of software and hardware manufacturers, PC User Groups, PC Publications, etc.

Glossary of Terms at the end of the book has a complete list of all the related terms that you can look up when and if you need an explanation.

Index is where you look for the location of specific topics or words. It's simply a road map of where all the key topics can be found.

Your feedback is very important to enhancing the PC GUIDE series. Please complete and mail the Registration Card at the end of this book.

What Do You Have?

(This information is for your own use)

As you read this book, you will come across certain topics that require you to have some knowledge of your own PC. Take a couple of minutes to complete this page. If you don't know the answer to some questions, ask a friend who is familiar with PCs.

Don't forget to take this page with you when you go shopping for software and other PC related products. This information will be very valuable to you.

What is the manufacturer's name on your:

PC:_____   Monitor:_____   Printer:_____

What is your microprocessor: 486____   486-SX____   386____   386-SX____   286____

How much memory do you have: 1 MB____   2 MB____   4 MB____   8 MB____

What size hard disk do you have: 40 MB____   80 MB____   120 MB____   200 MB____

What size floppy drive(s) do you have: 3-1/2"_____   5-1/4"_____   Both_____

What type of video card do you have: Super VGA____   VGA____   EGA____

What type of monitor do you have: Color_____   Monochrome_____

What type of printer do you have: Laser____   Dot Matrix____   Ink Jet____

What type of pointing device do you have: Mouse_____   Trackball_____

What type of modem do you have: 2400 BPS____   9600 BPS____   14,400 BPS____

What version of DOS do you have: 6.0____   5.0____   4.0____   3.3____

What version of Windows do you have: 3.1____   3.0____   None____

Table of Contents

Chapter 10. Troubleshooting Guide 181

Introduction

Few things in life affect us as much as a personal computer. If you have never used one before, you may find this hard to believe. But, if you are one of the millions who use a PC every day, you'll agree that it does make work easier and adds a little pleasure and entertainment to your leisure time.

If you still feel somewhat intimidated by your PC, don't think that you are dumb or lack something that others have. PCs are so new to most of us that we still haven't had time to absorb them into our lives the way we have done with most other things. Compare your PC to an automobile. Whether you are 18 or 80 years old, you can probably remember how difficult it was the first time you learned to drive a car. In spite of the fact that you grew up around cars since the day you were born. PCs on the other hand, have only been around since the early 1980's.

In the United States alone, there are over 70 million PCs. Every year over 12 million more PCs are bought by all sorts of people, businesses and various organizations. You are going to see PCs mushroom all around you. The cash registers at most supermarkets and fast-food restaurants are modified PCs. Banks, State, Local and Federal Government offices all use PCs. Medium-sized businesses and large corporations are close to putting a PC on every work-station. Pretty soon, if you are computer illiterate, you will be at a great disadvantage. You may have been able to avoid learning to program your VCR all these years. The end result is that you miss some interesting TV programs. In the next five years, not knowing how to use your PC will end up costing you more when you have to use various services such as banking, telephone directory assistance, shopping by mail, paying bills, etc.

I'll do it by hand, even if it kills me!

What used to cost over $5,000 ten years ago, is now available for under $1,000. It's even faster and more powerful. Think about it! Soon every home and office will be equipped with at least one PC. This is quite a change from the early days of PCs. In 1981, when IBM introduced the original IBM PC, their top executives thought that they could probably sell as many as 250,000 units over the life of the PC. Since then, IBM alone has sold over sixteen million PCs.

One way or another you are going to learn to use your PC and enjoy doing it. In order to get there from here, you have several options. You can just muddle through without learning the basics. You can study your PC manual, your DOS manual and everything else that you can get your hands on. Or, you can relax and read this book at your leisure.

Always remember that you learn by doing. Don't be shy around your PC. A famous Silicon Valley philosopher laid down two important Golden Rules for PCs:

Rule #1: Don't be afraid of your PC! It won't bite and it won't blow up!

Rule #2: If you do something dumb and get stuck; look up Rule #1!

What makes this book so special and useful to you, is that it's easy to read. Every term is clearly explained in a non-technical manner. Whenever possible, abbreviations are not used so that you can jump chapters without worrying about passing over the description of a strange term. Certain basic terms however will be explained at the very beginning of the book and you are asked to remember their meanings. Imagine how it would be like if we had to explain the meaning of PC, DOS, etc. hundreds of times throughout this book.

You want to learn to use DOS, because you want to use your PC. DOS is just the means to an end. Learning to use your PC is not really that difficult. DOS on the other hand

Please ... do something! I told the boss I speak DOS fluently!

is a whole different matter. There are a number of commands, error messages, short-cuts, etc. If you are a studious type of person, you may decide to read every book and manual on this subject, from cover to cover. At the end you may qualify to call yourself a real "NERD!" Or, if you are somewhat lazy, you may wish for a DOS pill that will make you an instant expert! If you are more realistic, you may realize that you don't get something for nothing. In order to use your PC better, you do have to learn DOS. With PC GUIDE you'll learn only what you need to know. The rest of the stuff is also here in this book, but you only need to look it up if you get stuck and need help.

The best thing you can do for yourself is to believe that you can easily use DOS, if you just learned a few common sense parts of it. If you believe that you are capable of learning things that make sense to you, then relax, because this book was designed for someone just like you.

This book covers a lot of information. Some of it you'll need to learn in order to use your PC. Most of it you should be familiar with so that you can look it up when you need help.

Have fun, and enjoy your PC.

Chapter 1. To DOS or Not To DOS?

Remember years ago, when life was much simpler? If you wanted a toaster, you had a choice of two brands and nothing else. If you wanted a car, you had a choice of five manufacturers and a few models for each. Today, you are faced with dozens of choices for almost everything. Have you looked at how many different bars of soap there are! It shouldn't surprise you that when it comes to PCs, you'll be facing the same dilemma. What kind of PC should I buy, what kind of software do I need, etc.? One of the most important questions you've probably asked yourself is how to get around DOS.

Let's find out what kind of role DOS plays in your PC. The name PC or personal computer is a very broad term. It refers to any small computing device that's bigger than a quarter and smaller than a refrigerator! These days that may include an eight ounce calculator or a fifty pound box with a monitor, keyboard, etc. In the mid-1970's, when the PC was invented, there were several different types on the market. Each type of PC used its own unique method of operation. When IBM introduced the original IBM PC in 1981, it created a standard that led to the explosive growth of the PC

industry. Within a few years, most PC manufacturers joined the IBM standard and became known as IBM compatibles. That means that IBM and compatibles use very similar or sometimes identical parts and run the same programs. Today, there are two major standards: IBM and compatibles versus the Macintosh produced by Apple Computer, Inc. There is a third and lesser known standard called Amiga produced by Commodore. IBM and compatibles by far outnumber all others by at least ten to one.

1.1. If You Have a PC, You Don't Have a Choice!

DOS stands for Disk Operating System. In simple terms, DOS is what makes your PC do what you want it to do (although sometimes you may wonder about that!). If you think of your PC as a car and yourself as the driver, DOS is like the gasoline you need to have to drive the car. Without gasoline you can sit in your car all day long and not move an inch. Without DOS you can stare at your PC all day long and it will simply stare back at you. DOS works as a medium between you and your PC. When you power up your PC, it's just a machine that doesn't know what it's supposed to do. DOS is a series of instructions that let you tell your PC what you want it to do. Don't be alarmed. You don't have to tell your PC what to do every second you use it. That's why there are programs that do specific things like word-processing, accounting, etc.

When you use a PC you have to use an operating system. You don't have a choice. Otherwise, you'll end up writing your own programs! When it's all said and done, DOS is not so bad. Do you know that the wealthiest man in the United States, Bill Gates, the Chairman of Microsoft Corporation got his start by selling DOS? DOS is the operating system used by all IBM and compatible computers. Since 1981, it has been improved and upgraded several times. Every upgrade is called a version. The latest version, MS-DOS 6 was introduced in 1993.

Depending on when you purchased your PC, the version of DOS installed in your computer may vary. MS-DOS version 4 was introduced in 1988. It was later upgraded to version 5 in 1991. PCs produced prior to that period used even earlier versions of DOS. DOS versions 5 and 6 are significantly easier to use, more powerful and more efficient than their earlier versions. If by chance you are currently using a DOS version prior to MS-DOS 5, you should seriously consider upgrading to version 6. You will definitely get your money's worth with all the new and added benefits that the latest version of DOS offers. To continue to use an older version of DOS, is like riding a horse and buggy in the middle of interstate highway.

1.2. If You Ignore it, it Won't Go Away!

Learning to use DOS is not anybody's idea of having a good time. The typical DOS manual or book is at least 300 pages long and covers at least fifty strange commands that you are expected to learn. On top of that, there are about fifty error messages that occasionally pop up on your screen just to annoy you.

Unlike a headache, if you ignore DOS, it won't go away. If you plan to use your PC, you have to learn DOS. In this book we are going to do something that should please you. We start by learning a little bit about DOS and what it does. Then we'll learn a little about your PC. Afterwards, you choose which parts of DOS you want to learn and which parts you'll want to ignore for now.

1.3. How Much is Enough?

When you start learning about DOS, the first thing that crosses your mind is "OK, when do I stop learning all that technical gibberish?" The nice thing about this book is that you can skip the stuff that you don't like. As long as you know that it's covered somewhere in this book, and you can find it when you need it. You know your capacity to learn better than anyone else. Just make sure that you read this book. Whatever stays with you afterwards is the gravy! The general things that you will remember are the stuff that will help you find the answers when you get stuck.

1.4. How do You Remember All That Stuff?

If you simply read a whole bunch of words like RAM, FORMAT, ICON, DELETE, etc., you'd probably panic. Lets get serious. These are not words that you use in everyday conversation with your friends and associates.

The key to learning DOS is not trying to memorize the important stuff. Rather, you should learn the meaning of various DOS commands. If you learn why you need to FORMAT a disk, you'll also remember how to FORMAT one when and if necessary. If you don't remember it right away, all you have to do is look it up in this book and do it. You'll learn by doing, not by avoiding! After you do something a few times (even if it's with the help of this book), it'll become second nature to you. Just like riding a bicycle.

Chapter 2. Computer Basics for the Real Beginner

You don't have to be a mechanic in order to drive a car. And you don't have to be a technical wizard in order to use a PC. But a general knowledge of what your PC does and how it works, is essential for your understanding of DOS.

2.1. The Real Meaning of a PC

A personal computer system is defined as the big PC box, plus the monitor, printer, modem, mouse, software, etc. In this book we refer to the whole thing as the PC or the system. Ten years ago, personal computers had a standard look and configuration; today, they come in all shapes and sizes.

Hardware (The Real Nuts and Bolts)

The term hardware refers to all the physical parts and components of your PC, including the main unit, monitor, mouse, modem, printer, and disk drives.

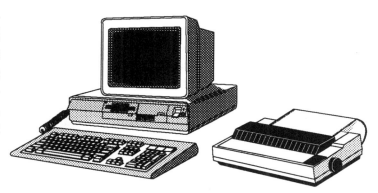

Software (The gasoline for Your PC)

Programs that tell your computer what to do and how to do it are called software. Software is a classification for various sets of instructions that run a PC. The only physical parts of software are the instruction books and the diskettes that the programs are stored on.

2.2. The Binary System (The Way Nerds Count!)

The most important discovery that led to the development of electronic computers was the binary system. The binary system is based on the two digits, 0 and 1. These days you hear a lot about different digital equipment like digital watches, digital TV, digital music, etc. They all use the digits 0 and 1 to transmit or store various information like music, data, TV signals, etc.

"Bi" means two (as in bicycle) which refers to a two-wheeled device. The binary system is a method of counting in which a number or a letter of the alphabet is represented by a combination of zeroes (0) and ones (1). In our daily lives, we use the decimal system (based on the digits 0 to 9) to express an infinite combination of numbers. We also use the 26 letters of the alphabet (from A to Z) to express ourselves. In the binary system, we only have 0 and 1 to describe the same numbers. Expressing numbers in binary is not as easy as it is in decimal; for example, the decimal number 1992 is expressed as 11111001000 in binary form.

Fortunately, we don't have to know the binary numbers or use them with our computers. Just remember that the "0" and "1" of the binary system can be expressed as the "ON" and "OFF" switches in the PC. By turning switches on and off a certain way, the computer knows exactly what you are talking about. Programs are the medium or the interpreter between you and your PC. They translate the information you express in English, into the binary language that's understood by your PC. When the computer responds with the information you have requested, the software translates the binary information back to English. The earlier generation of computers used vacuum tubes and switches to work with the binary system. Today's computers use microprocessor chips containing hundreds of thousands of microscopic switches to accomplish the same thing.

2.3. Key Components of a PC

A PC consists of several small and large components. PCs now come in so many different shapes and sizes, that it's important to understand the function of various components. The key items are described here in general terms:

System Unit (The Main Box)

The system unit, sometimes called the Central Processing Unit (CPU), houses the brains of your computer. It connects to the other components, like the keyboard, monitor, mouse, and printer. The system unit houses several key components, including the mainboard (motherboard), power supply, adapter boards, floppy drive, hard disk drive, and, possibly, other items.

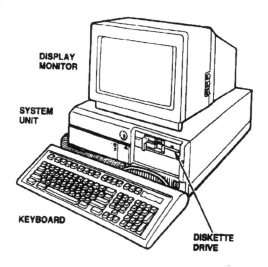

Case

The computer case is a metal or reinforced plastic enclosure that covers the system unit. The original IBM PC case was designed to sit flat on top of a desk. Millions of IBM and compatible PCs are still using the same design. These cases are often made of sheet metal and consist of two parts: the base unit and the cover. The various components inside the PC are attached to the base unit by metal screws. The cover is then attached to the base unit. Computer cases

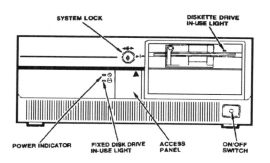

are made from materials that prevent electronic frequencies from interfering with nearby radios, televisions, and telephone systems. The Federal Communications Commission (FCC) has set up specific guidelines for computer emissions. PCs for home use should have FCC class B approval, and PCs for office use should have FCC class A or B (more strict) approval.

Power Supply

Personal computers either use AC power from a wall outlet, or operate on batteries. Battery-operated PCs are usually the small portable units that we will describe later in this chapter. PCs don't use the AC power that flows directly from the wall outlet into the computer. Instead, the 110-volt power is fed to a transformer that converts it to 12-volt DC, much like a car battery. Most power supplies are made of stainless steel and house the transformer and a small fan. The fan cools the various parts of the transformer, as well as circulates air inside the computer.

Motherboard (The Mother of All Boards)

The mainboard of your PC is the real nerve center of the whole system. The processor, memory, and other components of the unit are either located on the

motherboard or are connected to it. To better understand what a motherboard is and what it does, you should first become familiar with the computer circuit board.

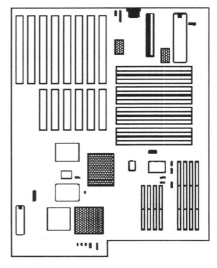

A computer board, often called a printed circuit board, is a green, flat surface, usually about 1/8 inch thick. It's size ranges from about the size of your palm to slightly larger than a sheet of letter-size paper. The board is often green with gold colored veins running throughout the surface. The veins act like hundreds of feet of wire.

Your motherboard often contains the microprocessor, memory chips, the instructional chips (called ROM BIOS), expansion slots, and miscellaneous other components. Although brands and types vary greatly, most motherboards follow the original IBM PC standard for locating drilled holes for screw attachment, expansion slots, keyboard connection, power connection, etc. This standard feature makes it easier to replace defective parts or upgrade a system in the future.

Microprocessor (The Brains!)

The microprocessor which is sometimes called: Central Processing Unit (CPU) is the brains of your system. It's usually a small matchbook-sized, dark gray item with silver legs. Some microprocessors are rectangular with tiny legs along the two longer sides, while others are square with legs on all four sides. The exterior of the chip is simply a protective shell that encloses the microprocessor itself.

The microprocessor chip is about one inch square. It contains hundreds of thousands (or sometimes millions) of microscopic switches that are etched on silicon wafers in a process somewhat similar to the way boards are made.

Math coprocessor (The tiny math wizard)

A math coprocessor is a microchip specifically designed to work in tandem with a CPU. It takes over the mathematical calculation functions from the CPU, thus freeing up the CPU to perform its other tasks faster. The math coprocessor can be purchased separately as an option. Every motherboard has a built-in socket for adding a math coprocessor. Some new generation microprocessors, like the 80486, have the math coprocessor functions built into the CPU chip.

Memory

Your PC needs memory in order to work. Think of the combination of microprocessor and memory as a calculator and a sheet of paper. You take information from the paper and feed it into the calculator. Afterwards, you take the results from the calculator and write it on the paper.

Computer memory is often called Random Access Memory (RAM). Because when your PC is powered up, it can randomly store information in the memory chips. The design of memory chips is somewhat similar to the design of microprocessors.

They consist of thousands of microscopic switches. As you type something on the keyboard, it's first transferred to RAM. The switches in the memory chip turn on or off according to the information you type in. The information is then transmitted to the microprocessor for interpretation and further processing. The feedback from the microprocessor is sent to the memory to be stored or displayed on the monitor to indicate the results of the processing and await new input from you.

Memory chips are data storage devices that actively keep information for as long as the power is on. When the power is turned off, all information stored in the chips is wiped out. The switches go back to their off position. When the computer is turned back on, the chips are blank and ready to accept new information.

ROM BIOS (Chips That Remember)
ROM (Read Only Memory) is a special kind of chip that can be programmed to retain a certain amount of information that can only be read. Once it's programmed, it retains that information and can reproduce it every time your computer is turned on. BIOS (Basic Input/Output System) is the set of instructions stored in ROM chips by PC manufacturers.

ROM BIOS chips store programs that are used to start the computer, perform diagnostic routines and tests, instruct various components on how to communicate with the microprocessor and with each other, and govern the internal operations of the PC. ROM BIOS chips are usually inserted in sockets on the motherboard, that make it easy to update the chip, if and when necessary.

Expansion Slots
One of the best features of IBM and compatible computers is the expansion slot, which is the medium for interface between the PC motherboard and other

adapter boards. It also allows for future expansion and growth of the system. Expansion slots, located on the motherboard, are about four inches or longer. An opening about one inch deep runs the length of the slot. Two rows of gold colored teeth run along each side of the slot opening. Adapter boards with plated strips that match the teeth in the slots are inserted into the expansion slots to connect to the motherboard. The original IBM PC (and its compatibles) had eight expansion slots. Newer PCs have many of the interface functions built into the motherboard, thus reducing the need for that many expansion slots.

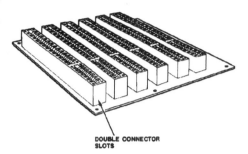

DOUBLE CONNECTOR
SLOTS

One important advantage of the expansion slots has been the ability to upgrade a PC to higher levels of performance by adding boards that have newer microprocessors.

Adapter Boards

When the IBM PC was introduced in 1981, the motherboard contained the microprocessor, memory chips, and ROM BIOS chips. Other functions, such as additional memory, the controller chips for drives and video, interfaces with other devices such as printers and modems, etc. were all placed on adapter boards.

These boards contain the appropriate chips to control specific functions. The bottom of each adapter board has a protrusion the size of the expansion slot, covered with gold colored connections that correspond to the gold colored teeth in the slots. Adapter boards are inserted into the slots and secured to the computer case with a screw.

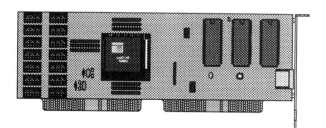

Memory Board

Various PC motherboards are designed to contain a certain amount of memory capacity. If you need more memory than that capacity, a memory board must be installed in your system unit. Different classes of PCs use different types of memory boards. Memory plugged in directly on the motherboard is always faster than memory accessed on a memory board.

Drive Controller

The drive controller is a printed circuit board that contains the appropriate chips that control the operation of up to two floppy and two hard disk drives. During the 1980's there were several different types and sizes of floppy and hard disk drives. PC manufacturers did not traditionally include the hard disk drive and controller with the PC. The computer dealer often installed the hard disk drive and controller, based on the buyer's needs and requirements. Today, more than half the systems are sold with the hard disk drive and the controller installed at the factory.

Video Graphics

The video graphics controller is a printed circuit board that contains the appropriate chips to create the required images and graphics on the screen of your monitor. Since there are several different types of monitors and video graphics standards, some PC manufacturers leave out the video controller and monitor so that it can be installed by the dealer.

Parallel and Serial Ports

PCs need a special set of controller chips to enable them to interact with other devices attached to them. Some peripherals, like printers, modems, and mice, are attached to the interface board. Many new generation PCs incorporate the parallel and serial interfaces on the motherboard. A parallel interface, often used for communication between your PC and a parallel printer, is a special preset standard that permits very fast transfer of data between your PC and the printer. A serial interface is a flexible communication standard, that typically runs at less than half the speed of a parallel interface, and needs to be set up on both ends.

Game

The game controller board contains a set of chips that control the function of one or two joysticks. Joystick is a handheld device similar to the gear shift of a car. It lets you move objects on the screen of your monitor while playing games. The game controller chip is sometimes built into certain brands of motherboards.

Other

Various devices (now and in the future) can be attached to your PC by using an existing or new interface board. The advantage of expansion slots in a PC is that adapter boards can be added as long as there are free expansion slots left in the system. One of the new innovations that will be popular in the 1990's is a multi-media board that turns your PC into a powerful center for computing, live video, high quality sound, and many other yet-to-be-developed uses.

Floppy Drive (Store it and Carry it Around)

Floppy drives were the first devices designed for storing information in PCs. A floppy drive is a magnetic storage device similar to a cassette tape recorder. In fact, the first generation of personal computers in the 1970's used cassette tape recorders for storage. Gradually, floppy disk drives were developed for PCs. Their size and cost have been decreasing while their capacities have been increasing.

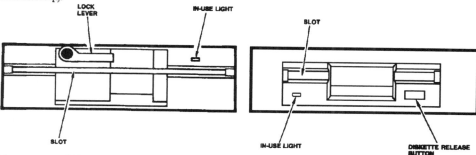

The name "floppy disk" refers to the soft, flexible structure of the disks themselves. Floppy disk is a round piece of thin mylar-type material coated with a magnetic compound on both sides. It is housed in a square 5.25" x 5.25", flexible plastic enclosure or a 3.5" x 3.5", hard shell disk. When the floppy disk is inserted into the floppy drive, a unit called the drive-head comes in close contact with both sides of the disk. The head has magnetic code reader/writers on each side. As the floppy disk spins inside the drive, the head moves back and forth to read data from or write data to the disk.

Hard Disk Drive (Small Box, Big Appetite)

A hard disk drive is a distant cousin of the floppy drive. As the name implies, instead of using a soft, flexible material, the data storage surface is made of rigid material. Hard disk drives are also somewhat different from floppy drives in other respects. They are much faster, store much more data, cost more, and are more sensitive to handling. Unlike a floppy drive, the hard drive is in a sealed enclosure to protect it from dust particles and mishandling.

The storage medium is called a "platter." It's made of thin, rigid metal with magnetic coating on the surface, and concentric circles on both sides, somewhat similar to a music record. The platters range in size from 2 to 5 inches in diameter, depending on the type of drive. Depending on capacity, brand, and storage technique used, the hard drive may contain one or more platters. For every platter, the drive has two read/write magnetic heads which work like the needle on a record player, except that the heads don't touch the platters, but operate microscopically close. They are so close, in fact, that a human hair could not fit in the gap. The platters rotate at approximately 3600  RPM (Revolutions Per Minute), faster than a car driving at 55 miles per hour. Because of the high speed of the platters and the closeness of the heads, the entire assembly is constructed with shock resistant mountings. This is quite incredible for a device about the size of a bar of soap! Newer hard disk drives also include the components that were formerly on the hard drive controller, thus eliminating the need for a separate controller board.

Tape Backup Drive (To be on the Safe Side)

A tape drive works very similar to a cassette tape recorder. Used for backup purposes, it can record and play back the information stored on specially designed cassettes. The data on the hard disk drive is copied onto cassette tapes that can be stored for many years. In the early 1980's, hard disk drive technology was not as reliable as it is today. Therefore, hard drives were in danger of malfunctioning and losing all the data they stored. Tape backup drives were primarily used to copy important data periodically. If the hard drive failed, the data on the tape could be copied to a working hard drive.

Businesses that rely on PCs for important data, use tape drives to backup critical pieces of information. Another use for tape drives is the storage of data that's seldom used. Once that data is stored on tape, it can be deleted from the hard disk, thus freeing up more space on the drive for other purposes.

CD Drive (Books, Sound and Video on a Tiny Disk)

The CD (Compact Disk) technology that has revolutionized high-fidelity music is rapidly becoming popular with PC owners. A CD can store the equivalent of thousands of pages of information on a single Compact Disk. The average CD stores about 600 Mega Bytes of data on both sides (equivalent to 300,000 typed pages). CDs use a different principle to store and read information than the magnetic method used by cassette tape players, floppy, and hard disk  drives. CD drives are substantially slower than hard disk drives. The CD is coated with a special material that consists of microscopic dots. When data is recorded on the CD, the dots are converted to a series of black and white dots corresponding to the information being stored. The CD player uses a laser head to move on the surface of the spinning disk to read the black and white dots. The dots are then interpreted, and the information is fed back to the PC in a series of "ON" or "OFF" signals using the binary system.

Most commercially available CDs can only read from prerecorded CD disks. They are called "Read Only Memory" (CD-ROM) drives. Another, more expensive CD drive can record data only once on a CD, but that disk can be read an indefinite number of times. They are called "Write Once, Read Many" (WORM) drives. Some CD drives are capable of both reading from and writing data to the CD. These CD drives are currently very expensive, and are often used by organizations that need to store thousands of pages of information. The cost of various CD drives is rapidly declining, and should become more affordable for the average PC owner in the next few years. It is possible that as the cost of read/write CD players decline and their speeds increase, they may; at some point in the future, replace both floppy and hard disk drives.

Input Devices (Telling Your PC What to do)

PCs communicate with people by receiving instructions and information (Input) and giving information back (Output). PC output is either displayed on the screen of the monitor, sent through a modem, or printed on a printer. Input, on the other hand, is provided by several different means. Input devices translate instructions or information supplied by you into electronic codes that the computer understands. Some input devices, like a keyboard, input numbers and alphabet characters; others, like a mouse, are used for pointing at items on the screen. Others, like scanners, are used for taking snapshots of printed information and feeding that to the computer.

Keyboard (The Traditional Tool)

Every PC has a keyboard that looks somewhat like a typewriter keyboard. The keys consist of five different groups, as illustrated in the following diagram.

The main and largest group looks very similar to the arrangement of keys on a typewriter. The central part consists of letters of the alphabet arranged according to the standard typewriter called "QWERTY," named after the arrangement of the top row of left hand keys.

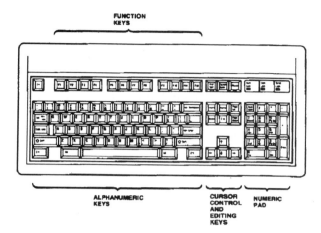

The keys marked F1 through F12 in the top row are called "Function Keys." Today, many programs use each function key to provide a command shortcut. For example, most programs use the F1 key for Help. Therefore, if you press the F1 key, a set of explanations will appear on the screen describing the topic you are currently working on, just as they would have appeared if you typed the command "help."

The group of keys on the right side of the keyboard look very similar to a calculator. These "Numeric Keys," are usually used in accounting and spreadsheet programs where the input is large amounts of numbers.

The two groups of keys between the numeric keys on the right and the QWERTY keys on the left are the arrow keys and instruction keys. The arrow keys tell the blinking cursor on the screen which direction to move. The instruction keys (Insert, Delete, Home, Page UP, etc.) tell the PC the commands to execute.

Mouse (The Tiny Computer Pest)

Mouse is a pointing device that can speed up using a PC. It operates with programs that are designed to accept signals from a mouse. It's a small handheld device the size of a bar of soap. The top of the mouse has two or three

buttons, depending on the manufacturer or model.

Under the mouse is a smooth ball about the size of a cherry tomato. The user's hand rests on top of the mouse. By moving it on a flat surface near the keyboard, the ball under the mouse turns and sends signals to the PC about the direction and distance the mouse is moving. As the mouse moves, the blinking cursor on the screen also moves in the same direction as the mouse moves.

Trackball (Upside Down Mouse)

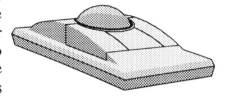

Trackball is a mouse turned upside down. The ball and the keys are on top of the device. The advantage of a trackball over a mouse is that it doesn't require space to move. Different manufacturers use the same general idea with different designs that create their own unique shape and feel.

Pen Mouse

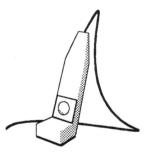

The pen mouse is like a miniature mouse inside and a fat pen outside. Held like a pen, the signal from its movement on a flat surface is sent to the PC just like the movement of a mouse.

Digitizer (Draftsman's Pencil)

A digitizer is a special device that is used for giving special coordinate data to the PC. Used primarily by organizations that create drawings for engineering and construction purposes, digitizers operate on a principle somewhat similar to a mouse, but offer greater precision. As the unit, often referred to as the "puck," is moved on a flat tablet, the blinking cursor moves on the screen. The keys on the digitizer perform many special functions. There may be from 4 to 16 keys on the unit. A major use for digitizers is tracking the shape of an existing drawing. By moving the cross hair to the various points of a drawing on paper and clicking the appropriate keys, the computer can re-create that drawing on the screen.

Digitizers are often used with Computer Aided Design (CAD) programs. These programs facilitate the work of designers and draftsmen on the computer screen.

Scanner (From Paper to PC in one Step)

A scanner is a device that can transfer an image of a photograph or written information to the computer. Scanners emit a special light onto the subject. The intensity of the light that is reflected back to the scanner based on the darkness and shape of the image is interpreted and sent to the PC.

The Plastic Surgen said I can design my new nose right on the PC!

Scanners can scan typed or handwritten text, graphs, diagrams, and photographs. The resolution and quality of the scanned subjects vary according to the type and quality of the scanner.

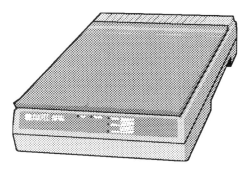

Flat-bed scanner

Handheld scanner

Joystick (The Ultimate Game Handle)

Joystick is a handheld device used for playing PC games designed for use with a joystick. It plugs into the game port of the PC. By moving the handheld stick, the subject on the screen moves in the desired direction. The buttons on the joystick are used to issue specific commands to the PC, depending on the game.

Output Devices

PC output is either produced on the screen or on a printer, or sent via modem to another device or computer. Output can also be produced from a combination of all three, if necessary.

Monitor

Monitor is a computer's window to the world. It displays both the instructions and information being given to the computer and the response from the computer. Monitors look much like a TV set and operate on the same basic principle. The size of the screen and the number of colors it can show are the most common ways of differentiating monitors. Desktop PCs use stand-alone monitors. When purchasing a desktop PC, you can choose among different types of monitors. That choice is governed by your budget, your application, and your needs.

Portable and smaller computers use monitors that are integrated into the system unit. If you purchase one of these units, the model you choose determines the type of monitor that comes with it. The monitors that come with the current generation of portable PCs are flat and often use the LCD (Liquid Crystal Display) technology that is used in digital watches and calculators. Most portable PCs have the capability to plug into an external color monitor. Recently, a number of manufacturers have introduced small, portable PCs with color displays. These PCs cost almost twice as much as the non-color versions.

Monochrome Graphic

Monochrome means "single color." A monochrome monitor displays one color on a solid background. The display color may be white, amber, or green on a black background. Monochrome graphic monitors were the first generation monitors used with computers, and were the only choice available until the early 1980's. These monitors display sharp images of text and certain graphics. However, they cannot take full advantage of the new generation of graphic environment programs, like Windows. Consequently, they have become less popular because of these limitations .

VGA (Video Graphics Array)

The VGA standard was introduced by IBM in 1987. This has quickly become the most popular video standard ever. Currently, over 90% of PCs are sold with some form of VGA monitor. VGA uses a different method for displaying characters and graphics on the screen. It's capable of showing up to 256 colors, making its output close to that seen on a TV. VGA monitors use an analog signal input that is somewhat similar to a color TV.

SVGA (Super VGA)

Super VGA is based on the same technology as VGA, but, it has from 50% to 100% better resolution. The small difference in cost between a super VGA monitor and a VGA monitor, and their respective video controller boards, has made Super VGA the current video standard of choice.

Printer (The Power of the Written Word)

Printer is a device that produces written images (numbers, alphabets, graphs, etc.) on paper. Almost everybody has seen a printer of some form: in an office, in a supermarket check-out line, in school, or in other places that provide a written document or receipt. Printers have been available and in use longer than PCs. Printing technology has evolved almost as radically as PCs. The price, performance, and quality of output from the current generation of printers is significantly superior to what was available only five or ten years ago.

Printers come with many different shapes, sizes, and printing technologies. This section provides an overview of different printer technologies. Although owning a printer with your PC is not an absolute necessity, having a printer is becoming increasingly important.

Dot Matrix (The Popular and Affordable Technology)

Dot matrix printing technology was developed in the 1960's for mainframe computers. In recent years, dot matrix printing technology has advanced to

the point where printed matter looks sharp and crisp, similar to that produced by a typewriter.

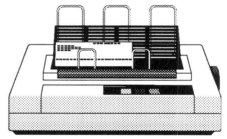

A small unit the size of a pencil containing several thin wires is pointed toward the ribbon. When the printer is instructed to print a character, the small pins hit the ribbon against the paper in a way that creates the image of that character with those dots. Obviously, the smaller the dots and the closer they are together, the sharper the character. Dot matrix printers can print at speeds of more than 300 characters per second.

Ink Jet

Ink jet printing technology was developed in the 1980's as a quieter, faster alternative to dot matrix printers. It uses a technology similar to dot matrix printing. However, instead of pins in the print-head, there are microscopic holes. Instead of using a ribbon, ink is forced out of the tiny holes directly onto the paper to form the characters.

Ink jet printers are generally higher priced than most dot matrix printers, but their print quality is closer to that of a laser printer. They make up a small percentage of the printers sold annually.

Thermal Transfer

Thermal transfer printers are somewhat similar to ink jet printers, but instead of squirting dots onto the paper, heat is used to transfer dots from the ribbon to the paper.

Laser (The Ultimate Printing Machine)

Laser printers are the top-of-the-line printing technology for PCs, but their prices are still higher than most other printers. Laser printers use a sophisticated technology for printing, similar to that of a copying machine. When the computer instructs the laser printer to print a page full of characters or graphics, the laser printer waits until it receives an image of the entire page. The instructions tell the printer what characters and sizes to use. The printer forms an image of the whole page in its memory. Then, using a laser beam and special mirrors, the image is reflected on a cylindrical device called a drum. The drum is electronically charged to attract fine ink powder particles where the images are. When the ink powder forms an image of the page on the drum, a sheet of paper is electronically charged to attract the ink powder from the drum as it passes under it. After the ink powder is transferred onto the 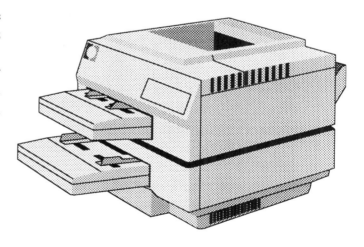 paper, the paper passes under a heating element that melts the ink and fuses it to the paper. Most commercially available laser printers for PCs can print from 4 to 12 pages per minute.

Modem (Your PC's Window to the World)

Modem is a communication device for computers. Using the telephone lines and a modem at each end, two computers can communicate back and forth no matter where they are located. As long as there is a proper phone connection, PCs using their modems can transfer data to each other anywhere in the world.

Modem communication is achieved by using special programs developed for this purpose. Recent technological breakthroughs have permitted the addition of Fax capabilities to modems with only a slight increase in price.

Type

Modems come in many different shapes and sizes. There are two types of modems: internal and external. Internal modems look like an adapter board and fit inside the PC in one of the expansion slots. External modems come in a small case and connect to the serial port of the PC. All modems for PCs follow a communication standard pioneered by Dennis Hayes founder of Hayes Microcomputer Products, of Atlanta, Georgia. To ensure that they follow that standard, most PC modems are designed to be "Hayes compatible."

Speed

Modem speed is based on data transfer rate. That rate is measured by the number of bits per second (BPS). If you recall the description of the binary system ("ON" and "OFF" switches), a bit is a digit (0 or 1) that is part of the combination that represents a number or a letter of the alphabet. PC modems range in speed from 300, 1200, 2400, 4800, 9600, to 19,200 BPS. The 300 and 1200 BPS modems are no longer manufactured. Faster modems can slow down to communicate with an older, slower modem. If you have a slow modem, get rid of it.

2.4. Different Types of PCs

In the 1970's and early 1980's, there was only one type of personal computer, and it was designed to sit on top of a desk. The shape and look of desktop PCs was further solidified with the introduction of the IBM PC. In the mid 1980's, creative designers introduced PCs in all shapes and sizes. In spite of the appearance of a PC, the components inside and outside the unit perform a standard operation. For example, a desktop PC has a separate monitor that, like a TV set, may sit on top of the base unit. In a portable PC, on the other hand, the monitor is incorporated inside the base unit. Both monitors still perform the same function, but their shape has been modified to accommodate their intended purpose. The same thing applies to other PC components described earlier.

Desktop

Desktop PCs commonly share one major feature: They consist of a base unit, a separate monitor, and a separate keyboard. The shape of the base unit depends entirely on the type of case that's used. As the following figures illustrate, the case may have different shapes and sizes.

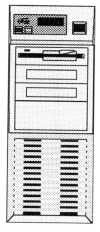

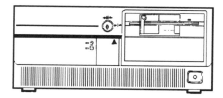

Desktop PCs are somewhat bulky to move around frequently. On the other hand, they generally offer more room for growth and expansion by providing for new or replacement components. Most desktop PCs use off-the-shelf (standard size and shape) components that make repairs and upgrades easier and less expensive. Desktop PCs are expected to remain popular and their sales are projected to grow at approximately 10% to 15% a year through 1995.

Portable

Portable PCs are getting smaller, more powerful, and more affordable. Currently, portables account for 30% of PC sales. That market share is expected to grow to 50% by 1995.

Notebook (A PC in Every Briefcase)

Notebook PCs are the new generation, high performance, lightweight units that are the size of a hard-cover book. They weigh between 4 and 7 pounds, and pack all the powerful features of desktop PCs. They are all battery operated. The batteries generally last 2 to 5 hours. For people who must have color, most units plug into desktop color monitors. The rapidly declining price of powerful notebook PCs makes it possible for people to use the same computer at work and at home. If a color monitor is needed, it's possible to have desktop color monitors at both locations and still save money, compared to having a complete desktop systems at each location.

Physically, different brands of notebook PCs look very similar. The components of notebook PCs, are often proprietary designs of the manufacturers. Notebook PC sales are projected to grow at approximately 25% a year through 1995. In 1992 they amounted to approximately 25% of total PC sales, a share expected to grow to 50% by 1995.

Palmtop

A new generation of small, lightweight PCs introduced during 1990 are called "Palmtop" because they weigh from 10 ounces to 2 pounds and can be held on the palm of one hand. Some of these units pack more power than the original

IBM PC. They currently don't have all the powerful features packed into notebook PCs. Creating a unique market for themselves, they have enough word processing and data storage capability to serve as a personal time management tool and note pad for businesspeople who have a larger computer at work or at home. By hooking the two units together, data can be transferred back and forth, thus getting around the smaller capacity limitations of the palmtop.

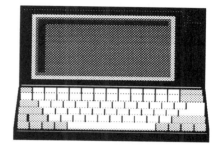

Pen PC

Keyboardless computers were introduced in 1991. They are constructed somewhat like a notebook PC, with a touch-sensitive screen but without a keyboard. They rely on specially developed operating systems that permit using them without a keyboard. They are primarily targeted for specific applications, such as delivery businesses, food servers, hospitals, inventory checkers, etc. Some models are being offered with handwriting recognition software that allows the user to write directly on the screen with a special pen.

2.5. Major Software Categories

The greatest advantage of the standard established by IBM PC compatibility has been the availability of thousands of software programs that can operate indiscriminately on the millions of IBM and compatible PCs throughout the world. Earlier we discussed the issue of IBM compatibility in relation to the PC hardware. This section gives you an overview of software, and the role software plays in your PC.

All right ... let's see you do it!

Computer hardware, by itself, is not capable of doing very much. The microprocessor, memory, floppy drive, hard drive, keyboard, and monitor (among other things), need special instructions to operate as a unit. They also need to have a means of communicating with you, unless you want to spend several years learning programming and computer language. Programs are developed by computer scientists and programmers so that when you work with your PC using their programs, you can communicate with your PC in English. The program translates your instructions or questions to computer language and then translates the computer's response from computer language to English. In the 1970's, when PCs were introduced, there were no programs available, so, users had to develop their own.

Current programs are very different from those in the 1970's and 1980's. Programs are written to simplify using the PC. Most programs are designed for specific functions and have simplified the task of using them basically to filling in the blanks or answering yes or no to questions. Some people who are afraid to use PCs may be thinking about the difficulties involved in the 1970's and early 1980's. In the 1990's, the emphasis is on "user friendliness."

Operating Systems

Operating system is the program that instructs the PC how to work with its various components. Over the years, operating systems have been upgraded and simplified

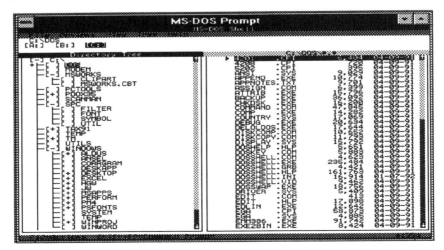

to make using the PC easier. Currently, only two major operating systems are available for IBM and compatible PCs. MS-DOS is developed by Microsoft Corporation. MS-DOS version 6 was introduced in 1993. DR-DOS is developed by Digital Research Corporation. DR-DOS version 6 was introduced in 1992.

Operating systems contain various commands for instructing the PC to perform different functions. Recent versions of operating systems provide so much help that you no longer have to try to remember any of the commands. The commands you use most frequently will eventually become second nature to you.

User Environments

In the past few years the use of IBM and compatibles has become much easier by using "Graphical User Interface," or GUI ("gooey") for short. GUI basically converts your PC screen to a pictorial representation of whatever function you are performing. For example, if you are using a word processing program to type a letter, the screen will have small pictures of single or double spaced lines. To use them, all you have to do is choose the one you want and point at it with your mouse. Small boxes containing pictures of various commands make it easier to use GUI programs. A GUI environment helps standardize the general look and feel of programs that function under it. The most popular GUI program is Microsoft Windows 3.1, which was introduced in 1992.

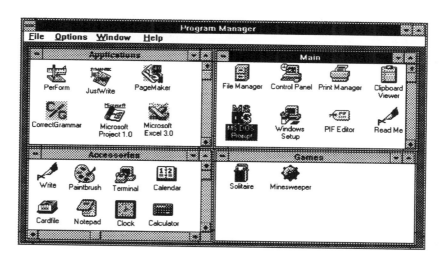

Application Software (Programs That do it All)

One of the major forces behind the tremendous popularity of PCs at home and office has been the availability of software for specific applications. Called application software, these programs perform specific tasks. Literally thousands of programs are available for almost everything imaginable: writing letters, manipulating and storing data, number crunching, accounting, tax preparation, recipes, wine lists, publishing, matchmaking, etc. They are available with various capability levels, and range in price from a few dollars to hundreds of dollars.

Word Processing (Writing Made Simple)

Word processing programs help you in writing and composing various written documents like letters, reports, memos, books, newsletters, flyers, etc. These programs contain a tremendous number of essential and convenient features. As far as you are concerned, these programs make the screen resemble a blank sheet of paper with help and other useful commands around the page. You can easily set up the margins on each page or the entire document, decide if you want your text to be single or double spaced, indicate whether you want automatic page numbers, etc. When you type in your material, if you make a

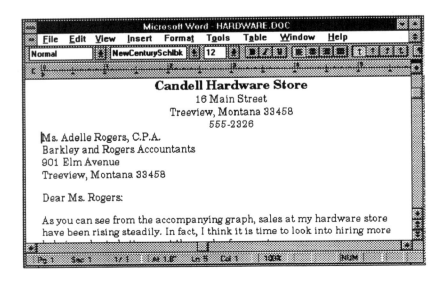

mistake, you can go back on the screen and correct the error; if you want to delete or move a paragraph, you can simply do that. After the shape of the document appears satisfactory, you can have the program check your spelling and point out suspicious words that it cannot find in its dictionary of over 100,000 words. Some programs even have a thesaurus that allows you to find words comparable to what you are using.

Some word processing programs have the ability to check your grammar and suggest a more acceptable approach to your writing. Some of the more powerful programs even allow you to compose your document complete with headlines, graphs, and art work.

Database Management (Easily Manipulate Information)

Database management programs help store and sort information in many different ways. In effect a database management program is like a huge sheet of paper with a large number of rows and columns. Each box created by the intersection of rows and columns is called a "cell." The cells can contain

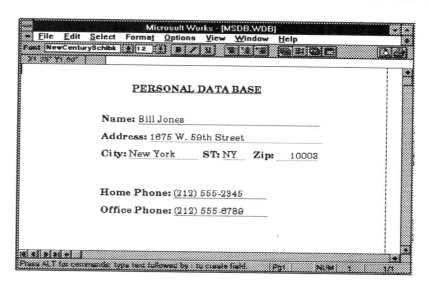

numbers, names, addresses, zip codes, etc. The program can organize the information and sort it by whatever criteria you want. For example, if you enter names and addresses of your friends or customers into the database, the program can sort them by last name, zip code, city, state, etc., in a matter of seconds.

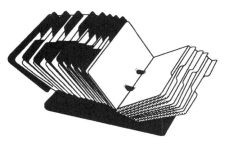

Some organizations customize powerful database management programs for their inventory control and accounting needs. Database programs have a great deal of flexibility and can be programmed to perform customized tasks.

Spreadsheet (Number Crunching and Massaging)

Spreadsheet programs are somewhat similar to database programs, except that various numerical analyses can be performed on the contents of individual cells. For example, your home budget can be set up in the spreadsheet. Based on certain assumptions, you can create a simple formula to have the computer forecast your future expenses.

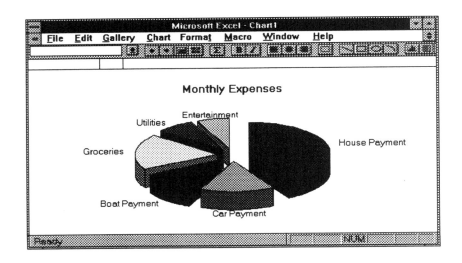

Data Communication and Information Exchange

Your computer's reach can extend far beyond the doorway of the room in which it's located. Hooked up to a modem and using a communications program, your computer can connect to any computer with a modem anywhere in the world. Communication programs are used together with modems to provide a link between two computers. In order for two modems to connect, a protocol allows the two devices to recognize each other. These programs also provide a systematic method for checking for errors and correcting those errors in data transmission.

Discover a whole new world!

Integrated Packages (Jack of all Trades!)

Integrated programs contain the essence of several programs in one package. Typically, an integrated package includes word processing, database, spreadsheet, and communication programs. For some users, especially those with limited needs or little experience with PCs, integrated packages offer an

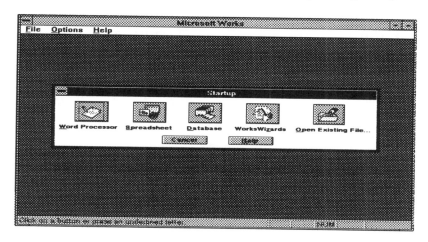

excellent value. They are often less expensive than purchasing each package separately. Their other advantage is that the commands and operation of each program in the package is consistent with the others, so they are easier to learn and to use.

Personal Finance and Income Taxes

PC programs that help you run your house-
hold finances, keep track of your assets and
investments, balance your checkbook, and
prepare your income taxes are available in
many different shapes and forms. These
programs are designed to help you manage
personal finances as easily as entering check
and deposit amounts in a checkbook. They
produce an image on the screen of your
monitor that may look like your checkbook
or a notebook that you would have designed
for this purpose yourself. Often the companies that produce these programs

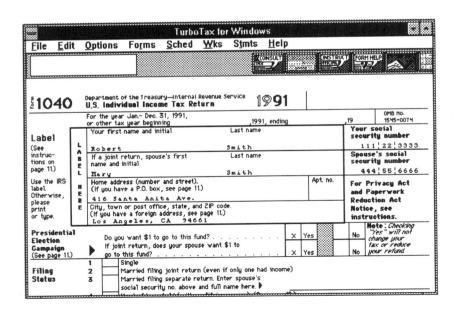

seek the opinions of many people regarding their needs and requirements. Then they design the program to meet those requirements. You benefit from the input of experts as well as ordinary people in the design of these programs.

Business Accounting (Painless Way to Manage Your Business)

Large corporations have been using computers for accounting since the 1950's. Medium sized companies started using them in the 1960's and 1970's. Small businesses (of which there are over 15 million), started using PCs in the 1980's. Today they are the largest purchasers of PCs. Still, millions more are waiting for computers to get easier to use and their prices to drop even further. Unfortunately, some of them may wait for a very long time, because computers do get easier to use and their prices do keep coming down continuously. The trend doesn't seem to stop.

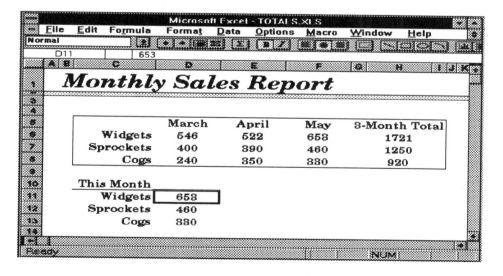

Businesses that have been using PCs for their accounting have a clear edge over their competitors who do not. PCs help organize vital information and provide timely status reports at the touch of a button. Business accounting programs keep track of income and expenses, keep up-to-date inventory, issue invoices and purchase orders, calculate payroll checks and tax deductions, and perform literally hundreds of other functions for the business owner or manager.

Large or small chains of supermarkets, department stores, and discount stores often use PCs instead of cash registers. As you buy certain food items from your local supermarket, most stores use scanners to read the special code on the items or key in a code from the price ticket into the register. That information not only helps print your receipt, it also helps the store know how many of each item were sold that day. The computer can automatically order more items if they run below a certain level on the shelves, and by keeping track of sales volume at different times of the day, the manager can schedule more people for the peak periods.

Desktop Publishing (Create Your Own Publication)

A few years ago if you wanted to publish a flyer, newsletter, or illustrated manual, you had to go to a special printer to explain what you wanted, go back and forth to proofread the work, and finally have the document produced. PCs have changed all that with special programs called "desktop publishing." These

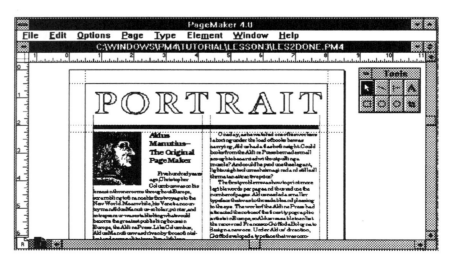

programs are designed to help you create an entire document right on your computer screen. They can create professional quality columns, large and small character sizes in a variety of shapes, graphs, illustrations, etc.

Desktop publishing programs take word processing one step further. They allow you to move text around on the page, compose the look of the printed page, and create letters and characters of various sizes. A laser printer can print high quality pages that rival professionally prepared material. Most newspapers and magazines are now using PCs to compose their publications. Businesses, schools, churches, individuals, and other groups and organizations are increasingly using PC desktop publishing for their printed materials.

This is cut and paste?!

Education (Learning is More Fun With a PC)

The impact of PCs on the education of the younger generation is tremendous.

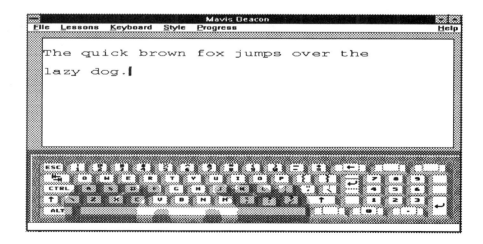

Already, children exposed to PCs are performing unimaginable work with these machines. They can learn almost any topic by using PCs interactively. Educational programs are designed to ask the right questions and lead the students to think and analyze for themselves.

Thousands of educational programs are currently available for PCs. Topics range from mathematics, geography, biology, chemistry, and history, to economics, finance, etc.

Games and Entertainment (Fun! Fun! Fun!)

Some people buy home PCs simply for playing games and helping with their hobbies. However, as you have seen so far, that is just one of the many functions of a PC. Games and entertainment are the largest categories of software available today. The enhancements made to color monitors and powerful PCs make the games more vivid, like those in video arcades.

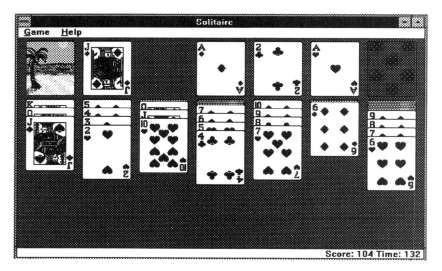

Parents are discovering that a home computer can help their children do a lot of things in addition to playing games. PCs play games that are more realistic than those played on video game systems. Spending around $200 for a TV video game system and $50 per game cartridge can soon add up to over $1,000. For that amount, most people can buy a home computer.

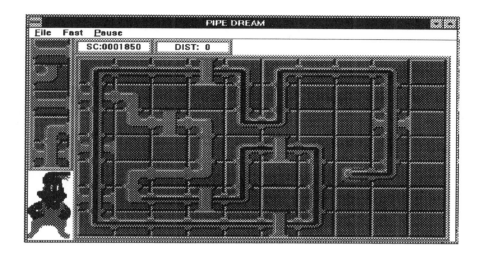

Entertainment programs for hobbyists and others are rapidly covering all areas from stamp collecting, and wine lists to gourmet recipes, genealogy, and personal diaries, etc. Every day new programs are developed to address unique areas of interest.

Utilities (Handy Little Programs)

Utility programs are those which help facilitate using a PC or various programs.

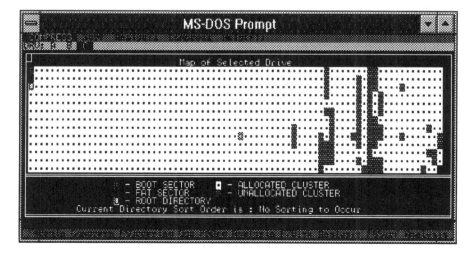

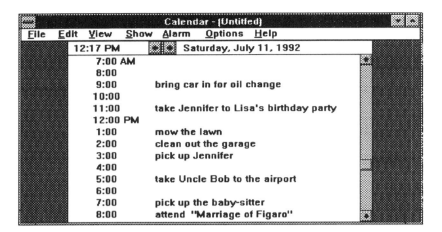

Some utilities are designed to act like an activity calendar, scheduler, or calculator. Others help you speed up your memory, hard disk, etc. Some others analyze your system's configuration and give you a status report as well as diagnose any problems your PC may have.

Other

Virtually every topic imaginable has been addressed by computer enthusiasts. Still people continue to develop new programs for activities that were formerly

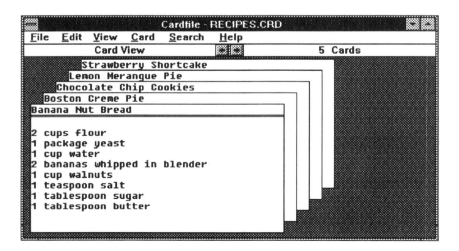

unknown. There are PC programs that help you with your family tree, matchmaking, employee interviews and testing, encyclopedia, world atlas, etc.

Chapter 3. Understanding the Basic Terms

Computer users have their own language. You may be surprised to find out that after reading this book, you'll be able to at least understand what they are talking about. You don't need to speak the language, just develop a feel for what the basic terms are.

3.1. DOS is Not as Bad as it Sounds!

Do you remember ever trying some exotic dish for the first time? Think of the concern that you had before taking the first bite. After you tried a couple of bites, you probably realized that it was not as bad as you first thought it would be (although some exotic foods can be worse than you can imagine)! DOS is much the same way. The whole concept of learning the language long associated with "Nerds" may not be your idea of having fun in your spare time. Relax! When you finish this book, you'll learn only a few new words but a whole new way of using your PC. DOS doesn't have to be a real pain in the neck.

3.2. The Eighty-Twenty Rule

A famous Italian philosopher who is credited with the invention of Pizza, came up with the well known 80/20 rule. He noticed that a few people in a group always ate most of the Pizzas ordered by that group. After extensive studies he concluded that 20% of the people were eating 80% of the Pizzas. Later on, he discovered that the same simple rule applied to most other things in life.

We use 20% of what we know, 80% of the time. That same rule applies to DOS as well. Most of the time we may only use about 20% of the DOS commands. In this book we are going to learn the 20% that you will need to know. Then you will simply read about the other 80%, so that you know where to find them when you need them.

File

Your PC needs some way to keep track of information that you feed it. At some point in your life, you have probably visited a library. Remember the way books are organized by topic and category so that you can easily find what you are looking for.

When you type a letter to your Aunt Millie, or organize your personal checking account in your PC, it needs a name to associate with the information that you have just created. Normally, you can just come up with a name like: "Letter to Aunt Millie," or "My Checking Account for 1993." Now you are going to find out why PCs are not yet 100% user friendly. Back in 1981, when they were laying down the rules for using an IBM or compatible PC, the machines were not as powerful as they are today. Therefore, they had to work within certain limitations. The name of a file could not be more than eight characters. We still have to live with the same limitation. So, your letter to Aunt Millie, can be called LTRAUNTM. You have to come up with a creative way to name the information that you generate with your PC.

From now on when you see something that looks as if it was created with alphabet soup, you know that it must be a file name. In the meantime, you can come up with your own style for creating file names. For example, all your letters can start with LTR followed by five characters made up of letters or digits. Letters to customers may be called LTRCUST1, LTRCUST2, etc.

Looking at a File

When you create a file on your PC, there will be occasions when you'll need to see a list of those files or actually look at the contents of a file. Using your PC, looking at a file is really easy. All you have to do is remember what you called it!

The main benefit of using a PC is to create files and then be able to re-use them, change them and expand them. This is a nice and handy feature.

Copying a File

Did you ever have to re-write an essay as a form of punishment when you were at school? Can you imagine how difficult it would be if you had to copy a multi-page document? Well, with DOS copying a file is as easy as copying a piece of paper on a copier.

There may be occasions when you'd like to copy a file you have stored in one place onto something else.

Renaming A File

There are a lot of neat things you can do with your PC. Among them is the ability to take a letter to Aunt Millie, and make a copy called letter to Aunt Helen. Once you copy that letter then you can make whatever changes you need to make to the copy of that first letter. All you have to do is give it a name different from the first letter.

Saving A File

When you create a new document on your PC or work on an existing one, all your work is performed in your computer's memory. When you are through, you need to save that document to your hard disk drive so that you can use it again in the future. To save a file, you have to give it a name. It's important to remember that if you save a file with a name that already exists, the newer file will replace the old one. One of the biggest mistakes most novice PC users make is to inadvertently save an unwanted file over a file with the same name.

Deleting A File

How often do you go through your drawers or closets and throw away the old, useless papers you have accumulated? Well, with your PC, you can easily do the same thing. Except, here you simply tell your PC to get rid of one or more files. This can be done with just a few keystrokes. Sometimes you have to delete some old files to make room for new ones.

Directory

You are going to discover that your PC can store a whole bunch of information. Think about the hard disk drive that's inside your PC. More than likely, it can store the equivalent of more than 20,000 pages of information in something the size of a bar of soap. All that information is stored in the form of files that can be awfully hard to organize. Imagine trying to find a file name from among hundreds.

There is a simple way for organizing information inside your PC. Think of the way books are organized in a library. All the history books are together, business books are in a separate area, etc. Within each group the books are arranged alphabetically. In the PC world, this is called making a directory.

A directory is where you store similar information. For example, all your letters can be in a directory called LETTERS. All your bills can be in a directory called BILLS. This way you can easily find what you are looking for. You can even create a directory inside a directory. For example, in the directory called WORK, you can have a directory called LETTERS. And others called CUSTOMER, BOSS, etc.

Creating A Directory

Creating a directory is as simple as putting a name tag on a filing cabinet. All you have to do is type a few letters and you've gotten yourself a directory. Once you create one directory, it's easy to create others as you need them.

Deleting A Directory

Getting rid of a directory is as simple as creating one. You may decide to delete a directory if it's no longer needed or you need the storage space for more important stuff.

Clearing The Screen

Occasionally, you'll discover that there is just too much information on your computer screen and decide to clear it. There is a simple way to tell your PC to clear the screen. Lets say you are typing your resume and your boss walks by your desk. You can tell your PC to clear the screen in a snap! Your PC screen may not give you away, but the guilty expression on your face probably will!

Formatting A Disk

Your PC stores information on floppy disks and the hard disk drive inside your PC. This information is stored magnetically. That's much like recording on cassette tapes. When you record something on a cassette tape, if there are some minor problems in certain spots, you'll have a hard time detecting them. On the other hand when you use your PC to store information, even one tiny mistake may be disastrous. Imagine what would happen if the computer missed a zero while printing the amount on your paycheck!

Magnetic disks much like other magnetic storage devices have some flaws that can be detected by your PC. DOS has a feature that allows you to have it check the entire disk surface and locate the weak spots. DOS not only detects bad spots, but it also marks off all weak areas to make sure that your PC does not attempt to store anything there. Every disk needs to be formatted by your PC the first time it's being used. The disk retains a map of all the bad and weak spots your PC needs to avoid.

Copying A Disk

Your PC takes in information that you type on your keyboard or feed it by floppy disk or through the phone line. It gives you it's feedback on your screen, printer or floppy disks. These disks are the way you add new programs to your PC or transfer information from your PC to another PC.

Copying disks is a simple way for you to make duplicates of information you have on a disk.

Making A Backup Copy

When you have important information on your PC or on a floppy disk, it's so easy to make a copy just in case something happens to the original. In fact, it's recommended practice to have a copy for safekeeping. In the PC world, this is referred to as having a backup.

Getting Help When You Need It

You keep reading in this book that you no longer need to memorize DOS. The reason is simple. DOS places a lot of on-screen help at your fingertips. This book will help you understand what everything means so that when you need to get help from DOS on your screen, it won't confuse you.

DOS versions 4, 5 and 6 provide very useful help screens right on your PC. When you need to know how to use a DOS command, all you have to do is type the name of that command and all sorts of explanations appear on your screen.

Doubling Your Hard Disk Capacity

MS-DOS 6 offers you the ability to double the capacity of your hard disk drive. It's almost like having an extra closet in your room at no cost and with no construction mess. This version of DOS is capable of cramming twice as much information into your hard disk without sacrificing much speed or accuracy.

Doubling your hard disk capacity with DOS 6 is easy. You'll love the benefits, especially because it's free!

Keeping Viruses Away

Just when you thought that you could leave the crime and sickness behind with the Six O'clock News, here comes news of another wave of demented acts. Computer viruses, like human viruses are infectious. They can damage your PC or cause it to lose all the information you worked so hard to create.

The good news is that you can avoid computer viruses by practicing "Safe Computing!" Be careful whom you exchange PC information with. MS-DOS 6 has a built-in virus detection program that will warn you if it notices a virus. It will also try to disable it, if the virus is included in it's list. Keep in mind that some new viruses may escape detection by the virus check.

Putting Programs On Your PC

One of the nice things about owning a PC is that you don't have to be a programmer to use it. This is different from the 1970's when the early pioneers used to program their own home-made PCs. Now you can buy a program for as low as five dollars. When you buy a program, you generally get it on floppy disks. The process of transferring a copy of that program to your computer is called "installing a program."

Most programs that you buy today are written in such a way to make it almost painless to install. Most programs automatically check what you have in your PC and then install themselves with little or no input from you.

Memory

You hear a lot about computer memory, the RAM, Kilo Bytes, Mega Bytes, etc. Do you know what memory does? The best way to explain it to you is to relate it to something you've probably experienced before. Think of it as a counter top at a fast-food restaurant or a library. At a fast-food counter, you place your order and the person (or persons) behind the counter prepare your food, take your money and give you what you ordered.

In some ways your computer memory acts as a counter top where all the interactions between you, your software and your PC take place. At first, when you tell your PC that you want to type a letter in your word-processing program, it goes to your hard disk and makes an identical copy of the main parts of your word-processing program and puts it in your memory. When you create a file called LETTERS, it exists in your memory. As you go about typing your letter, all of that's done in memory. Finally, when you decide to save the letter you have created, the PC writes a copy of that to your hard disk. Now, if you turn the power off, everything is still saved on your hard disk. On the other hand, if you turn the power off while your letter is only in memory, everything will be lost. That's because your computer only remembers things while the power is on.

Microprocessor

Everything in your PC needs some sort of interpretation, analysis or computation. The microprocessor is the brains of your PC. It's sort of like the cooks and servers behind the counter at a fast-food restaurant. They prepare and cook the food as you order. And the counter acts much like the memory in your PC.

Your microprocessor does it's thinking only while the power is on. The speed of your microprocessor determines how fast your PC can perform what you tell it to do.

Batch Files

Every time you turn your PC on, it needs to know certain things. For example, it needs to know if you want it to show you where it is, at any moment. It also needs to know which information to keep handy just in case you need it. Batch files contain information that your PC needs at start up.

3. **Understanding the Basic Terms**   55

Chapter 4. Putting MS-DOS 6 On Your PC

Read this chapter only if you have to put MS-DOS 6 on your PC. Typically that implies one of two things; either you just bought a PC without version 6 installed on your hard disk, or you are upgrading from an older version of DOS.

If you are installing DOS for the first time, your task is a little easier. However, if you are upgrading your DOS, there are a few additional steps you need to take. We'll start explaining the process for upgrading DOS and point out things that you don't have to do if you are starting from scratch.

If you already have a PC with an older version of DOS, you must run the Setup program. This program is designed to do most of the work for you. It'll detect the type of PC components you have. It'll also recognize most of the software you already have on your PC. If it notices any incompatibilities or shortcomings, it'll let you know.

To be on the safe side, it's very important that you make a backup copy of important information on your hard disk before you upgrade your DOS. If you are installing DOS for the first time, you don't have to worry about backing up.

Setup essentially transfers MS-DOS 6 from the floppy disks to your hard disk. The program files are all compressed on the floppy disks. Setup uncompresses each file and copies it onto your hard disk.

Insert MS-DOS Disk #1 into your A: drive and change your prompt to A:. Type:

   A:\>SETUP and press ENTER.

You'll see a DOS message asking you to wait while it checks your system. Next, you'll see the welcome screen:

- To set up MS-DOS now, press ENTER.

- To leave press F3.

The next question has to do with networks. Since you are not connected to a network, press N. You are then informed that you'll need one (1.2 MB High Density) or two (360 K Double Density) disks. These should be marked UNINSTALL. Setup then proceeds with making a copy of important DOS commands on these disks. If you are installing DOS for the first time, you don't need these disks.

Setup shows the following settings:

DOS Type: MS-DOS
MS-DOS Path: C:\DOS
Display Type: VGA

If the settings are correct press ENTER. If something is not right, move the highlight with the up and down arrow keys, then press ENTER to see alternatives.

You'll be given the option to install the following programs:

Backup	901,120	Bytes
Undelete	32,768	Bytes
Anti-Virus	360,448	Bytes
Total space required for MS-DOS and programs:	5,494,336	Bytes
Space available on your hard disk C:	xxx,xxx,xxx	Bytes

To install press ENTER, or use the up and down arrow keys to change the selections. You can press F3 anytime you want to leave Setup.

Setup proceeds with Disk #1 and after about a minute it will ask you to insert the first formatted UNINSTALL disk. Take out DISK #1 and replace it with the UNINSTALL

disk, close the door and press EN-
TER. If you use 360 K disks, after a
couple of minutes you will be asked to
insert the second UNINSTALL disk.

Feed Me

While Setup proceeds, you'll see a
graphic progress report showing "xx%
complete." Your screen informs you
that you can double your hard disk
capacity by typing DBLSPACE at the
prompt after Setup is completed.

When Setup is completed, you'll be
advised that your old AUTOEXEC.BAT and CONFIG.SYS files have been saved to
your UNINSTALL disks. To restart with the new MS-DOS, press ENTER.

If you reboot your PC, you'll get to the prompt. Type DIR and you'll see:

```
COMMAND   COM
DOS                 <DIR>
OLD_DOS   1         <DIR>
AUTOEXEC  BAT
CONFIG    SYS
WINA20    386
```

This is a good time to install DoubleSpace on your PC and double your hard disk
capacity. If you are currently using a disk compression program, don't install
DoubleSpace, get help from a PC expert.

To install DoubleSpace, at the prompt type:

C:\>DBLSPACE and press ENTER.

The DoubleSpace Setup screen informs you that the program takes up about 40 K of
your memory. Press ENTER to proceed or F3 to quit.

You will be given the option to use Express or Custom Setup. Choose Express and press ENTER. Process takes about three minutes. Press C to start the compression. The program will examine your drive and restart your computer. It will show you "xx% complete" progress report.

After compression is completed, it will also use DEFRAG to bring all your existing files together. It'll then show the new size of your hard disk. And inform you that a new drive H (uncompressed) with about 2 MB has been created for programs that can't be compressed.

Are we having fun yet?!

Chapter 5. Doing Simple Things With DOS

You've heard the famous "walk before you run" line before. When it comes to DOS, it only makes sense to start learning about simple things you can easily do by yourself. As you start to feel more comfortable with everything, you can go on to the next chapter and be a little more adventurous. You can use your PC almost like a pro, by just learning this chapter. If you don't understand something, go back and read it again. Then, sit at your PC and practice.

All roads lead to the prompt

To your PC the prompt is like the (sometimes!) smiling face of the server at a fast-food restaurant asking "How may I help you?" Your PC is trying to tell you that it's ready to take your order. The prompt also tells you which drive or directory is currently active. If you are at the main (or root) directory of your hard disk, your prompt looks like this:

C:\>

If you happen to be working with a particular directory like your word-processing program, your prompt may look like this:

C:\WORDPRO>

If you work with your floppy drive your prompt may look like this:

A:\>

There are several ways to make other information appear with the prompt, but we'll leave those for when you'll become a real pro.

When you want to tell your PC to do something, you type your command at the prompt. The only way your PC will know that it has to do something, is after you press the ENTER key. You can change your command before pressing ENTER by using the "Backspace" key that's on the top right hand corner of your keyboard and is usually an arrow pointing to the left.

☞   DOS is very sensitive to the way you spell your commands. Make sure that your typing is correct and you don't put extra spaces where you shouldn't and take out a space where it should be.

Clearing the screen

It's hard to come up with a logical list of reasons why you'd want to clear your screen but you'd find occasions when you just want everything cleared quickly. When you decide to clear the screen, all you have to do is type:

C:\>**CLS** and press ENTER

Repeating commands

There will be occasions when you'd want to repeat a command that you just gave to your PC. In cases like that, all you have to do is press the F3 key. For example, if you are looking for a file somewhere in one of your floppy disks, instead of retyping everything over and over again, you can use this simple repeat key. Put the disk in drive A: and type:

C:\>**DIR A:** and press ENTER

After DOS displays the contents of your disk in drive A:, if the file is not there, take the disk out and insert another. Press the F3 key and DIR A: will appear again. You can use the repeat key for any command.

Canceling commands

Everybody has a right to change their mind. When you are working with your

PC, specially at the beginning, there will be occasions when you'd like to change or cancel the command that you just typed in. If you've not pressed the ENTER key yet, all you have to do is use the "Backspace" key (the one with the left arrow). If you want to change the command, simply type what you want. Another way to cancel the command is to press the "Esc" key. The prompt will jump down a line and show a "\" backslash. You can type your new command after the backslash.

If you have pressed the ENTER key, and decide to stop the PC from carrying out your command, all you have to do is hold down the CTRL-C (CTRL key is at the bottom left side of your keyboard) keys simultaneously. You can also do the same thing with the CTRL-BREAK keys. The BREAK key is the same as the PAUSE key on the top right corner of your keyboard.

Creating a file

Creating a file is not something that you normally do with DOS. A file is a document that you create using a program. For example, you produce a letter with your word-processing program and give it a name. That becomes a file. Handling files is what DOS is all about.

Looking inside a file

Looking inside a file is probably not your idea of having a good time. But there may be occasions when you need to quickly glance at a file that you may have created. DOS has a TYPE command which will let you do just that. If you use the TYPE command with a file that you have created, chances are that you'll recognize most of what you've put in the file. At the prompt type:

C:\>TYPE LETTER1.EXT and press ENTER.

If on the other hand, you try to use TYPE with some DOS command, it may show a whole bunch of gibberish that you won't recognize.

Most programs come with a README file which often contains the most up-to-date information that they may not have been able to print in the manual. Most shareware programs do not have a printed manual. Instead, the manual is in a file on the program disk.

If you use TYPE to see the contents of a file with multiple pages, the pages will scroll rapidly on your screen. To see one page at time use the following command:

C:\>TYPE README.EXT | MORE and press ENTER.

The | MORE makes DOS show one page at a time. The "|" character is located at the top right corner of your keyboard near the backspace key.

Copying a file

One of the DOS commands that you'll be using often is used for copying files. Fortunately the command is also called COPY (pretty clever ha!). The COPY command is used for a number of things such as:

- Copying a file for safe keeping. This is a sure way of guaranteeing that in case of a problem, you'll have a copy of an important letter, document, list or design.

- Copying your documents to transfer to another PC. This is one of the common ways that people move their files from one PC to another for different reasons.

- Copying files from the hard disk to floppy disks, in order to get them out of the way. There are some files that you'll create and use but then stash away on your hard disk for a very long time. You can simply copy them to floppy disks and then take them off your hard disk.

When you are copying files, there are several things you should remember:

☞   You can't copy a file into another file with the same name and extension within the same directory. Your PC needs to be able to differentiate between the original file and the copy.

☞   To copy a file you need to have the name of the file you are copying, where you are copying it from and where you are copying it to.

☞   If you misspell the name of the file, it won't copy.

☞   If you copy a file to another file that already exists, the copy will write over the existing file.

☞   When you copy a file onto another, you need to indicate where each file is located.

☞   After DOS copies a file successfully, it gives you a "1 File (s) copied" message.

Following are some examples of the various ways to copy a file or group of files.

Making a Copy of a File

The simplest use of the copying feature is to copy a file into another file with a different name.

C:\>COPY FILE1.EXT FILE2.EXT and press ENTER.

If you look at the command carefully, you'll notice that it has the copy command followed by a space, then the full name of the "Source" file and it's extension, followed by a space and then the full name of the "Destination" file and it's extension.

Copying A File From One Drive to Another

One of the most frequent uses of the COPY command is to copy a file from one drive (usually the hard disk), to another drive (usually the floppy drive). The main reason is peace of mind. If you have important information that you'd like to preserve in case a disaster hits your PC, the copies of files can be used to get you back in business in a jiffy. To copy a file to another drive is very simple, all you have to do is tell your PC where to find the "Source" file and where to make the "Destination" file.

C:\>COPY FILE1.EXT A: and press ENTER.

Note that in this case there is no destination file name necessary if the name is the same. If you want to give the file a different name then you have to type:

C:\>COPY FILE1.EXT A:FILE2.EXT and press ENTER.

Copying A File From One Directory to Another

When you copy a file from one directory to another, you need to tell your PC which directory to find the "Source" file and which directory to copy the "Destination" file. Remember that your PC needs to be told exactly what to do, how to do it and where to do it. To copy a file from directory DIR1 to another directory called DIR2 you need to type:

C:\>COPY C:\DIR1\FILE1.EXT C:\DIR2 and press ENTER.

Copying More Than One File From One Drive to Another

The "*" symbol is called the "Wild Card." It takes the place of one or more characters. One place where the * is used a great deal is when you copy multiple files. If the files have something in common, you can use the * to reduce typing every file name. To copy all the files with the names FILE1.EXT, FILE2.EXT, FILE3.EXT, etc. from your hard disk to a floppy disk in drive A:, you can use the *:

C:\>COPY FILE*.EXT A: and press ENTER.

In the above command, the star takes the place of the numbers in the file names.

It can be used anywhere in the file to represent one or more characters. For example, to copy all the files in one directory to a floppy disk you can use the wild card:

C:\>COPY C:\DIR1*.* A: and press ENTER.

Copying A File From A Floppy Disk to the Hard Disk

There will be many occasions when you'll want to copy a file from your floppy disk to your hard disk. The copy command can do it easily:

C:\>COPY A:FILE1.EXT and press ENTER.

Note that here you didn't have to tell DOS to copy the file to drive C:. That's because you are typing your command at the C:\> and DOS assumes that's where you want to copy.

Renaming a file

There is a simple command called RENAME (or REN) that will allow you to change the name of a file. Sometimes you may want to change a file name because you want to use that name for another file. To rename a file you have to have the current name and the new name:

C:\>REN FILE1.EXT FILE2.EXT and press ENTER.

To rename a file from a different directory you need to specify the path to that file:

C:\>REN C:\DIR1\FILE1.EXT FILE2.EXT and press ENTER.

To rename a group of files, you can use the wild card * but you have to be careful not to confuse your PC.

C:\>REN FILE*.EXT FILE*.BAK and press ENTER.

Deleting a file

You'll love and hate this command at different times. It allows you to get rid of files that you no longer need. Deleting files opens more space on your disks and actually reduces the time your disk spends searching for files. However, there may times when you delete a file and later discover that you needed that file. Or, you may want to delete file "1" and instead delete file "2" by mistake. When you use this command you have to be careful and pay attention to what you tell your PC to do. The command is DEL short for DELETE.

C:\>DEL FILE1.EXT and press ENTER.

There are several rules you have to remember when using DEL.

☞ Never delete files that you have not created, unless you know exactly what you are doing.

☞ Never delete files that end with .COM, .SYS, .EXE.

☞ If you are not sure that you'll need the file later, copy it to a floppy disk, then delete it.

Deleting a group of files is just as simple as deleting a single file. You use the * to group them together.

C:\>DEL FILE*.EXT and press ENTER.

Be careful about using the *.* which means delete everything. If you unknowingly use the *.* and delete everything on your hard disk, you'll have nothing left, ZILCH, NADA!

You may run into a file that you won't be able to delete. These are called read-only files. They have been specifically marked to be viewed only and you can't change or delete them. To delete those files there is a different command, but you better get expert help before doing that.

Undeleting a file

At the end of every cloud there is a silver lining. The delete command is very handy, but it may be dangerous if you aren't careful. Fortunately, when you delete a file your PC doesn't completely erase the file from your disk. Instead, it changes the name of the file, makes it invisible and makes the space available to other files. If you have not yet saved something else over the deleted file you can use the UNDELETE command that is part of MS-DOS 5 and 6. This command changes the deleted file's name back to it's original.

C:\>UNDELETE FILE1.EXT and press ENTER.

If you have copied a file over the one you deleted, your PC will come back with a message telling you that the file can't be recovered.

If you want to undelete a bunch of files that you just deleted with a *.* you can use the same thing to undelete them:

C:\>UNDELETE *.* and press ENTER.

Creating a directory

If you have ever organized your paperwork in folders and file cabinets you are almost an expert in using directories. Basically, you use a directory to organize your files. Computer programs create their own directories when they are installed on your PC. Therefore, all you have to do is create directories for your own files.

Naming your directories is just as important as creating one. Generally, you have three types of files. Files that you'd like to keep, those that you'd like to delete shortly after you create them and those that you'd like to keep for a few months and then delete.

Directories for files that you'd like to keep should be named so that you can easily recognize them. Use names like LETTERS, CHECKS, BOOK, etc.

Remember that a directory name can't be more than eight characters.

Directories for files that you'd like to delete very shortly after they are created, should have names that remind you to get rid of them. Use names like DUMP, JUNK, GETRID, etc.

A large number of files are those that you keep for a few months. The easiest way to remember to delete them is to store them in directories named after the month the files are created. Use names like JUNKAUG, JUNKSEP, JUNKOCT, etc. This way for example, you'll know that in September or October you can delete the files in JUNKAUG.

In addition to directories you can also create subdirectories which are basically a directory within a directory. The root directory is the main directory on a disk. It's identified by the backslash "\". For example, the hard disk root directory is shown as:

C:\>

The command for making a directory is MD. To make a directory or subdirectory you'll need to go to the directory which you'd like to make the new one in. At the prompt type:

C:\>MD NEWDIR and press ENTER.

In the example above, the new directory called NEWDIR is made in the main (root) directory because you are typing at the C:\>. If you'd like to make the new directory in your word-processing directory, first go into that directory (see moving from one directory to another), then type:

C:\WORDPRO>MD NEWDIR and press ENTER.

Looking at directories

To look at directories or contents of a directory all you have to do is type:

C:\>DIR and press ENTER.

This tells your PC to show a list of everything in your hard disk root directory (remember that C:\ means the root directory on drive C:). Usually there are more directories and files that can fit on your screen. Therefore, you'll see a long list scroll up on your screen. In order to see one page at a time, you need to type:

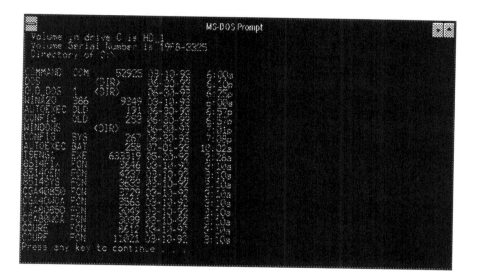

C:\>DIR/P and press ENTER.

The /P tells your PC to show one page at a time and pause. At the bottom of your screen you'll see your PC asking you to "Press any key to continue". Don't start looking for the "ANY" key on your PC! It's not there. It really means anyone of the keys. The safest keys to use are the two "SHIFT" keys located at both sides of your keyboard.

If you want to see the files all together and don't need to see the size and date of the file, type:

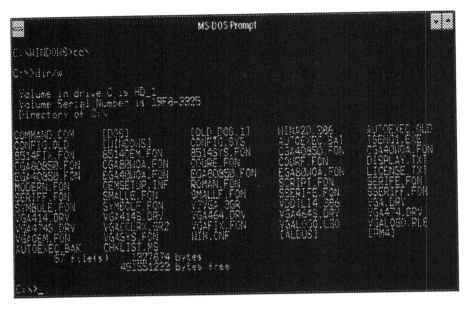

C:\\>DIR/W and press ENTER.

DOS versions 5 and 6 have a TREE command that shows your directories like a tree with all sorts of branches.

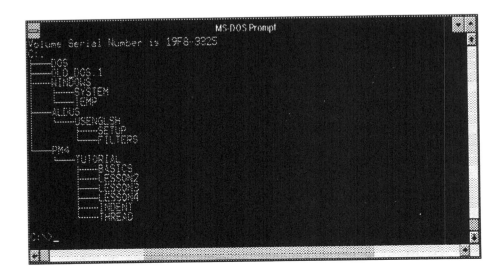

Renaming a directory

MS-DOS version 6 gives you the ability to rename a directory by using the MOVE command. Why would you want to change the name of a directory? There aren't that many good reasons to change the name of a directory. But if you need to use it, type:

C:\>MOVE C:\DIR1 C:\DIR2 and press ENTER.

Going from one directory to another

One of the most popular DOS commands is used for going from one directory to another. As you become more familiar with your DOS and your PC, the change directory command plays an important role. But before you get there, the command is also a harmless way for you to boost your ego and show-off to your friends, that you can actually make your PC do something! The only hard part about the command is remembering what it is. This is one of those "PC Things" that once you learn, you'll be considered a "PC Expert." Remember that "CD = CHDIR = Change Directory."

To go from one directory to another all you have to do is type CD followed by a backslash "\" and the name of the file you'd like to get into:

C:\>CD\DOS and press ENTER.

This will take you to the DOS directory. If your prompt is setup properly, you'll see:

C:\DOS>

When you are inside a directory and you like to get into a subdirectory within that directory, all you have to do is type CD followed by a space and the name of the subdirectory:

C:\WORDPRO>CD LETTERS and press ENTER.

You'll get inside the subdirectory:

C:\WORDPRO\LETTERS>

When you are inside a directory or subdirectory and want to get back to the root directory all you have to do is type CD followed by backslash "\":

C:\WORDPRO\LETTERS>CD and press ENTER.

Telling DOS the path to follow

Your PC needs to be told what to do and how to get where you want it to go to. The DOS commands tell your PC what to do. The path tells your PC how to move around. At first it may seem a little hard for you to remember all these directory and subdirectory names. But, if you look at it logically, you'll notice that it will start to make sense to you very quickly.

The DOS prompt tells you and your PC that you can tell it to do things in the directory shown at the prompt. For example, if you are at the root directory, it will look like this:

C:\>

Whatever you type at this prompt, your PC will try to do in the root directory. But, what happens if you want your PC to do something in your word-processing directory? For example, to copy a file from your word-processing directory to your floppy disk, you either have to go into that directory or define the path to that directory.

C:\>CD\WORDPRO and press ENTER.
C:\WORDPRO>COPY FILE1.EXT A: and press ENTER.

The other alternative is to simply define the path:

C:\>COPY C:\WORDPRO\FILE1.EXT A: and press ENTER.

Which way is the best? You be the judge. As you become more proficient with DOS you'll be able to use the shortcuts with ease.

Removing a directory

When you are finished using a directory that you have created specially for a particular task or project, you might decide to get rid of it. Removing a directory that you no longer need, helps open up more space on your hard disk and reduces the time your hard disk spends searching for information. To remove a directory, you have to use the RD command (Remove Directory). If you use MS-DOS versions prior to 6, before a directory can be deleted, it needs to be completely empty of any files and subdirectories. First check the directory to make sure that it's empty:

C:\>CD\DIR1 and press ENTER.

When you get into the directory type DIR to see it's contents.

C:\DIR1>DIR and press ENTER.

If the directory has some files, use the DEL *.* to delete them all. If it has any subdirectories, use the CD command to get into those subdirectories. Keep going deeper and deeper until all the subdirectories are empty. Now, type:

C:\DIR1>RD SUBDIR1 and press ENTER.

When the directory DIR1 is empty, use CD\ to get back to the root directory and type:

C:\>RD DIR1 and press ENTER.

If you have MS-DOS 6, removing a directory is much easier. The DELTREE command let's you delete the whole directory with everything in it. This is very convenient and also very dangerous. If you don't know exactly what you have in a directory and delete it in one clean sweep, you'll have a hard time recovering it later. If you choose to use it, at the prompt type:

C:\>DELTREE DIR1 and press ENTER.

Moving files around

There may be occasions when you'll need to move a file from one place to another. Let's say for example, that you want to get rid of a directory but you want to move a couple of files from there to another directory. If you use MS-DOS 6, there is a simple MOVE command that you can use. For prior versions of DOS, you'll have to copy the file to the new location, then delete the old file.

In MS-DOS version 6, the MOVE command simply requires that you tell your PC to take a file from one place and move it to another:

C:\>MOVE FILE1.EXT A: and press ENTER.

This will take FILE1.EXT from your hard disk and move it to your floppy disk. After the move is completed, your PC displays a confirmation note that the file was successfully moved and deleted from the original location.

Previous versions of DOS require that you copy the file first:

C:\>COPY FILE1.EXT A: and press ENTER.

Afterwards, you can delete the original file.

C:\>DEL FILE1.EXT and press ENTER.

Now you have the file on drive A: and have removed it from the original location.

Searching for files

Looking for files is relatively easy with DOS. It'll be helpful if you know the full name of the file, but even that is not much of a problem. All you have to do is tell DOS to search it's directories for the file you are looking for:

C:\>DIR C:\FILE1.EXT /S /P and press ENTER.

This command will tell DOS to show you a list of everywhere the file named FILE1.EXT is located. The space, slash "/", S tells your PC to look at all the directories and subdirectories under the root directory. The space, slash "/", P tells it to show one page at a time, if there is more than one page.

If you don't completely remember the full name of the file, don't worry. All you have to do is remember something about the name of the file. For example, if you remember the first letter of the file name, you can use the wild card * to get the rest:

C:\>DIR C:\F*.* /S /P and press ENTER.

This will list all the files with the first letter F in all the directories and subdirectories.

Getting disks ready for use

You have already read about the FORMAT command in Chapter 3, and the reasons why you need to format your disks before you use them for the first time. You have to be very cautious when you use FORMAT. It completely clears your disk of all previous programs and data it stores. There are several do's and don'ts with this command:

☞   Never use the FORMAT command without specifying the drive name.

☞   Never format your hard disk (get expert help).

☞ Never use FORMAT on a used disk, before you know what's on it.

☞ Never format a disk without specifying it's capacity.

☞ Never format a high density disk in a low density drive.

When you tell your PC to format a disk, it thinks that you have a disk with the same capacity as the floppy drive. This is important to remember. In Chapter 2, you read an explanation of different size and capacity floppy drives. Here is a brief review of that:

There are two types of floppy disks. The soft kind is 5-1/4" square. It has a hole in the center. The capacity that is most frequently used on newer PCs is called High Density. That is 1.2 MB of storage. The Double Density disks hold only 360 K.

The smaller, hard shell disks are 3-1/2" square with a metallic window shutter. The capacity that is most frequently used on newer PCs is called High Density. That is 1.4 MB of storage. The Double Density disks only hold 720 K.

If you have a high density floppy drive and you want to format a high density disk, all you have to do is type:

C:\>FORMAT A: and press ENTER.

If you want to format a disk in drive B:, simply type:

C:\>FORMAT B: and press ENTER.

If on the other hand, the capacity of your floppy disk is less than the capacity of your drive you have to use a different command.

For 5-1/4" drives if you have DOS versions 4, 5 or 6, type:

C:\>FORMAT A: /F:360 /V and press ENTER.

For 3-1/2" drives if you have DOS versions 4,5 or 6, type:

C:\>FORMAT A: /F:720 /V and press ENTER.

After your PC formats the disk, it will come back with a message on your screen, asking you if you want to give your disk a name. You can type up to eleven characters, or simply press ENTER for no name. It will then show you the total disk capacity and if there are any bad sectors, it will also show the amount of the bad sectors.

Going from one drive to another

You can easily move from one drive to another by typing the drive name. For example, to go from the hard disk to a floppy disk, simply type:

C:\>A: and press ENTER.

☞ The most important thing to remember is that before you tell your PC to go to the floppy drive, you should have a disk in the drive and have the door closed.

Copying disks

Copying disks is just as easy as copying files. There are many instances when you'd need to make a copy of one or more disks. When you buy any software, the first thing that you have to do is make a copy of all the program disks as backup so that in case something happens to the backup set of disks, the original set can be used.

Most of the time you'll need to make an exact copy of a disk. In that case you'll need to use the DISKCOPY command. This command requires that your Source (original) and Target (copy) disks be of the same size and capacity. One nice thing is that the Target disks don't need to be formatted when you use them with the DISKCOPY command.

If you have two floppy drives of the same size and capacity, you can type:

C:\>DISKCOPY A: B: and press ENTER.

If you only have one floppy drive or one of each size and capacity, you can type:

C:\>DISKCOPY A: A: and press ENTER.

Just follow the instructions on your screen as your disk is being copied. Your PC may ask you to take out one disk and put in the other a couple of times.

Making a backup of important information

One of the most important parts of life is it's unpredictability. You don't know from one minute to another what may happen. Your PC is one of the most reliable machines around, but that's no guarantee that it won't experience a problem or accident. DOS has a backup feature that allows you to make a copy of important data on floppy disks for safekeeping. Backup is different from copy in that your files get compressed in order to cram more data into fewer disks. It also means that you can't simply work with files that have been backed up. You need to use the RESTORE command to uncompress them first.

There are two types of backups:

● Full backup

●   Incremental backup

A full backup means that you copy the entire contents of your hard disk onto several floppy disks. This is the easiest form of backup. However, these days with the enormous size of most programs, it's not practical to use a whole bunch of disks to copy a hard disk.

If you have MS-DOS 6, the process is quite simple. At the prompt type:

C:\>MSBACKUP and press ENTER.

This command will activate the MS-DOS 6 backup feature. If you are using the command for the first time, it will run a few test programs to understand your PC. It will also ask you to use a couple of disks to test and to record configuration files. Just follow the instructions on the screen. Then you'll get the following screen:

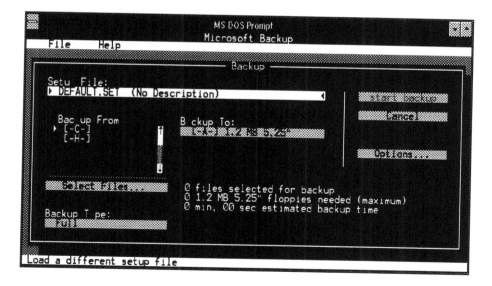

Choose BACKUP from the two choices on the screen and press ENTER. The next step is to choose the drive that you'd want to backup from. Use the TAB key (the key with the left and right arrows), to highlight the "Backup From" box. Use the arrow keys to move the highlight over "[-C-] All Files" and press the SPACEBAR to select it. Next, press the TAB key to move the highlight to the "Backup TO" box. Move the arrow keys to highlight over the destination drive. Press the SPACEBAR to select it.

Another box called "Backup Type" is set on Full. You can leave it alone for now. When you are ready to start the backup, press the TAB key to get to "Start Backup" and press ENTER when you are ready.

An incremental backup gives you a lot more flexibility and lets you backup only specific files, or files that have been changed since your last backup.

At the prompt type:

C:\>MSBACKUP and press ENTER.

When the backup screen appears on your monitor, you can move the highlight to choose the drive you want to backup from, the drive you want to backup to, and then if you want to select files, go to the "Select Files" box to select the files to backup.

If you want to incrementally backup from the last full backup, move the highlight to "Backup Type" and choose "Incremental".

If you are using DOS versions prior to MS-DOS 6, you need to use the BACKUP command with all the little cryptic messages. To backup the entire hard disk, type:

C:\>BACKUP C:*.* A: /S /L and press ENTER.

You are telling your PC to back up everything in drive C: and make a log of the files that are backed up. The space, slash "/" S tells your PC to start with the root directory. The space, slash "/" L tells your PC to make a log of all the files backed up.

If you want to tell your PC to only backup those files changed since your last full backup, type:

C:\>BACKUP C:*.* A: /S /M /A /L and press ENTER.

You are telling your PC to backup all the files on drive C: that have been modified since the last time you ran a full backup. Also, add the changes to the full backup and make a log of the backed up files.

Restoring backed up information

When you backup your files you hope that you will never have to use them. If you ever need to use the files you have backed up, you need to use the RESTORE command. You need to remember that if you use DOS versions prior to 6, you can only restore files using the same version of DOS that was used for the backup.

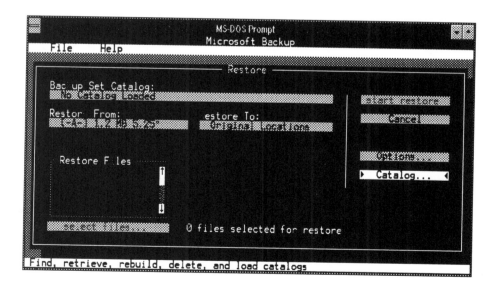

If you use MS-DOS version 6, restoring backed up files is easy. Put the backed up disk #1 in drive A: and type:

C:\>MSBACKUP and press ENTER.

When the backup screen appears on your screen, move the highlight to RESTORE and press ENTER. Move the highlight by using the TAB key to the "Restore From" and "Restore To" then press the SPACEBAR to select each item. Move the highlight to "Restore Files" and choose the "[-C-] All Files" that you want to restore. Then move the highlight to "Start Restore" and press ENTER.

If you want to restore only selected files, you need to move the highlight to "Select Files" and press ENTER. A different screen called "Select Restore Files" will appear on your monitor. Select the files that you want to restore by moving the highlight over them and pressing the SPACEBAR. When you are done, move the highlight to OK, and press ENTER. That will take you back to the "Restore" screen. Choose "Start Restore" and press ENTER.

If you have an earlier version of DOS, you need to type a few more commands. To restore all the files that were backed up, put the backed up disk #1 in drive A: and type:

C:\>RESTORE A: C:*.* /S and press ENTER.

The space, slash "/" S, tells your PC to backup beginning with the root directory. You will see instructions to insert each disk as your PC reads each one.

To restore only a selected file, you have to type:

C:\>RESTORE A: C:\DIR1\FILE1.EXT and press ENTER.

To restore the contents of only one directory, you have to type:

C:\>RESTORE A: C:\DIR1*.* /S and press ENTER.

Write protecting disks

Floppy disks have a built-in feature that will let you protect the data stored on them from accidental change or destruction. This is called write protection. There is a different method used for the soft 5-1/4" and the hard shell 3-1/2" disks.

3-1/2" disks have a small window in one corner with a moveable tab. The write protect feature is activated when you move the tab so that the window is open.

5-1/4" disks have a small notch on the upper corner. The write protect feature is activated when you place a small tape over the notch to cover it.

Printing

There are not going to be many occasions for you to use the DOS print command. All the programs that you will be using have their own print commands. Therefore, you don't really have to worry about learning to use this command. But if you have to use it, at the prompt type:

C:\>PRINT MANUAL.DOC and press ENTER.

This tells your PC to print a file called MANUAL.DOC.

Running programs

Getting programs started on your PC is very simple. Often, all you have to do is type a word that you can easily relate to that program. That word will automatically start your program running. For example, to run WordPerfect, you type WP and press ENTER, to run Lotus 123, you type 123, to run Microsoft Word, you type WORD. All you have to do is remember those few words.

If you use the DOS Shell, those command words will be on your screen and all you have to do is point at them with your mouse and double click. If your PC came with a menu program, then the names will be on your screen and all you have to do is to choose them.

Using DOS Help

MS-DOS versions 4, 5 and 6 offer on-line help. That means you can get to a help screen right on your PC. The easiest way to use the help screen is to type:

> **C:\>HELP COMMAND.EXT** and press ENTER.

It will describe the command you have specified and shows some examples of how it's used.

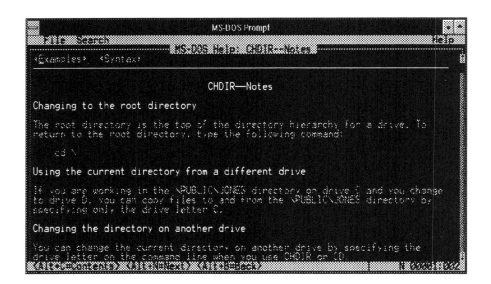

Chapter 6. Beyond Simple DOS

The stuff you have learned so far, is more than enough to get you well on your way to using your PC. This chapter gets into advanced topics that you can live without. Of course, there are some obvious benefits if you read and apply what you learn here. On the other hand, if your brain feels a little overwhelmed at this time, skip this chapter and come back to it later when you have practiced some more with your PC.

AUTOEXEC.BAT file

This is a batch file that tells your PC what to do as soon as you start up your computer. A batch file as you know by now, is a collection of instructions that your PC performs one after another.

MS-DOS versions 4, 5 and 6 create an AUTOEXEC.BAT file on your hard disk as they are installed. At first the files contain only a few basic commands like:

```
@ECHO OFF
PROMPT=$P$G
PATH=C:\; C:\DOS;
```

As you add more programs to your hard disk, they may add their own unique command lines. Most programs also add their directory to your "PATH=...." list. One of the advantages of having a program on the path list is that it can be accessed from anywhere. Normally, if for example, your word-processing software is WordPerfect, in order to use it, you'd have to change to the appropriate directory to type WP for it to begin. When WordPerfect puts it's directory in your path list, you can type WP from your root directory and it will start your WordPerfect program directly.

You can fine tune your AUTOEXEC.BAT file by adding a few lines to it.

However, because of the importance of the file, always keep a backup copy just in case something goes wrong with your changes. The easiest thing to do is to copy the file to another one with a different extension. For example:

C:\\>COPY AUTOEXEC.BAT AUTOEXEC.ONE and ENTER.

Once you have created a backup copy, changing your AUTOEXEC.BAT file is very easy with the EDIT command:

C:\\>EDIT AUTOEXEC.BAT and press ENTER.

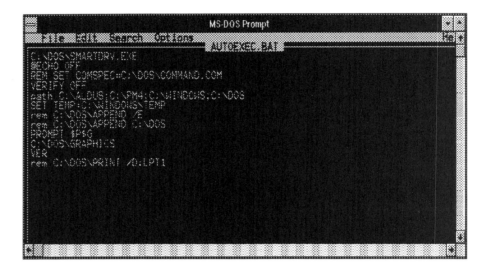

The EDIT screen will show the contents of your AUTOEXEC.BAT file on the monitor. You can use the up and down arrow keys to go to the line that you want to change. If you want to add a line at the end, simply go to the blank line after the last line and type your command. If you want to insert a line, simply move the blinking cursor to the line before the new line and press ENTER. Everything will drop one line from there and you can type your command. You can change your AUTOEXEC.BAT file to make it look like the following:

> **C:\DOS\SMARTDRV.EXE**
> **@ECHO OFF**
> **PROMPT=PG**
> **PATH=C:\; C:\DOS;**
> **SET TEMP=C:\TEMP**
> **LASTDRIVE=Z**

When you are through adding or changing lines, press the ALT key and then press the F key. A window will drop down on the top left corner of your screen. Use the down arrow key to move the highlight down to EXIT and press ENTER (you can also activate the EXIT command by simply pressing the key for the letter that is underlined, in this case the X). A little box will pop up on your screen and inform you that you have changed something and asks if you want to save the changes. Obviously you'll choose YES (Y).

CONFIG.SYS file

This is a batch file that contains specific system related files that give your PC information about various devices that are attached to it. These files are called device drivers and they are unique to each specific part. The device drivers for

```
                            MS-DOS Prompt
  File   Edit   Search   Options                              Help
╒══════════════════════ CONFIG.SYS ══════════════════════╕
 DEVICE=C:\DOS\SETVER.EXE
 BREAK=ON
 BUFFERS=20
 FILES=20
 LASTDRIVE=E
 SHELL=C:\DOS\COMMAND.COM C:\DOS\ /E:256 /p
 DEVICE=C:\DOS\ANSI.SYS
 INSTALL=C:\DOS\FASTOPEN.EXE C:=(50,25)
 DEVICE=C:\DOS\HIMEM.SYS
 DOS=HIGH
 DEVICEHIGH=C:\DOS\DBLSPACE.SYS /MOVE
 STACKS=9,256
 ─
```

most of the popular items are already built-into DOS. Therefore, it doesn't
need to be told how to interact with those. When you first install DOS on your
PC, it automatically creates a CONFIG.SYS file as it creates an
AUTOEXEC.BAT file. The file generally contains a few basic lines such as:

```
DEVICE=C:\DOS\SETVER.EXE
DEVICE=C:\DOS\HIMEM.SYS
DOS=HIGH,UMB
DEVICEHIGH=C:\MOUSE\MOUSE.SYS
BUFFERS=40
FILES=40
BREAK=ON
LASTDRIVE=Z
```

You can modify your CONFIG.SYS file exactly like you do with your
AUTOEXEC.BAT file.

Using multiple configurations

There may occasions when you may need more than one way to bring up your
PC. For example, you may have a CD-ROM drive that you use occasionally.
When you start up your PC with the CD-ROM active, the device driver for the
drive takes up a certain amount of your valuable memory. If you have better
uses for that memory at times when you don't need the CD-ROM, a different
configuration file will be very helpful. The same thing may apply to a scanner,
sound board, voice mail system, etc. MS-DOS versions prior to 6, required
you to start up your PC, change your AUTOEXEC.BAT and CONFIG.SYS
files, then re-start your PC all over again.

MS-DOS version 6 gives you the ability to create multiple AUTOEXEC.BAT
and CONFIG.SYS files. When you start your PC, it will show you a list of those
options and will execute whichever one you choose.

Setting up your start-up files for multiple configurations requires some
expertise. Let a PC expert do it for you. There is no simple way of explaining

it in this book. Even the MS-DOS 6 User's Guide, can be confusing to the novice.

Customizing the DOS prompt

The DOS prompt is your PC's way of telling you that it's ready for your order. Whatever you type at the prompt will be considered a command after you press the ENTER key. There are several ways to modify and customize your prompt. The most basic prompt looks like this:

C:>

Newer DOS versions automatically create a more helpful prompt by adding a line to your AUTOEXEC.BAT file. Your prompt will look like this:

C:\>

The backslash "\" is your root or main directory. If you change directories, this prompt will show where you are:

C:\DOS>

Which means that you are in the DOS directory.

You can also make your prompt show the date and time or other characters. But why would you want to waste your time with unimportant stuff like that?

If you learn everything you need to know about DOS and other programs, then get bored out of your skull, call your local "Nerd" and have your prompt changed into something funky!

Using check disk (CHKDSK)

You hard disk is a storage device just like your closet. Like your closet, over a period of time it can also accumulate bits and pieces of junk. Some of that junk is actually parts of files you created and saved but unbeknown to you, they got scattered, or lost their identity. These files wander about in your hard disk and make it more difficult to store information. The check disk command (CHKDSK) looks for these bits and pieces and then asks you if you want to save them for some sort of recovery. If you are not deep into file recovery, you might as well tell it to get rid of those pesky little things. Just remember this:

☞   Never use the CHKDSK command while Windows is running in the background. If you don't use Windows, disregard this warning.

☞   Never use CHKDSK if you use a disk compression software, unless the user's manual says it's OK.

Here is how you use CHKDSK:

C:\>CHKDSK /F and press ENTER.

Note the space, slash and F after the command. After a few seconds your PC comes back with a message saying "XXX lost allocation units found. Convert lost chains to files? Y/N". Since you want to get rid of those little files, press "N" for no. You will see a few pieces of information about the total memory in your PC, the capacity of your hard disk and the amount of space left on your hard disk.

Installing programs

The whole idea behind having a PC is to use software to get things done or to play games. When you buy software, it comes on floppy disks and somehow it needs to get into your computer. This process is called installing or setting up programs. After you do one or two, it becomes second nature to you. A few years ago, installing programs used to be a monumental task that meant lots of trial and error (mostly error!). Now most programs self-install.

There are several do's and don't that you need to remember before you try to feed your PC all these wonderful programs:

☞ Buy software that you need and plan to use. It's easy to get caught up in the excitement of ads and product reviews and buy a whole bunch of software that you won't need or use. It's not good for you, and long term it's not good for the software companies either.

☞ Buy software that works with your PC. If you completed the list at the beginning of this book, you should know what you have. When you buy software, check the package and make sure that under "System Requirements:" your type of system is included. Check for things like the microprocessor type, amount of memory, hard disk capacity, video graphics, sound board, etc.

☞ Make sure that the floppy disk size and type fits what you have. If you have both sizes (5-1/4" and 3-1/2") floppy drives then it doesn't matter which size you buy. Most programs have both size disks inside the package. Others use two different packages for these disk sizes. If you have an older PC, your drive type may not be high density. Check with the store to make sure that the right type of disk can be found.

☞ When you buy your new software, don't tear up the package and stick the disks in the floppy drive right away. If after reading the outside of the package or the beginning of the manual you discover that the software is not right for you, it'll be difficult to return an opened and damaged box. Most stores allow you to return a software if the plastic or paper envelope containing the disks is not opened.

☞ You're probably not that excited about reading a whole manual on how to use a software. At least try to locate the "Getting

Started" or "Read Me First" booklet that comes with the program to learn how to install it.

☞ Don't start installing the program before making a backup copy of the disks. You will save yourself a whole bunch of time, money and aggravation if you have a copy in case something happens to one set of disks.

☞ If you can convince a friend or associate who is an experienced PC user to stay with you while you install your first program, you'll do much better. But don't let the "expert" install it for you!

Verify What You Buy

When you buy software, you may be getting a number of things in the package. To make sure that you are not missing anything, always compare the contents of the box with what the manual says you should be getting.

Depending on what type of software you buy, where you buy it from and how much you par for it, the contents may vary. Some very inexpensive programs sell for as low as $5 and come with no printed manual or guide book. Instead, they have a sheet of paper that tells you how to install the program on your hard disk and how to print the manual that's on the disk.

Most software is packaged in complete sets of disks, user's manual, installation guide, registration card, etc. Generally, there is a list that tells you what you'd find in the box. Make sure that you locate everything you are supposed to find in the box.

Installing Shareware Software

Shareware programs often sell for less than $5 and contain everything on one or two disks. Most shareware suppliers create batch files that will install the program automatically. These programs are often compressed on the floppy disk and need to be decompressed as they are installed on your hard disk. If your program does not have an install batch file, it will probably have a README, README.DOC, README.TXT, MANUAL.TXT, or another file name ending in .TXT, .DOC, etc. You can read the file by first placing the disk in your drive A: (or B:), then changing to that drive. Next, you should try to read the contents of that file for instructions:

A:\>TYPE README.TXT I MORE and press ENTER.

With this command you are telling your PC to show you the contents of the README.TXT file and show one page at a time. Note the space after TYPE, TXT and the "I" character.

Installing Applications Programs

Most programs are now compressed on a few disks in order to save on disk costs. They generally use the commands SETUP or INSTALL to transfer the program from floppy disks to your hard disk. Most programs have a small booklet or a sheet of paper called "Read Me First", "Installation Guide", "Setup Guide", etc. The guide will have step-by-step instructions to install the program on your hard disk. If you can't find the guide or find it too complicated to understand, read the rest of this section.

- Find a disk called Setup, Install, or Disk #1. Insert the disk in your drive A: (or B:), close the drive door and change to that drive by typing A: and pressing ENTER.

- Find out from your installation guide what command to use in order to start the installation process. Often that command is SETUP or INSTALL. If you can't find those files, type DIR and look at the list of files on the disk. You may recognize another command which means something like install.

- Once you get the installation process started, the program may come up with several questions or give you some options. If the program offers you a quick install option versus custom install, take the easy way out.

- The program may ask you what directory you'd like to have it installed. Often, it offers you an option and asks if you agree with it. You don't really have any reason to change what the program suggests. So, agree with it's suggestion and proceed.

- Most new programs developed in recent years have the ability to ask DOS or Windows what type of system you have and consequently, ask you very few questions. The only questions you may be asked would be about your printer, monitor, CD-ROM, sound board, etc. In these cases the program often supplies you with a list of options and asks you to choose the one that matches yours or is similar to yours. After it's done, it may ask you if you want your AUTOEXEC.BAT and CONFIG.SYS files modified for the new program. Make sure that you have a backup copy saved and then let it modify your files.

- Frequently, once the installation process is finished the pro gram tells you to press a key to reboot the computer. Do it. If it doesn't suggest a reboot, hold down the CTRL-ALT-DEL keys and reboot anyway. Now your program is ready to be used.

Editing files

MS-DOS versions 4, 5 and 6 use an editor that lets you change files easily. There are only a few points you need to know about the editor: how to activate it, how to change a line, how to insert a line, how to save your work and how to get out.

How to Start the Editor

At the prompt type:

C:\>EDIT FILENAME.EXT and press ENTER

How to Change a Line

The editor screen will appear on your monitor. The blinking cursor will be at the top line. Use the up or down arrow keys to move to the line you want to change. Once you get to the desired line, use the left or right arrow keys to get to where you want. Use the delete key to take out the undesired characters.

How to Insert a Line

Move the blinking cursor to the line where you'd want to insert a new line and press ENTER. A new line opens up. If you want to insert a line at the end of the file simply move the cursor to the last line and then press ENTER.

How to Save Your Changes

Once you have finished making changes, press the ALT key. Press the F key to open up the File menu box at the top left corner of your screen. Move the highlight down to Save and press ENTER, or simply press the S key (underlined in Save).

How to Get Out

Once you are through using the editor, you need to get out. If you save your work, all you have to do is press the ALT key and then press F to get the File menu. Move the highlight down to Exit and press ENTER, or simply press X (underlined in Exit) to quit. If you haven't saved your work, when you choose Exit, a small box will pop up on your screen telling you that you have made a change and asks if you want to save it before you exit. Choose Yes and press ENTER.

Correcting time and date

Your PC has a built-in clock chip and a small battery that helps it keep track of time and date. The battery generally works for up to five years before it needs to be replaced. Replacing the battery in most PCs is relatively simple. In some PCs unfortunately, the battery is soldered to one of the boards. In that case you need to have a technician replace the battery for you.

The time kept by your computer is pretty accurate to within a couple of minutes a year. You only need to change your time during daylight saving periods.

The setup program in your PC has a simple method for changing the time and date. Since each PC is different, refer to your PC Operating Manual to learn how to change the time.

Having the correct time and date is important because your PC records the time and date each time you save a file or create a directory. This is very helpful when you need to compare various files and when they were last modified.

Optimizing memory usage

Today's programs rely on every bit of memory your PC can spare. One of the scarce commodities is the first 640 Kilo Bytes of memory. That's called Conventional Memory. When you run a program, it loads from the hard disk to your conventional memory. The more conventional memory you have left, the faster your program will work.

MS-DOS versions 5 and 6 have memory management capabilities. They both move the small, less important memory resident programs to areas above 640 K. MS-DOS 5 needs your help in optimizing your memory usage by setting up your AUTOEXEC.BAT and CONFIG.SYS files. MS-DOS 6 does everything automatically.

To see how your memory is being used, at the prompt type:

C:\>MEM /C and press ENTER.

This will show you a list of files occupying your memory.

If you are using MS-DOS 5, you can add the following lines to your CONFIG.SYS file in order to optimize your memory utilization.

DEVICE=C:\DOS\HIMEM.SYS
DOS=HIGH, UMB

If you have MS-DOS 6, then all you have to do is activate the memory management program and it automatically configures everything for you. At the prompt type:

C:\>MEMMAKER and press ENTER.

The program will give you a choice to use Express or Custom optimization. Choose the Express option and press ENTER. The program will ask you if want to use expanded memory. Since you will most likely not need it, choose no for an answer and press ENTER. You can always go back and modify your memory management setup later. After a few tests, MEMMAKER will modify your AUTOEXEC.BAT and CONFIG.SYS files. You are ready to go!

Optimizing hard disk performance

Your hard disk keeps storing and deleting, storing and deleting until someday it ends up with a whole bunch of files or file particles all over the place. You may remember reading earlier that when you store a file, DOS puts it on whatever empty spaces it can find on the hard disk. Of course, DOS keeps track of where everything is in the File Allocation Table (FAT). When you delete a file, DOS changes it's name slightly, and makes the space available for other files.

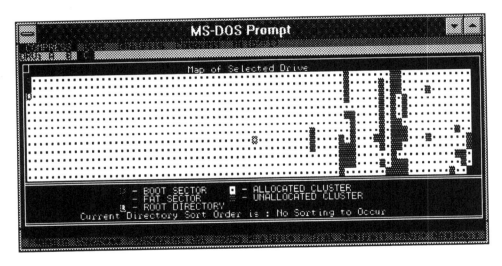

Chances are that a new file does not occupy the entire space made available by deleting an old file, or needs additional space. Consequently, it ends up scattered in different parts of the hard disk. Eventually, having a file scattered in many different parts of the hard disk makes the disk take longer to find files or store your files on the disk. There are programs called "Disk Defragmentation" or "Disk Optimization" software that analyze your hard disk and bring pieces of files together.

If you have MS-DOS version 6, you also have a free disk defragmentation program. All you have to do is type:

C:\>DEFRAG and press ENTER.

Depending on the size of your hard disk this process may take several minutes. You will see a map of your hard disk and a graphical progress report. If you have a defragmentation file, try to use it about once a month. You don't need to get carried away and use it any more often than that.

Doubling your hard disk capacity

Your hard disk can store tons of information. Every 10 Mega Bytes (MB) of your hard disk capacity is about 5,000 pages of information. So if you have a 100 MB hard disk, you can store about 50,000 pages of data. That may seem like a lot. Only a few years ago that was an astronomical amount only afforded by very large corporations. These days that's average. DOS takes over 5 MB and some programs may take from 10 to 20 MB on your hard disk. It's easy to fill up your hard disk in a short time.

Disk compression programs take the empty spaces out of your files and literally cram twice as much data in the same drive. There are several of these programs on the market. MS-DOS 6 contains a free disk compression program called DoubleSpace (DBLSPACE). If you have MS-DOS 6, installing DBLSPACE is easy and only takes a few minutes if your hard disk is empty, otherwise it may take between one to two hours. If you bought a new PC with MS-DOS 6 installed on the hard disk, the dealer or manufacturer may have already installed DOS and DBLSPACE for you. If you can power up your PC and get to C:\>, you definitely have DOS. At the prompt type DBLSPACE and press ENTER. If you see "Compressed hard drive", the program is already installed on your PC (make sure you were not sold a compressed 100 MB hard drive as a 200 MB drive). If you don't have DBLSPACE installed, you will see a start-up screen that will tell you to proceed with installing the program. You will need to press ENTER a couple of times to tell DBLSPACE to use the "Express Setup" and you are on your way. When your PC starts to setup DBLSPACE, just leave it alone for a while. When it's finished you'll see the setup screen again. This time it will inform you that DoubleSpace has finished compressing your drive C:. At this point press ENTER and let your PC restart.

You are now the happy owner of twice as much hard disk space than you started with. The nice thing about DoubleSpace is that you will not experience a noticeable loss of speed either.

☞   If you already have another disk compression program on your hard disk, don't try to install DoubleSpace by yourself. Get help from an experienced PC user who is knowledgeable about installing this program. If you are not careful, you may lose all your data on the hard disk.

Doubling your floppy disk capacity

DoubleSpace can also double the capacity of your floppy disks. There are many advantages to doubling the capacity of your floppies, but there is a little inconvenience that you need to be aware of. When you use DoubleSpace on your floppies, it literally makes your 1.2 MB 5-1/4" disks hold as much as 2.4 MB, and your 1.4 MB 3-1/2" disks hold up to 2.8 MB of data. You can use these disks to keeps copies of important files, etc. You can also use these disks to give your data to someone else. But the other PC also needs to have MS-DOS 6 on the hard disk.

A major inconvenience associated with using DoubleSpace on floppies is that before reading a compressed floppy disk you have to "mount DoubleSpace on the floppy drive" every time you put a compressed disk in there. In effect your drive needs to know that it's going to read a compressed floppy disk each time.

You can't simply use DIR to see a list of the contents of a compressed floppy disk. Instead it will have a single file called READTHIS.TXT, which you can look at using the TYPE command:

C:\>TYPE A:READTHIS.TXT and press ENTER.

You will see a message telling you that the disk has been compressed by MS-DOS 6 DoubleSpace. Simply change your drive to A: where the compressed floppy is located and type:

A:DBLSPACE /MOUNT and press ENTER.

After a few seconds you will see a message telling you that DoubleSpace is mounting Drive A:. When it's finished it will tell you that it has mounted Drive A:. Now you can do whatever you want with the contents of the disk in drive A:.

☞   If you take out the disk that you just mounted in drive A:, and replace it with another compressed disk, you will have to mount DoubleSpace for the new disk.

Keeping viruses away

Unfortunately, computer viruses have become as much a part of our PC life as crime and violence have become part of our social experience. A few brilliant minds who have the ability to create wonderful programs are instead, spending

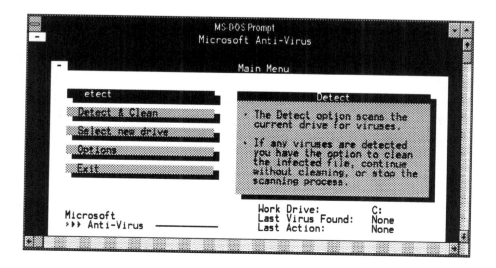

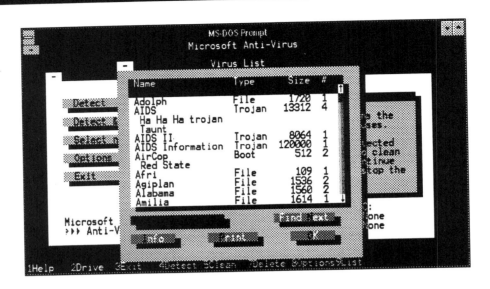

their time creating viruses that harm other people's PCs. Computer viruses only transmit through programs and data that you get from other people. Currently you may get a virus through floppy disks or through your modem. Practicing safe computing and knowing who and where you get your disks and modem information from is the key to keeping viruses away. However, it helps to have the ability to detect and disable viruses before they do any damage to your data or to your hard disk.

MS-DOS 6 has a free anti-virus program that will detect and disable most viruses. The key to remember is that new viruses are created every day and an anti-virus program written in Fall 1993 may not be able to detect a virus created in Spring 1994. So, in addition to practicing safe computing, you may need to periodically update your anti-virus program. Your MS-DOS 6 manual has a coupon for an inexpensive update. Keep these points in mind:

☞ Never get disks from strangers.

☞ Never download information from your modem directly to your hard disk. Always try to download to a floppy disk so that you can check it later.

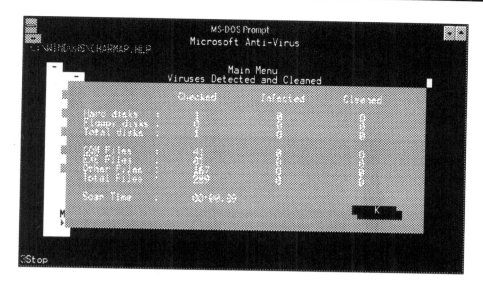

MS-DOS 6 has two virus programs to help you. Microsoft Anti-Virus (MSAV) can analyze your hard disk or floppy disks, detect viruses and disable them. Another program called VSAFE can run in the background and monitor your PC all the time for suspicious activities. If it detects a virus trying to change something it will warn you so that you can run MSAV to locate and destroy it.

Whenever you want to check for viruses you can simply type:

C:\>MSAV and press ENTER.

The program scans all your drives for viruses. If it detects a virus, it gives you the option to clear it. Choose that option and have the virus removed. You can run MSAV every time you want to use a new disk or you can run it every time you power up your PC. The latter option gets a little time consuming. To run MSAV every time you power up your PC, you need to add MSAV to your AUTOEXEC.BAT file. See the description of that file earlier in this chapter.

Another way of combating viruses is to have VSAFE roam around in your computer memory all the time. You can add a line with VSAFE to your AUTOEXEC.BAT file. Now, every time your computer is powered up, VSAFE is activated. If it detects that a virus is trying to change something on your hard disk, it warns you. You can then quit what you are doing and run MSAV to find the virus and destroy it. Running VSAFE in your memory does consume some of your precious conventional memory. You need to decide which is more important. If you get a lot of data disks from others, it's recommended that you load VSAFE in your batch file. If not, you can periodically run VSAFE to make sure that your PC is clear of viruses.

Using the MS-DOS diagnostics

MS-DOS 6 has a program called Microsoft Diagnostics which has the ability to analyze your PC and determine what types of devices are being used and the status of your communications channels. This is a very useful tool for determining what you have when you decide to add something else to your system. However, it does not tell you what the problem is if your PC won't start or acts weird. For that you need specific programs that are used for troubleshooting. To activate the Microsoft Diagnostics program, all you have to do is type:

C:\>MSD and press ENTER.

All the relevant information will be shown on your screen.

Connecting two computers together

MS-DOS 6 has a new program called Interlink which allows you to hook up two PCs together in order to move data from one to the other. Typically this is used if you have a portable computer that you take on the road with you and a desktop computer at the office that you use to gather various information, print your data, etc. Interlink allows you to hook up the two PCs with a cable and move data from your Client PC (the portable) to the Server PC (the desktop).

Chapter 7. Using DOS Shell

DOS is an operating system that uses a character based environment. You tell it to do things by typing what you want. A free feature that is included with MS-DOS versions 4, 5 and 6 is called the DOS Shell. It creates a nice-looking graphical environment on your computer screen. The graphics on the screen show various DOS commands in an easy to use manner. Basically all you have to do is use the arrow keys to activate a command. This saves you the hassles of remembering and typing commands.

DOS Shell offers an easier way to use DOS. You can make using the Shell even easier by using a mouse. This way you can simply move the mouse and make it point at the commands that you'd like to execute. Seeing the commands and various drives, directories and files on your screen, makes using DOS much easier.

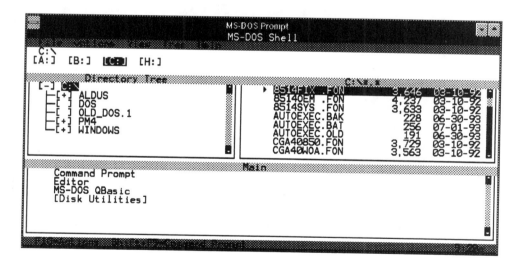

To Shell or not to Shell

Depending on who you ask, you may get different advice about using the DOS Shell. People who learned to use the old DOS the hard way, feel uncomfortable with the Shell and sometimes advise against it. But if are reading this book, you feel that you need help with DOS. Is there any reason you should also suffer like those who didn't have the DOS Shell available to them? If someone offers you a tool to make your life easier, would you refuse it? The DOS Shell is easier to use, more accurate and best of all, it's free.

Mouse or keyboard, which is better?

You can use your keyboard to work with the DOS Shell. However, it was really designed to be used with a mouse. Mice are so inexpensive these days that you can buy one for less than the cost of a dinner (of course, depending on your taste a dinner may range from $15 to $150). You'll enjoy the mouse longer than you'll remember the dinner!

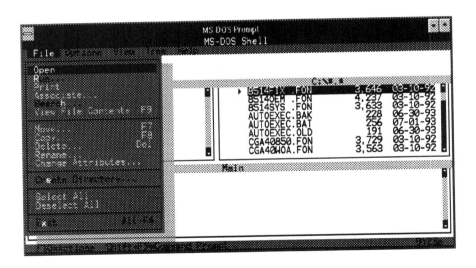

Getting the Shell started

Starting DOS Shell is really simple. You just type the command at the prompt:

C:\>DOSSHELL and press ENTER.

In a few seconds, the Shell will appear on your screen. If the Shell was not installed on your PC, you'll get an error message. Get expert help to install it for you.

Understanding the Shell

The DOS Shell occupies your entire screen. It's made up of a series of bars and boxes. At the top of the screen is a bar called the Menu Bar. In that bar you see the names of several menus like: File, Options, View, Tree and Help.

Below the Menu Bar is a box that shows the name of the directory that you are currently in. Below that you see little tiny boxes with the names of the drives in your PC. Below the drive letters are two boxes. One box, called the

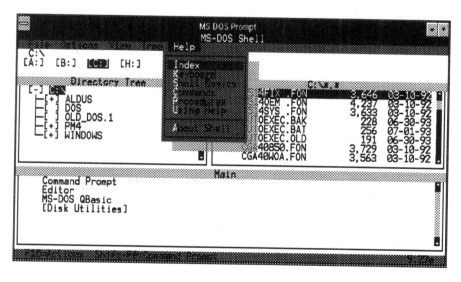

Directory Tree shows a list of the directories in the drive that you are currently in. The other box shows the drive you are currently in and a list of the files in it. Below those two boxes is another box called Main. It shows a list of a few key DOS commands you may need from time-to-time. It also shows your program commands.

Customizing the looks of the Shell

You can customize the appearance of the Shell by choosing one of the five layouts built-in the Shell. This is something that you can play with later, when you feel more comfortable with the Shell. The layouts show the following:

- All files: shows only files.
- Program list: shows only programs.
- Single file list: shows files and directories.
- Dual file lists: shows two sets of files and directories.
- Program/file lists: shows files, directories and programs.

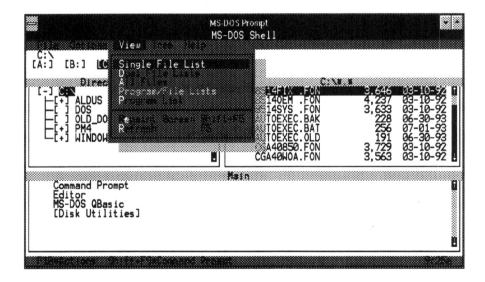

To change your Shell appearance you need to press the ALT-V keys or use your mouse to click on the VIEW menu on the Menu Bar. This will open up a list of options on your screen. Choose the layout that you'd like from the list of five.

Changing directories

Moving from one directory to another is rather simple. If you have a mouse, all you have to do is go to the Directory Tree box and click on the directory that you'd like. If you don't have a mouse, you'll have to press the Tab key (the key on the left of your keyboard with two arrows pointing in opposite directions) to move to the Directory Tree box. Then use the up and down arrow keys to move onto the desired directory.

Changing drives

Going from one drive to another is quite simple. If you have a mouse, all you have to do is move the mouse pointer onto the drive that you'd like to change and double click on the left mouse button. If you don't have a mouse, you need to hold down the CTRL key and then press the letter for the drive name you'd like to change to. For example, to go to drive A:, press CTRL-A.

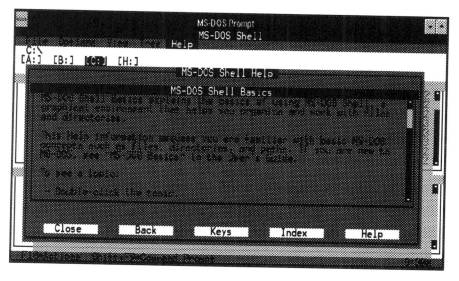

☞   If you want to change to a floppy drive, make sure that there is a disk in there and the door is closed. Otherwise, you'll get an error message.

Looking at files in drives or directories

To look at the files in a drive or directory, all you have to do is move your mouse pointer to the drive letter or directory name and click your left mouse button. This will display all the files in that drive or directory. If the drive has other directories, they will be displayed and you'll need to click on the appropriate directory.

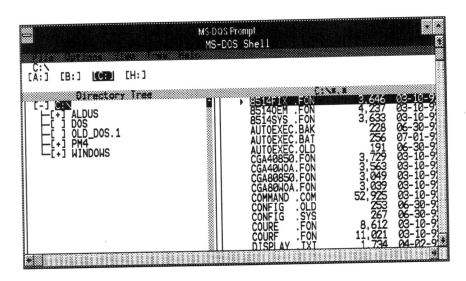

Working with files requires that you select which file you are interested in. Selecting a file or files is very easy to do with a mouse. Move the mouse pointer to the file name and click the mouse button. To select more than one file, hold down the CTRL key and click the mouse button as you move the pointer to each file.

Copying files

Copying a file with the Shell is as easy as moving a penny from one pocket to another. All you have to do is grab the file and move it to the other drive or directory. Simply use the mouse pointer to click on the file name, then hold down the CTRL key and hold down the left mouse button while it is on the file name and drag it to the drive letter or directory name of your destination (if you don't hold down the CTRL key, instead of copying the file, you actually move the file itself). Now, this dragging business will take a little getting used to. You may want to practice a little. At first you may let go of the button before reaching your destination, but you'll get a hang of it soon. After you move the file over and let go of the mouse button, a little box will pop up on your screen that will ask you if you are sure you want to copy that file where you dropped it. If you are, click in the yes button.

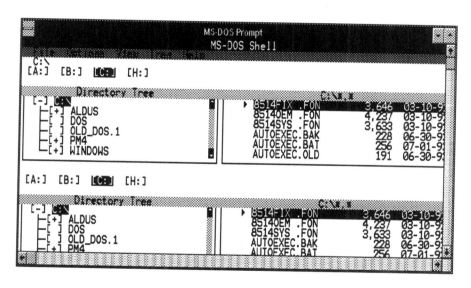

If you want to use a keyboard, first you have to move the highlight over it by using the spacebar. Now, if you press the F8 key, a little box will pop up on your screen that will ask you to type where you'd want the file to be copied.

Renaming files

There may be occasions when you may decide to rename a file. For example, to create a more current file with the same name. In that case, use your mouse to point at the file name and highlight it. Now move the mouse pointer to the "File" menu on the Menu Bar and click on that. A list will drop down. Choose "Rename..." and click your left mouse button. A little box will pop on your screen with the present name and a space for you to type the new name.

If you have to use your keyboard, after highlighting the file, press the CTRL-F keys to get to the "File" menu. From the list choose "Rename..." by pressing "N."

Deleting files

This is so easy with a mouse that it's almost dangerous! If you don't pay attention you may delete the wrong file. Simply move your mouse pointer over to the file name, click the left button so that it will be highlighted. Now, press the "Delete" key. A little box will pop up on your screen to ask you if that's what you want to do. Click on the yes button and the file is gone.

Using your keyboard, you have to highlight the file name then press the "Delete" key.

Searching for files

Finding files is a real snap with the Shell. All you have to do is move your mouse pointer onto the File menu and click the left button. A little box will drop down. Click on the "Search" and a little box will pop up on your screen asking you for the name of the file. Type the file name and press ENTER. After a few seconds the location of the file will be displayed. If it can't find the file it will come up with a message.

If you have to use a keyboard, press ALT-F to get to the File menu. On the list of choices type H or move the highlight by using the up or down arrow keys to Search then press ENTER.

Looking inside files

Sometimes you may want to look inside a file that you have created before you do things like copying, deleting, etc. Simply move your mouse pointer on the file name and click the left mouse button to highlight it. Now press the F9 key. It will show all the contents. If you do the same thing with a program file, the contents will be a whole bunch of funny characters. By pressing the "Page Up" or "Page Down" keys you can look at various pages. When you are done, just press the "Esc" key.

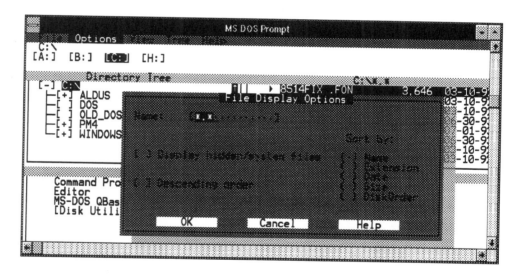

Moving files between drives and directories

Moving files is even easier than moving a penny from one pocket to another! You simply move your mouse pointer over to the file name, click the left button and hold it down while you move the file over the destination drive or directory.

If you have to use the keyboard, move the highlight over the name of the file and press the F7 key. A little box will appear on the screen with a place for you to type the new destination for your file.

Creating a directory

If you need to create a new directory in the main part of your hard disk (root directory) or in one of your existing directories (subdirectory), simply click your mouse pointer on the box containing the "Directory Tree" and then click on the drive name if you'd like to create the directory in root directory or click on a directory name if you'd like to create a subdirectory. This will highlight the new location. Now, click your mouse pointer on the File menu and choose the "Create Directory" command. A little box will pop up on your screen and you will be asked to type the name of the new directory. Remember that you can only use up to eight characters for the name.

Running programs

You'll love the way you can run programs from the Shell. The bottom box of your Shell should have a list of program commands. All you have to do is double click your mouse pointer on the program and off you go.

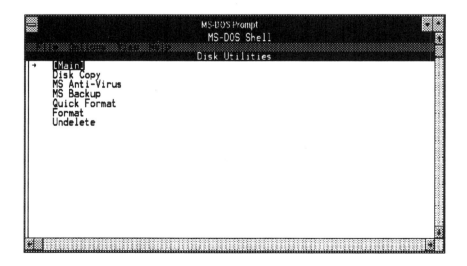

Quitting the Shell

All throughout this chapter you have learned that using your mouse is easier than the keyboard. Well, when you want to get out of DOS Shell it's easier to press the F3 key. If you want to use your mouse, click on the File menu and then click on the Exit command.

Chapter 8. Description of DOS Commands

Using your PC means that at some point in time you'll need to use an obscure DOS command you've never heard of. As much as we all like to ignore things that we don't like or find particularly difficult to understand or to remember, there is a need for this chapter to be in this book. However, that doesn't mean that you should read it and memorize it. Simply read it to know what other DOS commands are available and know where to look for them when you need them.

The descriptions that follow are kept as simple as possible. If you decide that you need more detail, then you need to look at your DOS manual, or at the DOS prompt type HELP COMMAND.EXT and press ENTER. Instead of COMMAND.EXT you need to type the name of the command you need help with.

APPEND

What does it do? This is an old command that has few uses these days. It basically lets you find files in a directory different than the one you are currently in. The path command does the same thing with fewer complications.

How is it used? If you have to use it, get a PC expert to set it up for you.

Warning: Don't use this command while you are running Windows.

ASSIGN

What does it do? This command tells DOS to assign one drive name to another. For example, if you only have one floppy drive but a program insists on using your B: drive, you can assign drive B: to A:.

How is it used? In your AUTOEXEC.BAT file add a line with:

ASSIGN B:=A:

BACKUP

What does it do? This command is used by all DOS versions prior to 6. It's a special command that compresses designated files and directories onto floppy disks. Backup can be in the form of a full backup or an incremental backup.

How is it used? When you want to backup your hard disk, you need a bunch of formatted floppy disks. At the prompt, type the BACKUP command and use *.* for all the files, or type the codes for all files changed since the last full backup. See Chapter 5 for details.

BREAK

What does it do? This command relates to the CTRL + C or CTRL + BREAK keys that you press in order to stop a program from running. When it's active, the breaking function works faster under most circumstances.

How is it used? It's typed at the DOS prompt (C:\>) or it's used in your CONFIG.SYS file. In CONFIG.SYS you type:

BREAK=ON or **BREAK=OFF**

to enable or disable the command.

BUFFERS

What does it do? This command puts aside some of your PC's memory and uses it as a buffer between the hard disk drive and the computer. The brains of your PC, the microprocessor, works faster than your hard disk drive, therefore, the buffer acts as a temporary holding area for information going into and out of the hard disk drive. The buffers have to be in the range prescribed in the next paragraph. If your buffers are too small, your hard disk may not work as efficiently. If your buffers are too large, you may not have enough memory left for other things.

How is it used? Buffers command is used in the CONFIG.SYS file. It appears as:

BUFFERS=XX

As a rule of thumb, if your hard disk drive is 40 MB, use 20 in place of the XX. If your hard disk is 100 MB or higher, use 40 in place of the XX. If it is between 40 MB and 100 MB, use a number between 20 and 40.

CALL

What does it do? This command is used in programming batch files. Batch files are mini programs that perform certain functions for you. For example, a batch file may start your word processing program soon after you turn your PC on. CALL allows you to run a second batch program while you are running another. For example, while your word processing file is getting ready to be started, another batch file is making your mailing list from a database program ready for use inside your word processing program.

How is it used? CALL is used in batch files that end with .BAT. It's a command that you'll rarely need to use.

CD (or CHDIR)

What does it do? This is one of the most frequently used DOS commands. CD or CHDIR means change directory. Since they both do the same thing, you just need to remember CD. This command displays the name of the directory you are currently in, or changes from the current directory to the one that you'd like to be in.

How is it used? At the DOS prompt type CD\ and press the ENTER key. This will show the name of the drive and directory you are currently in. If you type CD followed by the name of a directory, it will change to that directory. For example, if you type CD\DIRNAME and press the ENTER key, it will get you in the DIRNAME directory. Just remember that when this book says

DIRNAME, you don't type DIRNAME, you type the name of a directory on your hard disk drive.

CHCP

What does it do? This command lets you show or change the set of characters that are displayed on your computer monitor. You'd rarely ever need to use this command.

How is it used? Get help from a PC expert.

CHDIR

See CD.

CHKDSK

What does it do? This command is called Check Disk. It checks the status of a disk and displays a status report. While it checks a disk, it also tries to fix disk errors. It looks for documents and files that you may have created but for some reason were not stored where they are supposed to be. This may happen for example, if while you were in the middle of changing a document, power went out and your document was not properly stored.

How is it used? At the DOS prompt if you type CHKDSK and then press the ENTER key, DOS will analyze the drive that appeared at the prompt. It will also locate lost files on that drive. If it finds lost files it will ask you if you want them identified.

Warning: Don't use this command while you are running Windows.

CHOICE

What does it do? This MS-DOS 6 command prompts you to choose a batch file at start up. For example, if you want to start right into the word processing program you use almost all the time, or into Windows, you'll have multiple batch files. CHOICE will make your PC pause when it's powered up and asks you to choose a start up batch file.

How is it used? Get help from a PC expert.

CLS

What does it do? This command clears the screen and moves the prompt to the top, left corner.

How is it used? At the DOS prompt type CLS and press ENTER.

COMMAND

What does it do? This is the real thing! This command is the heart of DOS. It contains a number of key elements of DOS. This command appears in your main (root) directory as COMMAND.COM. Make sure that it's not deleted, because without it your hard disk won't know what to do.

How is it used? When you first install DOS on your computer, COMMAND.COM automatically transfers itself from the DOS floppy disks onto your hard disk drive. You really have no business fooling with this command, so leave it alone. As a precaution, keep your DOS disks handy in case you accidentally delete this command from your hard disk. If that happens, your hard disk will not be accessible. Insert your DOS disk called "Boot Disk" in drive A: and press the reset button to start your PC. This time it will read from the floppy drive and give you the A:\>. At this prompt type:

A:\> COPY COMMAND.COM C: and press ENTER.

COPY

What does it do? This is a frequently used DOS command. It copies one or more files from one disk or directory to another. It can also create a copy of a file or document.

How is it used? To copy a file from a floppy disk to your hard disk, put the disk in your floppy drive and change the prompt to that drive. For example, if you are using your A: drive, type A: and press the ENTER key to get to A:\>. At the prompt type COPY FILENAME.EXT C: and press the ENTER key. Substitute your file for the FILENAME.EXT. To copy all the files in the floppy to your hard disk, instead of naming each file, at the prompt type COPY *.* C: and press the ENTER key. The *.* (called star-dot-star) means all the files and file extensions are included. Another major use of the COPY command is to create duplicates of a file. For example, if you want to use an existing letter and by slightly modifying it send it to another person, you can make a copy of the first letter and make your changes to it to create the second letter.

C:\>COPY JOHN.LTR MIKE.LTR and press ENTER.

COUNTRY

What does it do? This command tells DOS what convention to use for date, time and currency. If you live in the United States, you won't need to use this command.

How is it used? When you first transfer DOS from floppy disks to your hard disk drive, DOS asks you what country to use. It will indicate that it will use the US unless you specify another country. If you specify another country other than the US, the COUNTRY command will appear in your CONFIG.SYS file. If DOS was already installed on your hard disk drive before you purchased your PC, this is already set up for you.

CTTY

What does it do? This command changes the way different devices that are hooked up to your PC communicate with the microprocessor. In other words, it's something you don't have to worry about.

How is it used? Get help form a PC expert.

COMP

What does it do? This is short for compare. It compares the entire contents of two files item by item and line by line. It's used to verify that the copy of a file is truly identical to the original. Latest versions of copy commands are so accurate that there really is no need to compare files.

How is it used? At the prompt type:

> **C:\>COMP FILE1.EXT FILE2.EXT** and press ENTER.

DATE

What does it do? This command shows the current date, and gives you the option to change it if necessary. If you change the date using this command, the change is not permanent and stays good as long as your PC is powered up. To permanently change the date, check the operating manual for your PC.

How is it used? At the DOS prompt type DATE and press the ENTER key. It will show the current date and give you the option to change it.

DBLSPACE

What does it do? This MS-DOS 6 command starts the disk compression process that doubles the capacity of your hard disk drive. Disk compression means that the computer squeezes your information so that it can store twice as much in the same amount of space. This command sets up or reconfigures compressed drives.

How is it used? This command is used during the MS-DOS 6 installation process. See Chapter 4, on "Putting DOS on Your PC."

Warning: Don't use this command while you are running Windows.

DEBUG

What does it do? This command lets you test and modify certain files. These files are called executable files that end with a .EXE extension. This command is rarely used and if you have a need to use it, better be very careful that you don't destroy any important files. Always make a copy of the file you want to change, onto a floppy disk in case you mess up the one on your hard disk.

How is it used? Get help from a PC expert.

DEFRAG

What does it do? This MS-DOS 6 command has a unique feature that lets you reorganize your hard disk drive. Over a period of time, different parts of a file get stored on different parts of your hard disk. When you use a file, if it's scattered, it will take your hard disk drive longer to locate the entire file and have it ready for your use. DEFRAG brings together scattered information in order to make it easier to read and write on the hard disk.

How is it used? Make sure that you have quit all other programs. At the prompt type:

C:\>DEFRAG and press ENTER.

Warning: Don't use this command while you are running Windows.

DEL (or ERASE)

What does it do? This command deletes the files that you specify. Believe it or not, you do delete files, the same way you go through your drawers and throw away old papers. Be careful when you delete files. Because often when a file is deleted, it cannot be recovered.

How is it used? At the DOS prompt you type DEL followed by the name of the file you'd like to delete. For example, to delete a sample file type:

       C:\>DEL FILENAME.EXT and press ENTER.

To delete a group of files with the same name but different extensions, at the prompt type: DEL FILENAME.* and press ENTER. To delete all the files with different names but the same extension, at the prompt type: DEL *.EXT and press ENTER. To delete all the files in a directory, first change to that directory by typing CD\DIRNAME and pressing ENTER. Now type DEL *.* and press ENTER. The *.* (called star-dot-star) means every file name and extension.

DELOLDOS

What does it do? This is the "Delete Old DOS" command which MS-DOS versions 5 and 6 place on your hard disk drive when they are first installed on your hard disk. When a new DOS version is installed, it creates an OLDDOS directory and places all the relevant files from the old DOS version in there. That file is created as a backup so that in case something goes wrong with the new DOS, you can re-install the old DOS and be able to use your PC. DELOLDOS simply deletes the old DOS directory when you are certain that the new DOS is working properly.

How is it used? When you are comfortable that the new DOS is working without any problems, simply type:

       C:\>DELOLDOS and press ENTER.

DELTREE

What does it do? This MS-DOS 6 command in one step deletes a directory and all the subdirectories and files in it. With previous versions of DOS, this used to be done in several steps. Be careful using this command. The directory that you delete may not be recovered if you change your mind later.

How is it used? At the prompt type:

C:\>DELTREE DIRNAME and press ENTER.

DOS will ask you for confirmation if you want to delete the directory named DIRNAME.

DEVICE

What does it do? This command loads the special driver you specify for a device that you have installed inside or attached to the outside of your PC. The device can be a printer, modem, mouse, CD-ROM, sound board, etc. The device driver is a special set of instructions that tell your PC how to communicate with a device. You probably won't need to use this command. Most devices are usually installed automatically by the software that comes with them.

How is it used? This command is installed in the CONFIG.SYS file as:

DEVICE=XXX

where the XXX's stand for the name of the device driver, etc.

DEVICEHIGH

What does it do? This command is used by MS-DOS versions 5 and 6. It loads the device drivers that you have specified for the devices you have attached to your PC, into a part of memory called upper memory. Upper memory is the area between 640 K and 1 MB. Loading the device drivers in upper memory frees up a valuable part of memory called conventional memory. That's the first 640 K of memory.

How is it used? In MS-DOS version 5, you have to place DEVICEHIGH in your CONFIG.SYS file to optimize your PC. For example, to place the driver for a mouse in upper memory in the CONFIG.SYS file, insert the following line: DEVICEHIGH=C:\MOUSE.COM. Refer to Chapter 6, "Beyond Simple DOS" to learn to fine-tune your computer. In MS-DOS 6, there is a command called MEMMAKER that will automatically move drivers to the most appropriate parts of memory.

DIR

What does it do? This is a very useful and harmless DOS command. It shows the contents of any directory that you specify. If you ever want to show off to other people unfamiliar with PCs (and don't really know what to do yourself), simply type DIR and press ENTER. A whole bunch of information will scroll on the screen. Between the Ooo's and the Ahh's, you can pretend that you know what you are doing!

How is it used? At a DOS prompt if you type DIR and then press the ENTER key, it will show the contents of the drive and the directory shown at the prompt. For example, if you type DIR at the C:\>, then it will show the contents of the main directory. If you type DIR at C:\DIRNAME>, then it will show the contents of DIRNAME. If the contents scroll too fast, you can type DIR/P and press ENTER. This will show one page at a time. At the bottom of the page you'll see a line telling you to "Press any key to continue..." If you want to see more file names on the screen, but don't want to see the other details such as file size, date, time, etc., you can type DIR/W and press ENTER. This will fill the entire screen with file names.

DISKCOMP

What does it do? This command compares the contents of two floppy disks. This is particularly helpful when you make a backup copy of a program disk or other important information and want to make sure that it was copied correctly. In the new versions of DOS the DISKCOPY command is so accurate that DISKCOMP is no longer necessary.

How is it used? At The DOS prompt type the name of the drive(s) you want to compare. For example, if you only have one floppy drive and want to compare two disks, you simply type:

C:\>DISKCOMP A: A: and press ENTER.

The computer tells you to put the original disk in drive A: and press ENTER. After reading the contents of that disk, the computer will prompt you to put the other disk in the drive. Depending on disk capacity, this process may be repeated a few times.

DISKCOPY

What does it do? This popular DOS command makes an identical copy of a disk by copying the entire contents of "source" disk to a "target" disk. This is an easy way to create backup copies of your important program and data disks. The important point to remember is that the two disks need to be identical in size and capacity. For example, you cannot use this command to copy a 5-1/4" onto a 3-1/2" disk, or a 720 K onto a 1.4 MB disk.

How is it used? At the DOS prompt, if you only have one drive, type:

C:\>DISKCOPY A: A: and press ENTER.

If you have two different size floppy drives, remember that DISKCOPY can only be used with identical size disks. Therefore, you can't use DISKCOPY A: B: to copy from drive A: to drive B:. On the other hand, if both drives are the same size and capacity, you can use the above command.

DOSKEY

What does it do? This is an advanced command which lets you edit DOS command lines and also helps you create macros. Macros are sets of keystrokes or commands that can be memorized by your PC, so that it can be recalled with only one or two keystrokes. For example, if you type your name and address on all your correspondence, you can create a macro for that so you won't have to type it every time.

How is it used? Get help from a PC expert.

DOSSHELL

What does it do? This command starts the DOSSHELL which is a graphical screen that lets you activate DOS commands by using tiny pictures (called icons) rather than typing commands. It is included in MS-DOS versions 4, 5 and 6. Chapter 7, describes DOSSHELL in detail.

How is it used? Simply type:

C:\>DOSSHELL and press ENTER.

The graphical screen appears on your monitor. The easiest way to take advantage of DOSSHELL is to use a mouse. Whatever command you choose, you can simply move the pointer of your mouse on the picture of that command and click your mouse button.

DRIVPARM

What does it do? This is an advanced DOS command which you will probably not have much use for. It defines certain parameters that control the operation of various drives.

How is it used? This command is used in your CONFIG.SYS file.

ECHO

What does it do? This command can either show or hide the information in your batch programs. It's very likely that you will not use this command. Certain programs that need to have it, will install it in your AUTOEXEC.BAT file automatically.

How is it used? This command is like a light switch. It appears as a line in your AUTOEXEC.BAT file as either:

ECHO=ON, or **ECHO=OFF**.

EMM386

What does it do? This command only works with 386 and newer generation PCs. It activates or deactivates a special memory management scheme that lets your PC take advantage of memory above 640 K (called expanded memory).

How is it used? This is added to your CONFIG.SYS file as:

DEVICE=EMM386.EXE

Warning: Don't use this command while you are running Windows.

ERASE

See DEL.

EXIT

What does it do? This command lets you quit the DOS activity you are using at the time and takes you back to the program you were running before going to that DOS activity. For example, if you are running Windows and temporarily access DOS while Windows is running in the background, you can go back to Windows by typing EXIT and pressing the ENTER key.

How is it used? At the DOS prompt type:

C:\>EXIT and press ENTER.

EXPAND

What does it do? This MS-DOS 6 command decompresses a compressed file. It's a companion command to DBLSPACE. Files or directories that have been compressed by DBLSPACE can be decompressed to their original size.

How is it used? At the prompt type:

C:\>EXPAND A:\COMP.EXT C:\DIR\FILE.EXT and ENTER.

DOS will uncompress the file COMP.EXT from drive A: and place it in directory DIR as file name FILE.EXT.

FASTHELP

What does it do? This command shows a list of all MS-DOS commands and gives a summary explanation for each.

How is it used? At the DOS prompt type:

C:\>FASTHELP and press ENTER.

FASTOPEN

What does it do? This command helps improve the performance of your PC. When you work on various documents, they are each represented by a file. As you use these documents, your PC keeps opening files for you. FASTOPEN helps keep the files you use in a state of readiness, so that they open up faster.

How is it used? You no longer need to use this command.

Warning: Don't use this command while you are running Windows.

FC

What does it do? FC stands for File Compare. It compares the contents of two files and shows the differences between them.

How is it used? At the prompt type:

C:\>FC FILE1.EXT FILE2.EXT and press ENTER.

FCBS

What does it do? This command specifies the number of File Control Blocks that can be open at the same time. You don't have to worry about using it.

How is it used? This command is used in your CONFIG.SYS file.

FDISK

What does it do? This command starts the Fixed Disk program which prepares and configures your hard disk drive for the very first time. Most new generation hard disk drives are configured at the factory and using FDISK might alter their configuration.

How is it used? This is a very sensitive DOS command and it is best if you sought expert help in case you ever need to use it.

FILES

What does it do? This command helps speed up the operation of your PC by specifying the number of files that can be accessed at the same time. The higher the number of open files, the faster your PC can find information. On the other hand, each open file consumes a certain amount of memory. Therefore, the number needs to be balanced properly. Unless otherwise advised by one of your programs, you can be safe with FILES=20.

How is it used? If one does not already exist, add a line for:

   FILES=20

to your CONFIG.SYS file. In most cases a FILES line is automatically added by DOS or one of your programs during installation.

FIND

What does it do? This command searches for text in a file or a group of files.

How is it used? At the prompt type:

C:\>FIND /I "SOMETHING" C:\>DIR\FILE.EXT and ENTER.

DOS will look for "something" and ignores capitalizations, in drive C:, directory DIR, file FILE.EXT.

FOR

What does it do? This is a programming command that you'll never need to use.

How is it used? Get help from a PC expert.

FORMAT

What does it do? This command prepares a floppy disk or hard disk for use. All disks are made of magnetic materials. The surface of any disk has certain impurities which are not capable of storing information accurately. Formatting lets your PC analyze the surface of a disk and mark off the weak zones so that information may not be stored there.

How is it used? Use this command with care. When you format a disk, all information currently stored on it is erased. To format a floppy disk at the DOS prompt type FORMAT A: and press ENTER. If you want to format a floppy disk and also give it the ability to start up your PC, type:

C:\>FORMAT A:/S and press ENTER.

To format your hard disk, type:

A:\>FORMAT C:/S and press ENTER.

Formatting your hard disk will erase everything you have stored on it, therefore use it only if you know what you are doing.

GOTO

What does it do? This command directs DOS to go to a specific line in a batch file. You'll rarely ever need to use this command.

How is it used? Use this command in batch files ending with the .BAT extension.

GRAPHICS

What does it do? This is an old command carried over from the earlier versions of DOS when there was a different video technology. This command lets your printer accurately print the information that is displayed on your computer screen.

How is it used? Get help from a PC expert.

HELP

What does it do? This command explains various DOS commands. It also shows how to use those commands.

How is it used? At the DOS prompt type HELP and press ENTER. It will show a list of all the DOS commands. By choosing a command from the list, you can see an explanation for that command. You can also get help with a command by typing the name of that command, i.e.:

C:\>HELP COMMAND.EXT and press ENTER.

IF

What does it do? This is a conditional command. It lets you set conditions for certain processes to take place.

How is it used? This command is used in batch programs that end with .BAT.

INSTALL

What does it do? This command is used for loading a program into memory or transferring it from floppy disks onto your hard disk for the first time.

How is it used? Each program has it's own way of using the INSTALL command. Generally, there may be an INSTALL.EXE file on the first disk of that program. All you have to do is insert that disk into your drive and at the prompt for that drive type INSTALL and press the ENTER key.

INTERLNK

What does it do? This MS-DOS 6 command allows two computers to be connected by cable through their parallel or serial ports. This command enables the computers to share and exchange information and use each other's hard disks and printers.

How is it used? Have a PC expert set up interlink for you the first time. You can then use it by yourself afterwards.

INTERSVR

What does it do? This MS-DOS 6 command is used with INTERLNK. It starts the server when you use interlink.

How is it used? At the prompt type:

     C:\>INTERSVR and press ENTER.

KEYB

What does it do? This command starts the keyboard program which lets you configure your keyboard for various languages. If you are using your PC in English, you won't have to fool with this command.

How is it used? Get help from a PC expert.

Label

What does it do? This command is used to change, modify or delete the name of a floppy disk or hard disk. The disk name is called volume label and can be up to eleven characters long.

How is it used? At the DOS prompt if you type LABEL and press ENTER, your computer will display the current name (volume label) of your disk and give you the option to type a new one, change the existing one, or press ENTER for no name. If you want to change the name of a disk other than the one at your prompt, for example a floppy disk in drive A:, put the disk in drive A: and type:

    C:\>LABEL A: and press ENTER.

You'll be given the option to create, modify or delete the label for the disk in drive A:.

LASTDRIVE

What does it do? This command tells your PC that you have a limited number of drives. You don't necessarily have to use this command.

How is it used? In your AUTOEXEC.BAT file insert the following line:

    LASTDRIVE=Z

LH (also LOADHIGH)

What does it do? This command moves special DOS commands and drivers that are necessary for operating your PC to the upper memory area (memory between 640 Kilo Bytes and 1 Mega Bytes). By using upper memory, it helps free your valuable conventional memory (the first 640 Kilo Bytes).

How is it used? Load High is used in your AUTOEXEC.BAT file.

LOADFIX

What does it do? This is a helpful command that requires some expertise in order to use it properly. LOADFIX checks the status of your programs to make sure that they are loaded above the first 64 Kilo Bytes of conventional memory.

How is it used? Get help from a PC expert.

LOADHIGH

See LH.

MD

What does it do? This command is called Make Directory. It's used to create a directory or subdirectory. You will be using this command from time to time. A directory is like a filing cabinet with several drawers and lots of file folders in those drawers. Each drawer is like a subdirectory. You use directories and subdirectories to organize your documents and the vast amount of data that you store on your hard disk drive.

How is it used? At the DOS prompt simply type MD followed by the name of the directory that you'd like to create. The prompt should be at the drive or directory you want to create the new directory in. For example, to create a directory for your personal information, type:

C:\>MD PERSONAL and press ENTER.

This will create a directory called PERSONAL. Type:

C:\>CD\PERSONAL and press ENTER.

Your prompt will change to C:\PERSONAL>. Now you are inside the

PERSONAL directory. If you type MD LETTERS and press the ENTER key, this will create a subdirectory called LETTERS inside your PERSONAL directory. It's like creating a folder called LETTERS inside a drawer called PERSONAL.

MEM

What does it do? This command shows the status of your memory usage and availability.

How is it used? At the DOS prompt type MEM and press ENTER. To see more detail, type:

C:\>MEM/C and press ENTER.

MEMMAKER

What does it do? This MS-DOS 6 command optimizes the memory of your computer by configuring various commands, device drivers and memory resident programs in upper memory (the area between 640 Kilo Bytes and 1 Mega Bytes). MS-DOS versions prior to version 6 require you to optimize your memory usage manually or with the help of software developed by other companies.

How is it used? At the DOS prompt type:

C:\>MEMMAKER and press ENTER.

Warning: Don't use this command while you are running Windows.

MENUCOLOR

What does it do? This command lets you define the colors in the menu that appear when you start your PC. It's not the sort of thing you have to worry about.

How is it used? This command is used in your CONFIG.SYS file.

MENUDEFAULT

What does it do? This is one of those commands that you don't have to worry about using. It lets you specify the various items in your start-up menu. For most of us, the default values (those determined to apply to most of us by Microsoft) are just fine and there is no need to change them.

How is it used? This command is used in your CONFIG.SYS file.

MENUITEM

What does it do? This command lets you define various items on the start-up menu. This is another one of those commands that you'll hardly ever use.

How is it used? This command is used in your CONFIG.SYS file.

MKDIR

See MD.

MODE

What does it do? This is one of those do it all commands that specify, set up or modify various items that deal with devices attached to your PC. It's rarely used these days.

How is it used? This command can be used at the DOS prompt if you want the change to be active only while your PC is powered up. It can also be part of your AUTOEXEC.BAT file so that it becomes active every time you power up your PC.

MORE

What does it do? This is a useful command that lets you see the contents of a file one page at a time.

How is it used? There are two ways you can use this command. At the DOS prompt you can type:

C:\>MORE < FILENAME.EXT and press ENTER.

At the bottom of each page a MORE prompt appears that instructs you to press the space bar to go to the next page. Another way is to type:

C:\>TYPE FILENAME.EXT |MORE and press ENTER.

The vertical bar key "|" is generally located at the top right corner of your keyboard near the backspace key.

MOVE

What does it do? This MS-DOS 6 command makes it easy for you to move a file from one location (directory or drive) to another. You can also use this command to rename a file or a directory.

How is it used? At the prompt type:

C:\>MOVE FILE1.EXT C:\DIR1 and press ENTER.

MSAV

What does it do? This is a great MS-DOS 6 command that checks your hard disk and floppy disks for viruses. It's like having a free X-Ray to check for diseases. Computer viruses are like diseases created by a few sick computer users who spread their viruses for fun. This command looks for viruses with known characteristics. Unfortunately, new viruses are created almost daily and a clean bill of health may not always guarantee that your PC is clean. The best policy is to practice "PC Abstinence!" Be careful when you get disks or data from other people.

How is it used? At the prompt type:

> **C:\>MSAV** and press ENTER.

You can also add it to your AUTOEXEC.BAT file.

MSBACKUP

What does it do? This MS-DOS 6 command makes it easier to backup a file, group of files, directories or an entire hard disk. There is a DOS and a Windows command in this version of DOS. Depending on which type you have installed on your computer, the way it starts varies slightly. Both versions work almost the same way.

How is it used? With the DOS version, at the prompt type:

> **C:\>MSBACKUP** and press ENTER.

A special backup screen appears and you can then simply type the name of the file(s) or directory(s) that you want to backup. With the Windows version, there is a tiny picture (icon) for backup. All you have to do is move your mouse pointer to that drive and click your mouse button.

MSCDEX

What does it do? This command is part of MS-DOS versions 5 and 6. It makes your PC capable of using a CD-ROM drive.

How is it used? This command is used as part of your CD-ROM drive installation process. The software drivers that come with your CD-ROM drive will automatically install everything for you.

Warning: Don't use this command while you are running Windows.

MSD

What does it do? This MS-DOS 6 command activates the Microsoft Diagnostics program. It's a handy program which analyzes your computer system and gives you a detailed report.

How is it used? At the DOS prompt type:

      C:\>MSD and press ENTER.

NLSFUNC

What does it do? This is a special command which you probably don't need to use. It lets you configure your PC to support the unique requirements of different languages other than US English.

How is it used? Get help from a PC expert.

Warning: Don't use this command while you are running Windows.

NUMLOCK

What does it do? This command will rarely be used, but it is there if you need it. NUMLOCK is a key on your keyboard. It controls the function of number keys on the right side of your keyboard. Those number keys have dual functions. Normally, when you power up your PC, it activates the NUMLOCK key and those number keys become active. This command allows you to over-ride that.

How is it used? This command is used in your CONFIG.SYS file.

PATH

What does it do? This command lets your computer find files from within other directories. Most programs automatically make themselves part of the PATH command. If one doesn't already exist on your PC, they even create one. This is a very useful command.

How is it used? This command is used in your AUTOEXEC.BAT file. At the DOS prompt if you type:

C:\>TYPE AUTOEXEC.BAT and press ENTER.

You'll see the contents of your AUTOEXEC.BAT file. Your PATH should look something like this:

PATH=C:\; C:\DOS; C:\PROGRAM1; C:\PROGRAM2;.

If you want to change your PATH, at the DOS prompt type EDIT AUTOEXEC.BAT and press ENTER. The contents of your AUTOEXEC.BAT file will appear on the screen. Move the cursor (blinking line) to the line where PATH is located and then type in your changes. When you are done, press the ALT key, then press F and a menu drops down. Move the highlight down to EXIT and press ENTER.

PAUSE

What does it do? This command causes a temporary delay in the processing of a program. At the bottom of the screen it tells you to press any key to continue processing your program. This is not something that you'll need to use.

How is it used? This is used inside batch programs that end with .BAT.

POWER

What does it do? This MS-DOS 6 command controls the power usage in battery operated portable computers. It's used to turn the power management feature on or off. It's also used to adjust the power conservation level.

Additionally, it shows the power management status.

How is it used? Add a new line to your CONFIG.SYS file:

DEVICE=C:\DOS\POWER.EXE

PRINT

What does it do? This is an old DOS command that is rarely used anymore. It is used to print whatever file you tell your PC to print. Current programs all have a built-in print feature that eliminates the need to use this DOS command.

How is it used? At the DOS prompt type:

C:\>PRINT FILENAME.EXT and press ENTER.

PROMPT

What does it do? This command changes the way the DOS prompt appears on your screen. DOS versions 4, 5 and 6 automatically setup the prompt to show the name of the directory that you are currently in. This is really all you need and other modifications of prompt are unnecessary.

How is it used? This command is used in your AUTOEXEC.BAT file. It's automatically activated when you power up or reset your PC.

QBASIC

What does it do? This is the programming language that made the "NERDS" famous! QBASIC is a command that starts the QBASIC program. Chances are that you'll never have to use this command.

How is it used? At the DOS prompt type QBASIC and press ENTER.

RD

What does it do? This command is used for deleting a directory. It stands for Remove Directory. You'll be using this command from time-to-time. It's important to note that you can't delete a directory that is not empty. DELTREE command introduced in MS-DOS 6 can delete a directory and all it's contents in one step.

How is it used? At the DOS prompt type:

C:\>RD DIRNAME and press ENTER.

If the directory called DIRNAME is empty, it will be removed from your disk. If it's not empty, you need to use CD\DIRNAME to get into that directory and delete all it's contents before you can remove the directory.

REM

What does it do? This is called the Remark command. It lets you add your remarks to batch files (those ending with .BAT) and the CONFIG.SYS file. You can also deactivate a command inside those batch files and prevent it from being executed.

How is it used? At the DOS prompt type:

C:\>EDIT FILENAME.EXT and press ENTER.

You'll see the contents of that file.

You can type REM followed by a space at the beginning of the line you'd like to deactivate or add a remark to.

REN (also RENAME)

What does it do? This is called the Rename command. It's used to change the name of a file. For example, you can rename FILENAME.EXT to FILENAME.OLD. Remember that you can't change the name of a file to one that already exists.

How is it used? At the DOS prompt type:

C:\>REN FILE1.EXT FILE2.EXT and press ENTER.

RENAME

See REN.

REPLACE

What does it do? This command is used to replace a file with another file with the same name. It's generally used for updating programs on your hard disk.

How is it used? Follow the instructions that came with your program update.

RESTORE

What does it do? This command is used in conjunction with the backup command. It places a file or files that were backed up on floppy disks earlier, back on the hard disk. Remember that the Restore command only works on a PC using the same version of DOS as was used to create the backup disk(s).

How is it used? At the DOS prompt type:

C:\>RESTORE A:FILENAME.EXT and press ENTER.

If you want to restore everything that is on floppy disks, then type:

C:\>RESTORE A:*.* and press ENTER.

RMDIR

See RD.

SET

What does it do? This is a programming command that establishes certain criteria for your PC. It's used in your AUTOEXEC.BAT file. If you type it at the prompt, it gives you a list of what has already been set.

How is it used? Add a line to your AUTOEXEC.BAT file stating that you have set up a temporary directory called TEMP.

SET TEMP=C:\TEMP

SETVER

What does it do? This command tells programs that were designed specially for earlier versions of DOS, what version to relate to.

How is it used? It is used in your AUTOEXEC.BAT file.

SHARE

What does it do? This command starts the share program. Share allows your files to be shared by various programs at the same time. It also locks access to your files when more than one program attempts to change the file at the same time.

How is it used? It's used in your AUTOEXEC.BAT file.

SHIFT

What does it do? This is one of those rarely needed commands which is used to change the position of certain parameters in batch files that end with .BAT.

How is it used? This command is used in batch files or programs.

SMARTDRV

What does it do? This command is used in DOS versions 5 and 6. It creates what is called a disk cache. The disk cache acts as a buffer between your hard disk and your microprocessor. Your hard disk is slower than the microprocessor in your PC. A disk cache takes a certain portion of your computer memory called extended memory (those above 640 Kilo Bytes), and uses it as a holding area. It keeps track of the information that goes into and out of your hard disk. A copy of the most frequently used information is held in cache memory for instant access by your microprocessor.

How is it used? This command is used in your AUTOEXEC.BAT file.

Warning: Don't use this command while you are running Windows.

SORT

What does it do? This command is used for sorting information. Sorting can be done alphabetically, by date, etc.

How is it used? At the prompt type:

>   **C:\>SORT C:\DIR1** and press ENTER.

DOS will sort the files in directory DIR1 alphabetically, from A to Z.

STACKS

What does it do? This is a technical DOS command that controls the way your computer interprets electronics signals. It's not something you'll be using.

How is it used? This command is used in your CONFIG.SYS file.

SUBMENU

What does it do? A menu in PC lingo is somewhat similar to a menu in a restaurant. It's a selection of items or activities on your screen. When you select an item, a series of predefined activities take place. Menus are designed to make it easier for you to use your PC. A submenu is a menu which is activated when you select an item on a main menu. You really don't have much use for this command.

How is it used? This command is used in your CONFIG.SYS file.

SUBST

What does it do? This is called the Substitute command. It substitutes a directory for a drive name and makes DOS think that it is dealing with a drive. It's not something you'll have to worry about.

How is it used? Get help from a PC expert.

Warning: Don't use this command while you are running Windows.

SYS

What does it do? This is a very important command. Your PC cannot operate without it. Unlike COMMAND.COM, this command does not appear as a visible file. This is not the type of command that you have anything to do with.

How is it used? When you format a disk, if you type:

C:\>FORMAT /S and press ENTER.

It will prepare the disk for use and place the SYS command as well as the COMMAND.COM on it.

TIME

What does it do? This command shows the time kept by the clock inside your PC.

How is it used? This command can be used either in your AUTOEXEC.BAT file or typed at the DOS prompt. Normally, you don't need to use it unless you want to know the time kept by your PC.

TREE

What does it do? This command shows the structure of a directory like the branches of a tree. Each subdirectory is like a branch off of a larger branch.

How is it used? At the prompt type:

C:\>TREE C:\ /F and press ENTER.

This will show a tree structure of your root directory and all the files.

TYPE

What does it do? This is a useful command if you want to see the contents of a file. The only exceptions are program files, those with .COM and .EXE extensions.

How is it used? At the DOS prompt type:

C:\>TYPE FILENAME.EXT and press ENTER.

If your file is longer than one page, the contents will scroll up on your screen. To make it show one page at a time, type:

C:\>TYPE FILENAME.EXT |MORE and press ENTER.

UNDELETE

What does it do? This command is used with MS-DOS versions 5 and 6. It helps you recover a file that you may have accidentally deleted. It's important to know that when you delete a file, it is not immediately erased from you disk. Instead, DOS makes the location available for other files to be stored. Therefore, if you decide to recover a deleted file, try to do it as soon as possible. Before anything else is written over it.

How is it used? At the DOS prompt type:

     C:\\>UNDELETE FILENAME.EXT and press ENTER.

UNFORMAT

What does it do? This command is used to recover what you may have erased from a disk by formatting it. It needs to be done before you store anything on that disk.

How is it used? At the DOS prompt type:

     C:\\>UNFORMAT A: and press ENTER.

This will return the disk in drive A: to the condition before it was formatted.

VER

What does it do? This shows the DOS version in your PC. You use it only if you need to know what version of DOS is running in your PC.

How is it used? At the DOS prompt type:

     C:\\>VER and press ENTER.

If you want your PC to display the DOS version every time it is powered up, you can add a line to your AUTOEXEC.BAT file with VER.

Warning: Don't use this command while you are running Windows.

VERIFY

What does it do? This command makes sure that the information you are storing on your disk is written correctly. It was somewhat useful with the earlier versions of DOS, however newer versions of DOS are very accurate and this command is unnecessary.

How is it used? It is used in your CONFIG.SYS file as:

VERIFY=ON.

VOL

What does it do? This command simply shows the name of the disk and serial number (volume label), if it has any.

How is it used? At the DOS prompt type: VOL and press ENTER.

VSAFE

What does it do? This is a virus detection command that when activated, constantly monitors your PC for viruses. If it finds a virus, it will pop a warning on your screen immediately.

How is it used? You can either type this command at the prompt or add it to your AUTOEXEC.BAT file.

XCOPY

What does it do? This is a more powerful command than the simple COPY. It copies files, subdirectories and directories.

How is it used? At the DOS prompt type:

C:\>XCOPY A:\DIRNAME C: and press ENTER.

Chapter 9. DOS Error Messages

As sure as night turns into day, just when you think that you understand the plain English meaning of what DOS is all about, you are confronted with pesky error messages. These are not simple messages, mind you! They are cryptic! When you see "Abort, Retry, Ignore;" or "Bad or missing command interpreter," you'd probably want to smash everything in sight.

This chapter is exactly what the Doctor ordered! You don't have to read this chapter now if you don't want to. Just browse through it to know what's in it. When you get stuck with an error message and don't know what to do, simply grab this book, get to this chapter and alphabetically locate the error message. Viola! It's as simple as ABC.

As you look for the answer to an error message, you may be wondering why the messages are so cryptic. The reason is that they try to conserve memory and disk space. They assume that after a few times you'll know what the message means.

Abort, Retry, Ignore

What caused the problem? You see this message more than any other. Generally, it happens when you tell your PC to do something and it realizes that you don't have all your ducks in a row! You often see another message before this line. For example, it may tell you that it can't read from drive A: and then advises you to abort what you told it to do, retry your command again, or simply ignore it and it may work. Most often, if you change directory, say from your hard disk to drive A: and there is no disk in that drive or the drive door is open, you'll get this message.

How do I solve it? If your problem is because there is no disk in the drive, then simply put a disk in there and close the door. If it is because the door was open, then close it. When you correct the cause of the message you can type "R" for retry. If what you do to correct the problem still doesn't work, then press "A" to abort your command. There is a danger in pressing "I" for ignore because it may compound your problems. Try not to use ignore if you are not sure of what you are doing.

Access denied

What caused the problem? Some files are set up with special protection as a "read-only" file. That means you can't change or delete that file. If you attempt to rename, write to, or delete that file you will get this message.

How do I solve it? Unless you're itching to do something to that file, leave it alone. Generally when a file is protected, there is a good reason for it.

Bad command or file name

What caused the problem? You just told DOS to execute a command or a file to fetch and it has no earthly idea what you're talking about.

How do I solve it? Your PC can't read your mind (yet!), so if you told it to do something but didn't spell it right, or asked for something that doesn't exist, then your PC simply tells you that it doesn't understand what you want. First check your spelling. Then make sure what you told it to do is something your PC is supposed to do. Also make sure that the file you are referring to is in the same directory that you are operating from.

Bad or missing command interpreter

What caused the problem? DOS can't find a file called COMMAND.COM. This is one of the important DOS files that contain a whole bunch of instructions for your PC. It may have been either accidentally erased from your hard disk, or you had started your computer with a floppy disk in drive A: and later removed the disk before you got done with what you were doing.

How do I solve it? If you had started your PC with a floppy and removed the disk before you were done, the only way out is to reset your PC by pressing CTRL-ALT-DEL keys together. If on the other hand, COMMAND.COM has been deleted from your hard disk, you need to put it back on. Find your DOS boot disk (usually disk #1) and place it drive A:, then close the drive door. Now, press CTRL-ALT-DEL keys together to reset your computer. This time your PC is going to show an A:\>. Type: COPY COMMAND.COM C: and press ENTER. This way you'll copy the file from drive A: onto drive C:.

Cannot find a hard disk on your computer

What caused the problem? Well, you either don't have a hard disk, your hard disk is not working, or the one that you have is not recognized by MS-DOS 6. Hopefully, this will be the last time you'll buy a hard disk in a dark alley from a suspicious character for $10!

How do I solve it? If you don't have a hard disk, you have a serious problem. If you have a hard disk and it's not working, then you have a much more serious problem. If MS-DOS 6 does not recognize your hard disk, then you need to call Microsoft Product Support Services at (206) 646-5104.

Check mouse compatibility list

What caused the problem? This message appears only if MS-DOS 6 notices a problem with your mouse the first time you start the DOS Shell. The vast majority of mice sold these days are Microsoft Mouse compatible, therefore it is rare to find a problem.

How do I solve it? On the same screen DOS will show the mouse driver version on your computer. Check your DOS manual for the list of compatible mouse versions. If your mouse is on that list, then choose the <Use Mouse Anyway> option. If your mouse driver is incompatible, choose <Disable Mouse>. You need to call your mouse manufacturer for their latest mouse driver program.

Code page not prepared for all devices

What caused the problem? If you receive this message, either you are over your head or you know what you are doing! If you don't know what you are doing, then you are messing with character sets. which is too advanced for you. If you know what you are doing, then refer to the MS-DOS manual.

How do I solve it? Just get out of there and go to your other programs.

Code page operation not supported on this device

What caused the problem? See the preceding message!

How do I solve it? See the preceding message.

Current drive is no longer valid

What caused the problem? If you try to tell your PC to do something with a disk drive, but there is no disk in that drive, you end up getting this message.

How do I solve it? Simply put a disk in that drive and you are back on track.

Device error during prepare

What caused the problem? This is a little too advanced for the level of this book. If you came up with this accidentally, get out of it quickly.

How do I solve it? You have specified too many character sets. Reduce the number and proceed.

Directory not empty

What caused the problem? You are trying to get rid of a directory which still has one or more files or subdirectories in it.

How do I solve it? Change directory to the one you want to delete. Check the contents by typing: DIR and pressing ENTER. If there is a file other than two lines, one with a single dot and the other with two dots, try to delete it. If there is a subdirectory there, you need to delete it to empty your other directory.

Disk boot failure

What caused the problem? This may happen if for some reason your hard disk drive is not functioning properly or is not working at all.

How do I solve it? Hopefully, this may be a temporary glitch. Try to reset your computer by pressing CTRL-ALT-DEL keys together. If that doesn't work, turn your PC off and wait a few minutes before restarting it. If you get the same message, then your hard disk may need to be checked by a professional.

Disk error reading drive x

What caused the problem? DOS is trying to tell you that it's having a problem reading from your drive x. This could be due to a number of factors. One likely scenario is that the information you want is on a bad part of the drive.

How do I solve it? Tell your drive to read another file. If you still get the same message, then you may have a serious problem. If the problem is with a floppy disk, see if you can copy it's files to another drive one by one. If the problem is with your hard disk, you can either call a professional for help or buy one of those hard disk utility programs that analyze and correct most hard disk problems. They don't guarantee that they can fix all hard disk problems, but they are pretty successful with most.

DMA buffer size too small

What caused the problem? This problem may only occur if you are trying to use the MS-DOS 6 backup program and you also have Windows installed on your PC. If you don't have enough memory, this message may appear on your screen.

How do I solve it? This is a little more advanced than the level of this book, therefore refer to your MS-DOS 6 and Windows manuals for instructions on how to increase your DMA buffer size.

Duplicate file name or file not found

What caused the problem? This may happen when you try to rename a file. If the new name that you specify already exists, or the name of the file that you want to rename is not spelled right, this message pops on your screen.

How do I solve it? If the name already exists, simply try another name. If you didn't spell the file name correctly, try again.

EMS page frame not found

What caused the problem? This may happen if you run a program that needs expanded memory and you have not allocated any. Expanded memory is a part of your computer memory that can be turned off when you first setup your PC. Few programs need to use it. Therefore, in most cases it is turned off to save memory for other important tasks.

How do I solve it? Go to your DOS prompt and type: MEMMAKER to activate the MS-DOS 6 memory management program. When the setup screen is displayed choose "YES" for expanded memory.

Expanded memory unavailable

What caused the problem? See the previous message.

How do I solve it? See above.

Failure to access code page font file

What caused the problem? This is an advanced error message that has to do with character sets. If you stumbled upon this by mistake, get out real fast. If you got here knowingly, check your DOS manual.

How do I solve it? Check your DOS manual, the solution is too advanced for this book.

File allocation table bad on drive x

What caused the problem? This is like losing all the street signs in a city! The file allocation table (FAT), is like a detailed map that keeps track of where everything is on your hard disk. If the table is damaged for some reason, your hard disk will not store or retrieve anything.

How do I solve it? This is a serious problem. You can either get professional help, or use a hard disk utility program to restore your FAT.

File cannot be copied onto itself

What caused the problem? You probably made a spelling mistake or forgot to complete the COPY command. If you tell DOS to copy a file to another file with the same name, or if you simply type: COPY FILENAME.EXT and press ENTER, you'll get this message.

How do I solve it? Correct your spelling or complete the copy command by specifying a file name to copy to.

File creation error

What caused the problem? This means that DOS can't create your file. One possibility is that your disk is full and doesn't have enough room for this file. The other possibility is that your drive is losing it's ability to write a file to the disk.

How do I solve it? Check the size of the file and the remaining capacity of your disk.

File not found

What caused the problem? Your PC is trying to tell you that it can't find the file that you want it to get. Either you didn't spell the file name correctly, or the file is not where you told your PC to look for.

How do I solve it? Check your spelling to make sure it's correct. If your spelling is correct, then make sure that you are in the proper directory.

File was destroyed by virus

What caused the problem? This MS-DOS 6 message pops up if the virus detection program detects that a virus has destroyed a file. In this case it is recommended to remove the file to avoid further corruption of your other files.

How do I solve it? If the corrupted file is important, copy it to a floppy disk and then delete it from your hard disk. Afterwards you may use a more sophisticated virus program or a file recovery program to restore that file.

Font file contents invalid

What caused the problem? This is an advanced problem that comes up if you mess with your character set. It is beyond the level of this book and you should consult your DOS manual.

How do I solve it? See your DOS manual.

General failure reading drive x

What caused the problem? This is a catch-all message that covers a lot of problems like not having a disk in the floppy drive, leaving the drive door open, trying to read from an unformatted disk, the disk is damaged or trying to use the wrong type of disk in the drive.

How do I solve it? The solutions to this problem are quite simple. Make sure you have a disk in the drive when you want to use that drive. Make sure that the door is closed when there is a disk in the drive. Don't try to read from or write to an unformatted disk. Don't use high density disks in low density drives.

Incompatible hard disk or device driver

What caused the problem? This MS-DOS 6 error message may come up during setup if your hard disk is not on the compatible list of Microsoft.

How do I solve it? This is pretty advanced stuff and may require a change of your hard disk partition. Some drives are partitioned at the factory and should not be changed by the user. The safest course is to contact your PC manufacturer for help.

Incompatible partition

What caused the problem? This MS-DOS 6 error message only comes up during setup if you have a partition by the Speedstor Bootall program.

How do I solve it? Check your MS-DOS 6 manual for installing DOS manually on your hard disk.

Incompatible primary DOS partition

What caused the problem? This MS-DOS 6 error message only comes up if your hard disk is not compatible with the Microsoft list. The main problem is caused by the hard disk partition.

How do I solve it? Don't mess with your hard disk partition. Get help from your PC manufacturer.

Insufficient disk space

What caused the problem? Bet you know what this means! You are trying to put more on the disk than it has room for.

How do I solve it? If the problem is with a floppy disk, simply get another disk. If the problem is with your hard disk, then you should examine all the files on your hard disk and start deleting old data files you don't need and delete programs you don't use frequently.

Insufficient memory

What caused the problem? This means that you have some memory resident programs that collectively leave little memory for your other programs.

How do I solve it? Use MEM/C to see a list of programs that consume your memory. You need to delete some of the less frequently used programs from your AUTOEXEC.BAT or CONFIG.SYS files.

Invalid code page

What caused the problem? You get this message if you incorrectly try to define the characters on your keyboard for a foreign language like French, Spanish. German, etc.

How do I solve it? This is an advanced topic that most of you will not run into. Get help from a PC expert.

Invalid directory

What caused the problem? You probably spelled a directory name incorrectly or specified a non-existent directory name. Another possibility may be your incorrect use of slash "/" versus backslash "\." Remember that when you change directories by using the CD command, you have to use the backslash. For example: CD\DIRNAME and press ENTER.

How do I solve it? Check your spelling and the backslash. If none of them is a problem, make sure that the directory name that you specified actually exists.

Invalid drive specification

What caused the problem? You don't need this book to tell you what this message means! Your PC is trying to tell you that the drive you specified for it to do something with, does not exist. For example, if you only have one floppy drive called A:, and you tell your PC to do something with drive B:, it will tell you to go fly a kite!

How do I solve it? Check your typing and make sure that you are specifying a drive that already exists on your PC.

Invalid file name or file not found

What caused the problem? You just told your PC to do something with a file and your PC is telling you that it either can't find the file or the name is not valid. You may have misspelled the file name or used an illegal character in the name. This happens if you tried to use the REN command. Another possibility is that you were trying to use the TYPE command, but in the file name you used the wild card "*".

How do I solve it? Make sure that the file name is spelled correctly. If you are trying to rename a file, use the letters of the alphabet A through Z, and the digits 0 through 9. If you are trying to see the contents of the file by using the TYPE command, you need to spell out the full name of the file.

Invalid media, track 0 bad or unusable

What caused the problem? You are trying to put five pounds of candy in a three pound bag! You are trying to format a disk in a drive with a different capacity. For example, you may be trying to format a 720 K floppy disk in a 1.4 MB drive without using the correct command.

How do I solve it? If you are trying to format a 360 K floppy disk in a high density, 1.2 MB drive, use the FORMAT A: /F:360 command. If you are using a DOS version prior to 4, you need to use FORMAT A: /4. If you are trying to format a 720 K floppy disk in a high density 1.4 MB drive use the FORMAT A: /F:720 command. For DOS versions prior to 4, use FORMAT A: /N:9/ T:80.

Invalid number of parameters

What caused the problem? DOS is trying to tell you that it can't understand the command that you just typed. It may be misspelled or may have too many characters.

How do I solve it? Check the command to make sure that it's spelled correctly.

Invalid parameter

What caused the problem? See the previous message.

How do I solve it? Check the command.

Invalid path

What caused the problem? Several mistakes may have led to this message: you may have misspelled a directory name or a path to a directory, or you may have tried to remove the directory that you were in by using the RD command.

How do I solve it? Check your spelling of the directory name and the path. Make sure that you are not inside a directory that you are trying to remove.

Invalid Signature

What caused the problem? Your PC is not trying to tell you that it doesn't recognize your signature! This MS-DOS 6 message is trying to tell you that a virus has been detected and it's identifying characters are not in the current version of VSAFE that came with your DOS.

How do I solve it? Microsoft encourages you to purchase their updated virus detection program.

Invalid switch

What caused the problem? You may have mistyped a command option which is a slash followed by a letter.

How do I solve it? Type the command again, but this time ask for DOS help to figure out what to use. If for example you get this message with the COPY command, with MS-DOS 5 and 6, type HELP COPY. With DOS 4, type COPY /?.

Non-system disk or disk error

What caused the problem? When you started your computer, you had a disk in your floppy drive A:, and that disk did not have the boot part of DOS.

How do I solve it? Simply take the disk out or just open the floppy drive door and then press the SHIFT key on your keyboard to restart your PC.

Not enough space to install MS-DOS

What caused the problem? This MS-DOS 6 command is trying to tell you during setup that it can't install DOS on your hard disk because there is not enough space left.

How do I solve it? Exit setup by pressing the F3 key twice. Examine your hard disk to see if you can delete some unnecessary files to make about 5 MB available.

Not enough space to install selected·programs

What caused the problem? This MS-DOS 6 command is trying to tell you that it doesn't find enough space on your hard disk to install all the programs that you want.

How do I solve it? Refer to the previous message.

Not ready reading drive x

What caused the problem? You tried to tell your PC to do something with one of your floppy drives and it realized that either there was no disk in the drive or the drive door was not closed.

How do I solve it? Either put a disk in the drive or close the door.

Parity error

What caused the problem? This is bad hardware news. It means that when your PC performed it's self-diagnostics when it started, it noticed a problem with one or more of your memory chips.

How do I solve it? If the message appears just once, simply reset your computer and hope that it won't show up again. If it shows up repeatedly, then you may have a bad memory chip or one of the chips or chip modules may not be seated properly. Check Chapter 12 regarding opening up your PC. After opening up your PC, touch the metallic power supply to ground yourself and then gently press the chips into their sockets.

Program is trying to modify memory

What caused the problem? This MS-DOS 6 message is trying to warn you that a virus is trying to mess things up royally.

How do I solve it? Run MSAV to remove the virus.

Program is trying to stay resident in memory

What caused the problem? This MS-DOS 6 message is trying to warn you that it has noticed another program trying to hang around in your memory. It could be a virus.

How do I solve it? If you know that another memory resident program is supposed to be there, just choose the continue option. Otherwise, run the MSAV program to get the virus out.

Program is trying to write to disk

What caused the problem? This MS-DOS 6 message tells you that a program is trying to write to your hard disk. This message appears only if you have activated the virus detection program to warn you of any program trying to write to your disk.

How do I solve it? If the program that's trying to write to your hard disk is supposed to do that, press continue. Otherwise press stop and then run MSAV to detect and remove the virus.

Resident programs were loaded after VSAFE

What caused the problem? This MS-DOS 6 message appears if you try to remove the virus detection VSAFE program from your hard disk and it notices that you had installed some other memory resident programs after VSAFE. When you install VSAFE on your PC, there is a sequence that you are supposed to follow. When you decide to delete any memory resident program including VSAFE from your hard disk you are supposed to follow the reverse of that sequence.

How do I solve it? While the VSAFE error message is on your screen, choose the stop button to leave it active in your memory. Now, you can remove the other memory resident programs. Each program has it's own way of being removed from memory. Check the user manual for each program. If all else fails, at the DOS prompt type: EDIT AUTOEXEC.BAT and press ENTER.

Now, you can deactivate the start-up commands for those memory resident programs by typing REM followed by space before each line relating to those memory resident programs.

Root directory contains DOS files

What caused the problem? This MS-DOS 6 message may appear on your screen if you are upgrading to MS-DOS 6 from an older version and DOS detects that some of your old DOS files are in your main or root directory. This may only have happened if a novice had setup your old DOS for you. Normally, DOS is supposed to be in a directory by itself. DOS versions 4 and 5 create their own directory automatically. The new DOS needs to make sure that all the old DOS files are clearly tucked away before it will install itself.

How do I solve it? You need to create a start-up disk by using the FORMAT A:/S command. Now, you have to compare the list of new DOS files with those old DOS files already in the root directory of your hard disk. Type: DIR C:\>ROOT.TXT and press ENTER. This will create a file with a list of all the files in your root directory. Now make sure that your printer is on, type: PRINT ROOT.TXT and press ENTER. This will print a list of the files in your root directory. Place the Setup Disk #1 from MS-DOS 6 in your drive A: (or B:) and type EDIT A:\PACKING.LST and press ENTER. This will show you a list of all the files in each disk. Compare it with the list you just printed. Mark all the files with similar names (could be different extensions). Now, copy the files that you just marked, from your hard disk to the floppy disk and delete those files from your root directory.

This is not the correct disk

What caused the problem? This MS-DOS 6 message pops up during the upgrade setup. It's trying to tell you that the uninstall disk you just inserted in the floppy drive is not unformatted.

How do I solve it? Take the disk out and replace it with an unformatted disk then press the Shift key.

Too many primary partitions

What caused the problem? This MS-DOS 6 message appears if you are trying to upgrade to version 6 and it detects that you have too many partitions on your hard disk. This problem is a little too advanced for you to solve.

How do I solve it? Get professional help.

Virus found

What caused the problem? Guess what? MS-DOS 6 virus detection software has found a virus and is warning you to do something. You have four choices: Clean, Continue, Stop, or Delete.

How do I solve it? Choose "Clean" to have MSAV get the virus out of your program file.

Write protect

What caused the problem? You just tried to copy a file to, or change it on a floppy disk that has been write-protected. You write-protect disks to make sure that they can't be deleted or changed inadvertently. On 3-1/2" disks this is done by moving a little tab in the corner opening. On 5-1/4" disks you have to put a special sticker on the corner notch.

How do I solve it? If you really intend to write to that disk or change it's contents, simply remove the write-protection from the disk. On 3-1/2" disks move the tab to close the little opening. On 5-1/4" disks remove the little tape from the corner notch.

Your computer uses a disk compression program

What caused the problem? This MS-DOS 6 message appears during the installation of MS-DOS 6 DoubleSpace setup. It is trying to tell you that it needs more space to install itself. If you get this message and your PC stops working, you are in deep trouble, call Microsoft Product Support Services at (206) 646-5104. Otherwise, follow the instructions below.

How do I solve it? Exit setup by pressing F3 key twice. Review all your files and see if you can delete some that are not necessary to keep on your hard disk. After you open up some more space, run setup again.

Your computer uses password protection

What caused the problem? This MS-DOS 6 message means that DOS setup has detected a password protection scheme on your PC and wants you to disable it before it can proceed with installing your DOS upgrade.

How do I solve it? Exit setup by pressing the F3 key twice. Remove your password protection and run setup again.

Chapter 10. Troubleshooting Guide

This chapter will save your day when you are stuck and don't know what to do. All you have to do now is to become a little familiar with the problems and the solutions described here. This is a reference chapter and you don't have to memorize it. Just learn how to look up the solutions fast!

The rule of thumb is that when you are in trouble, always check the most obvious things:

● Are all the cables connected properly?

● Is the power switch turned on for all the parts?

● Did you change anything in the programs that control your PC?

● Did you add any new parts or programs?

Added a new part and now the PC won't start

Generally there are two types of parts that you can add to your PC. Those that you attach to the outside of your computer or those that you place inside it. If the part you added was attached to the outside of your PC, you need to double check the cables. If it was placed inside your PC, then you have to check several things in addition to the cable connections.

☞   Make sure that the board is properly inserted and seated inside the opening.

☞   Try to start your PC with a DOS floppy disk and see if it works.

☞   Take the part out and see if your PC will work without it. If you have MS-DOS 6, run MSD (Microsoft Diagnostic) or any other diagnostic utility to see a list of what is being used.

PCs are becoming more sophisticated every day. We keep adding more parts to do different things and increase the possibility of conflicts between these parts. Your PC communicates with various parts through special electronic channels. Just like a TV station, each part can occupy only one channel. If you add parts that are set at the factory for the same channel, then your PC will be confused and may refuse to work altogether. The solution is often simple. Almost all parts have settings that you can change to use an available channel. There are some important terms you should know as you try to correct this problem:

> Device Driver: is a mini program that is unique to each part or function in your PC. It tells your PC about the specific characteristics of that part and how your PC should work with it. Your printer, mouse, CD-ROM drive, etc. each have their own device drivers. Even the DOS memory management program called EMM386 has it's own device driver.

> DMA Channel: is a communications channel used for relaying signals between your PC and various parts.

> Interrupt: is the way your PC and various parts time their interactions. Inside your PC is a tiny crystal that beats millions of times per second. Every part in your PC is deigned to respond to a specific beat of that crystal. It's almost like the teacher who asks questions from students alphabetically based on their last names. When everybody has been asked a question, the teacher starts from the beginning again. This way every student knows exactly when a question is going to be asked from him/her.

Sometimes when you add a part to your PC, the factory setting on that part may be using the same DMA or interrupt as another part in your PC. In order to eliminate the conflict, you need to know which channels are currently used and by which devices. Once you run MSD or another diagnostic utility program, you can tinker with the part you just added. If you still have a problem or discover that the new part only gives you a few options and those are all taken by more important parts in your PC, you need to call the part manufacturer or the place of purchase.

Can't copy a file

If you have a problem copying a file, there can be several reasons:

☞ The disk you are trying to copy to may not have enough space and you get an error message. In this case either use a different disk or open some space on your disk by deleting some unnecessary files.

☞ You may be trying to copy a file to another file in the same place and with the same name. Simply change the new name.

☞ You may be trying to copy a file to a disk that is write-protected. The solution is simple. Remove the write-protection if you really want to copy that file onto that disk. If your disk is 3-1/2", move the small tab in the corner to cover the little opening. If your disk is 5-1/4", remove the tape that is covering the notch on a corner of the disk.

Can't delete a directory

Deleting a directory requires a little more care than deleting a file. There are two ways to create a directory. Either a program that you've installed has created a directory or you have created the directory to store a bunch of files in it. Either way, the directory may contain important information. Make sure that you will not need the contents of the directory. If you really want to delete that directory, there are a couple of situations that may have caused you a problem:

☞ If the directory is not empty, it can't be deleted. Look inside the directory by using CD\DIRNAME and then use DIR to see if it's empty. If it's empty, it should only have a dot "." and two dots "..". MS-DOS 6 has a simple command called DELTREE, that deletes a directory and all subdirectories inside it.

☞   You may have misspelled the directory name or did not type the path correctly. Retype everything.

Can't delete a file

☞   Check your spelling and make sure that you don't have blank spaces in the name.

☞   The file you are trying to delete may be designated as a read-only file. This means that either you or someone else has already gone through the trouble of protecting that file. It may be important!

Can't find a file

☞   The file may be tucked away in a directory somewhere. At the DOS prompt type: .

C:\>DIR\LOSTFILE.EXT /S and press ENTER.

With this command DOS will search your hard disk for the LOSTFILE.EXT and tell you in which directory it is located.

☞   You may have already deleted that file and it no longer exists.

Can't find a program

When you install a program, you go through an elaborate process of creating a directory, even some subdirectories, and a whole bunch of files. Losing a program is hard to do because there is so much stuff involved. If you delete a program, you will generally remember that. So, if you can't find a program, it's probably because of something really simple:

☞   Check your typing. Make sure the name is spelled right, spaces are where they should be, colons, slashes and backslashes are correct.

☞   Make sure that you are in the correct directory. If you normally start the program from the root (main) directory, make sure that your prompt looks like: C:\>.

☞   Check your AUTOEXEC.BAT file to make sure that the path to that program has not been changed. Your path should include the name of that directory:

PATH=C:\; C:\DOS; C:\MYPROG;

Can't restore old backed up file

Older versions of DOS, prior to MS-DOS 6 required that you restore a backed up file with the same version of DOS that you created the backup. MS-DOS 6 can restore a file backed up by an earlier version of DOS. If you have MS-DOS 6, refer to Chapter 5 to restore the file.

If you have DOS versions prior to 6, simply boot up using a floppy disk with the version of DOS used for backup, then insert the backed-up floppy disk in drive A: and type:

RESTORE A: C:*.* /S and press ENTER.

Delete at your own risk

Oops! You just deleted a file or used the *.* to delete all the files in a directory. Using the delete command is easy. Although DOS will ask you if you want it to delete a file or files with a yes and no (Y/N) answer, many people say yes before thinking about the consequences. Fortunately, there is an undelete command with DOS that will let you recover a file or files before it's too late.

☞   Make sure that you undelete your file(s) before you start saving other files. The new files may write over the old ones, making recovery nearly impossible.

DOS Shell won't start

This may be caused because your PC was given the wrong information about your video during setup, or the files containing information about your video were damaged somehow. In this case you need to re-install the DOS Shell.

☞   Make a copy of your DOSSHELL.INI file for backup. Simply give it a different name such as DOSSHELL.OLD. Now you need to copy your MS-DOS files from the DOS disks onto your hard disk. Place the setup disk in drive A: and type:

A:SETUP/Q and press ENTER.

After setup completes copying the files to your hard disk, copy your DOSSHELL.OLD back onto DOSSHELL.INI.

Floppy drive doesn't work

Floppy drives have a very good reliability record. In most cases they'll work flawlessly for many years. It's possible that something else may create a problem and you incorrectly blame the drive. If your floppy drive ever fails, it may stop working altogether or it may damage your floppy disks. There are several different scenarios:

☞   The disk you are trying to use in the drive is not formatted.

☞   The drive door is not closed.

☞   The disk is not inserted properly.

☞   The disk is formatted and inserted properly, the door is closed and the drive light is on but the drive just makes a spinning sound and nothing happens. Your drive may have failed. Place a formatted disk that has nothing or unimportant information in the drive and type:

A:\>DIR and press ENTER.

If it still doesn't work, get professional help to replace the drive or read Chapter 12 on how to do-it-yourself.

Formatted the hard disk by mistake

Throughout this book, in your manuals, etc. you have been warned not to use the FORMAT command without making sure that you are not targeting your hard disk. But you went ahead and did it anyway! If you have MS-DOS versions 5 or 6, you can use the UNFORMAT command to get everything back. Just don't turn your PC off. Type:

C:\>UNFORMAT C: and press ENTER.

If you don't have those versions of DOS, you need a utility program to unformat your hard disk. Without turning your PC off, get an expert to help you.

Getting lost is hard to do!

One of these days you are going to go from one directory to another, then another and finally wonder where you are. Or, you may be using a program and for some reason the program may quit and kick you out. Worst of all, your local "Guru" may have set up an easy to use menu for you (so you won't have to think), and one day you quit a program and don't see the familiar menu. When any of these happens to you, it'll feel like you have lost your car in a stadium parking lot and the crowd is about to come out the gates and run all over you. Don't panic. All you have to do is get back to the root (main) directory. You do that by typing CD\ at the prompt:

C:\WHATEVER1\WHATEVER2>CD and press ENTER.

This will take you right to the root directory. Now you can find your way around. If your prompt is not set up to show the directory name, type CD\ and press ENTER anyway. If you have been using a menu, try typing MENU at the prompt:

C:\>**MENU** and press ENTER.

Hard disk doesn't work

There are several ways that your hard disk may fail. It may simply refuse to power up when you turn your PC on, it may power up but refuse to read anything from the drive, or it may refuse to read or write every once in a while. Remember that your hard disk is probably one of the most expensive parts of your PC. Unfortunately, these days repairing a hard disk and getting a decent warranty costs almost as much as a new drive with a one year warranty. You should explore all avenues before giving up on your drive.

The problem can be due to a number of factors:

☞ Your PC was hit by lightning or a power surge and the hard disk got zapped. In this case you don't have much of a choice but to replace your drive.

☞ Your power supply is not working properly and is supplying less than necessary power to your hard disk. The solution is relatively inexpensive but an experienced person needs to diagnose it for you.

☞ You may have been doing something inside your PC recently and accidentally pulled on the signal cable that connects your hard disk to your controller board. Check the cable connections to make sure that everything is fully secured.

☞ Your hard disk may be full or full of scattered junk. Make sure that you are not running Windows in the background. Use the CHKDSK/F command at the DOS prompt to have DOS check your drive for lost or damaged areas. If it comes back with a lot of bad areas you may need to run a hard disk utility that will restore it for you.

HIMEM.SYS doesn't load

If you get a message that HIMEM.SYS is missing or not loaded, you need to check your CONFIG.SYS file to make sure that it's properly set up. Refer to Chapter 6 about editing files and the CONFIG.SYS file. Make sure that the following line is at the very top of the file:

DEVICE=C:\DOS\HIMEM.SYS

If it's not there, add it. If it's there, then the problem is something else, get help from a PC expert.

Keyboard doesn't work

Your keyboard is how you tell your PC what to do. If you press the keys and nothing happens it doesn't necessarily mean that your keyboard has a problem. Sometimes if your computer is stuck or confused, it won't respond to anything including what you type on the keyboard.

☞   Check the keyboard cable.

☞   Turn your computer off, wait 30 seconds and then turn it back on. At the beginning listen to the beeps. If your PC beeps just once, it hasn't noticed a problem with your keyboard. At the prompt try to type something. If nothing happens, your keyboard may be malfunctioning, but that may not be the only reason.

Keys on keyboard get stuck

After a few years (if you are a neat person), or a few months (if you are a slob) your keys may start to stick every once in a while. Dust, humidity, cigarette smoke, pieces of potato chips, etc. will eventually accumulate inside your keyboard and make your keys stick. If that happens, you can get a small can of compressed air and blow the grime away. Before you do that, make sure that your computer is turned off. Also, make sure that you follow the instructions on how to use the air can.

If the compressed air fails, you may need to open up the keyboard. If you are mechanically inclined. There is nothing to it. You need to turn the computer off. Turn the keyboard over and take out the screws in the back. Now hold the keyboard firmly and turn it over again. The top part of the keyboard frame should slide up. The keys and their bases will be exposed. Blow away the dirt. Use a few clean cotton swabs to clean around the base of all the keys. Put the cover back on and secure the screws. If your keys still stick, get professional help.

Lightning struck the PC

You know by now, that you need to have a surge protector in case of electrical surges or lightning. Sometimes, if your PC gets hit by direct lightning, there is nothing that can save it. Contact your dealer and have them replace the damaged parts.

If you live in parts of the country that experience severe lightning frequently, it would be a good idea to purchase a surge protector that is guaranteed to protect your PC and carries some sort of repair warranty.

Modem doesn't work

If your modem doesn't work, you may be able to fix the problem yourself. If you are just hooking it up for the first time, you need to follow the instructions in your Operating Manual. A few key points are:

- Attach a phone to the jack to make sure that it works.

- Make sure that you are properly connected to the phone jack.

- Make sure that the phone cord from the jack is inserted in the jack called "Line" in the back of the modem.

- If you have an external modem make sure that you have the correct cable between your modem and the serial port in the back of your PC.

- Make sure that you know which serial port (COM1 or COM2) your modem cable is attached to.

- If you have an external modem, make sure that the power cord is attached and the power switch is on.

If your modem has been working fine and then suddenly stops working, you need to check the following:

- Check the cable connections.

- Check your communications software to make sure nothing has been changed.

- Make sure that you have not added another device to your PC that is causing a conflict with the serial port used by your modem.

Monitor doesn't work

Your monitor is like a color TV. If you don't abuse it, it will work for many years. If your monitor ever fails, you can't open it up to fix it. Because of the high voltage that remains in a monitor, you should never attempt to open up your monitor yourself. Only a trained technician should do that.

There may be times when your monitor won't work and you'll find out that it was because of something really dumb, like the cable became loose or someone turned the knob and made your screen so dark that nothing could be seen. At least check those two before you call for help.

PC won't start

If your PC was working fine the last time you used it and now it won't even
start, check the following:

- Check all the cables. Make sure that they are all connected and
  secured.

- Make sure that your power outlet hasn't blown a fuse.

- If you are using a surge protector, make sure that it's on.

- When you turn the power on do you hear the fan inside your
  PC or the sound of your monitor? If you don't hear anything,
  then you may not be getting power.

- If your computer starts and your monitor shows that something
  is happening then your keyboard may be unhooked or your PC
  may be locked. Check the keyboard cable and also make sure
  that the PC key is in the unlock position.

PC can't run without stopping repeatedly

You may encounter this problem if you have upgraded to MS-DOS 6 and there
is a conflict in your CONFIG.SYS file. You have to reset your computer by
pressing CTRL-ALT-DEL keys or if that doesn't work by pressing the "Reset"
switch. When your PC shows:

"Starting MS-DOS ..."
Press the F5 key. You will see the following message:

"MS-DOS is bypassing your CONFIG.SYS and AUTOEXEC.BAT files"

You will then see the prompt. This will give you an opportunity to edit your
CONFIG.SYS file and take out the line that may be causing the problem.

PC gave out smoke and a burning smell

If this happens, quit your program immediately and at the prompt turn everything off. Check to see where the smoke or the burning smell is coming from. You need to have a technician look at your PC.

PC is frozen and won't do anything

You keep typing on your keyboard or moving your mouse and nothing happens. It seems as if everything is frozen on the screen. When this happens something has caused a conflict in your PC and it's confused. Try pressing the "Esc" key a few times. If that doesn't work, try pressing the CTRL-C keys together. If none of these work, you'll have to press CTRL-ALT-DEL keys to reset your computer. It's possible that even this command will not work. Your last alternative is to press the reset switch or turn your PC off. That should take care of the problem.

PC keeps running out of memory

If you load a lot of memory resident programs there may be certain occasions when you'll get a "Not enough memory" message. You have to remember that of the 640 K of conventional memory in your PC, DOS takes up a certain amount, VSAFE (virus detection program), screen savers, delete trackers, etc. each use up a certain amount of conventional memory. If there is not enough left for an application program to function properly, it will let you know.

You need to go to your AUTOEXEC.BAT or CONFIG.SYS files and disable one or more of the memory resident programs in order to free up more conventional memory.

Printer doesn't print

Your printer is one of the easiest parts of your PC. All you have to do is make sure that the cables are connected properly, paper is placed where it should be, the power switch is turned on, the on-line switch is on and your program knows what kind of printer you have.

If you have a problem with your printer the first time you hook it up, you may have a set-up problem. Make sure that when you install various programs, when they ask you for your printer type, you give the correct information. That tells your PC how to talk to your printer. To correct the problem, go to the program setup and check what type of printer it has listed. If you have a dot matrix printer, get a directory on your screen then press the Shift and Print Screen keys together.

If your problem developed after you have been using your printer for while, check the cable connections and the paper. If you have a paper jam, your printer will not do anything.

Printer prints slower than usual

When you tell your program to print something, it stores that information in your PC's memory and then sends it to your printer in small chunks. This will let you continue with other work while your printer is printing at it's own pace. If for some reason, something interferes with your memory, the pieces going to your printer may print one slow line at a time. There will be a noticeable slowdown. The best thing to do is to save the document that you want to print. Quit the program and turn your printer off. After a few seconds turn the printer back on, then reset your PC with the CTRL-ALT-DEL keys. This will give you a fresh start.

Program won't start

If you have just installed a program and it won't start, try the installation or setup procedure again. You may have missed something the first time.

If your program worked fine the last time and now you can't get it started, you may have either erased it or accidentally modified your path. Path is the line in your AUTOEXEC.BAT file that tells your PC where it can access various programs. If you have erased the program, obviously you already know about it. Install it again if you need it. If your path has been changed, use the EDIT command (refer to Chapter 6) to add the program back to your AUTOEXEC.BAT file. In the meantime, you can use CD\ to go to the program directory and get it started.

Spilled beverage on the keyboard

This is like driving under the influence. It's stupid but some people do it any way! Don't drink or eat around your PC. If you spill something on your keyboard, it may fry the keyboard circuitry and may also damage your PC. Once it's done, there is no easy solution. Have it serviced or replaced.

Time and/or date are off

Your PC is supposed to keep track of time with an electronic chip. Normally it does a good job but some clocks may end up being off by a few minutes a year. If it doesn't bother you, it won't bother your PC.

If your time and / or date are off on a regular basis then you have a serious problem. Your battery may be telling you that it's on the blink. Because your battery also keeps your PC's configuration information in memory, you'd better replace it as soon as possible. Make sure that you have recorded your PC's configuration and know how to recreate it. When the battery is replaced all of that information is cleared and needs to be setup again.

Chapter 11. Hints And Tips You Can Use

In many ways using your PC is like driving a car. When you use it on a regular basis, after a while everything becomes second nature to you. You'll notice that most of the things that may have been a little confusing or hard to remember at first will become more intuitive. The more you use your PC, the more things you will want to do with it. After a while, it's easy to take your PC for granted and forget to do the simple things that will prolong it's life and increase your enjoyment. This chapter covers a number of things that will be helpful to you and to your PC.

11.1. Setting Up your PC

Your PC and its peripherals offer the power and capabilities of a system that only twenty years ago required a large, specially built, chilled room and the constant care of several technicians. Although you no longer have to baby-sit your computer like the old days, you can't simply treat it like a TV set, either. The environment where your PC is going to be used should be set up properly with enough space to accommodate your PC and peripherals like the printer, mouse, etc. Your desk and chair are going to be very important in determining how comfortable you'll be, using your PC. Based on the type of system you have, you probably have an idea how you'd like to set up your PC. Your comfort and convenience are the most important factors. The PC is just a machine and it can be set up anywhere you have free space. The rule of thumb is that if you are comfortable then your PC is probably comfortable too!

Power

Your PC and its peripherals need to be connected to a 110 volt AC power outlet. You need to make sure a wall outlet is nearby. For added safety, you should check to make sure that the outlet is properly grounded. Also make sure that the outlet is not part of a circuit used by other major appliances (e.g. copier, air conditioner, refrigerator, etc.).

Phone

If you have a modem or a Fax, or plan to buy one in the near future, you should have a phone outlet nearby. Like the power connection, make sure you don't end up with phone wires running around on the floor.

Lighting

Proper lighting is very important to how well you will use and enjoy your PC. Make sure that the area where the PC is going to be used is well lit. Avoid light aimed directly at the monitor, because the reflections on the screen are uncomfortable, and will cause eye strain.

Ventilation

Components inside a PC create heat; if the heat stays inside the unit, it'll damage your system and cause malfunctions. The fan inside the power supply circulates the air inside the PC, pulls in cooler room air, and moves it past the heat-generating components. It's important that the path of the air flow remain clear. The room temperature should not be less than 50 or more than 100 degrees. Otherwise, the extreme cold or heat may damage some components or cause them to shrink or expand slightly, eventually leading to failure.

11.2. Protecting Your PC

Your PC is a marvel of technological innovations in all of its hundreds of components. Most components are made of solid state electronics, which means that there are no moving parts or parts that may fail easily. Under normal operating conditions, your PC should reliably perform its duties for many trouble-free years. You should take the following steps to make sure your PC is protected from various hazards:

Power Surges

The AC power current that flows through your home or office, fluctuates slightly. If several big, power-consuming appliances are connected to the same circuit breaker, whenever they start or stop, they can create a surge in electricity. PCs are sensitive to receiving a fairly steady flow of electricity, and may not operate properly without it. Air conditioning units, refrigerators, dishwashers, washers, dryers, copiers and laser printers are appliances that draw a lot of current when they first start up. If your PC is connected to the same circuit breaker 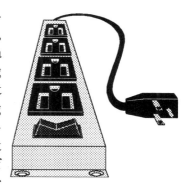 with one or more of these units, you may notice some irregularities in your PC's operation. You should use an outlet for your PC that does not share a breaker with one of these appliances. It's highly recommended that you use a surge protector to connect your PC and other peripherals to the wall outlet. Surge protection is a critical safeguard for your investment in the computer system. Another common cause of surges is electric "blackouts" or "brownouts."

By far, the most devastating damage is caused by lightning, which fortunately does not occur very often. Some areas of the country are more susceptible to lightning strikes than others. Parts of Florida have the potential for more than 100 strike days per year. The potential number of strike days per year gradually decreases as you move toward the West Coast. Southeastern states have between 60 to 80, Midwestern states have 40 to 60, northern and southern states have 20 to 40, and the West Coast has less than 20 potential strike days per year.

A surge protector is a small device that stands between the AC wall outlet and your computer system. Instead of plugging your PC, monitor, and printer directly into the wall outlet, you plug them into the surge protector, and then plug the surge protector into the wall. Certain models of surge protectors also have two outlets for connecting your modem or fax board to the phone line.

At least we have each other!

The inside components of a surge protector are the most important parts of the unit. A surge protector is supposed to have one or more fast action fuse(s) and a circuitry that prevents the power surge from going beyond the unit itself. Any surge protector you buy should definitely have the US UL (Underwriters Laboratory) approval. When comparing surge protectors, the two most important factors to consider are the clamp time, expressed in nanoseconds (typically 5 ns or less), and the highest spike voltage absorbed, expressed in volts (typically 6,000 volts or more). The smaller the clamp time and the higher the spike voltage, the better the surge protector.

Some of the other features you should look for when comparing surge protectors are as follows:

● The number of outlets on the unit

● Modem and fax phone line protection

● The number of circuit breakers (at least one 15 Amp breaker)

● An EMI/RFI (Electro Magnetic Interference/Radio Frequency Interference) noise filter

● UL 1449 listing (establishes the pass-through voltage at less than 400 volts)

● The number of switches (some units have one switch per outlet)

Static Electricity

Remember the little annoying zap you feel when you touch something, usually after walking on plush carpeting, on dry winter days? That zap is a result of the build-up of static electricity in your body. It doesn't harm you or the person you touch. However, computers are sensitive to static electricity and the results can be devastating. If you zap the case or the keyboard, the result may be that your computer will reset without any damage. On the other hand, if you zap while you are handling or touching a component inside your PC, the permanent information set by the factory in some ROM chips may be wiped clean. That could render a board or a hard disk drive totally useless. There are several precautions you should exercise to avoid both types of problems.

During normal use of your PC you can do one or more of the following to avoid static build up:

● Increase humidity in the room to above 30 percent by adding a plant to the room.

● Use an antistatic keyboard mat or floor mat.

● If you don't have a static mat, place a small 2 x 4 inch piece of aluminum foil near the case or keyboard and touch it first before touching any parts of your computer.

Magnets Cause Amnesia!

Several components in and around a PC use the magnetic principle to store information. Floppy disks, the hard disk, and data storage tapes are very sensitive to magnets. You should avoid putting anything with magnets near these items, or the data stored on them may be wiped clean.

Moisture and Humidity

Keep your PC away from areas with too much moisture or humidity. Similarly, keep liquids away from the PC and the keyboard. A small spill on the keyboard may cause a short circuit and damage it permanently. The same thing may happen to your PC. Eating, drinking, and smoking near the PC are not recommended.

Connecting and Disconnecting Cables

Your PC is the hub for a number of cable connections. Your monitor, keyboard, printer, mouse, modem, etc. are all connected to your PC by cable.

A certain amount of electric current flows in these cables. If you connect or disconnect any cables to any part of your computer system while the power is on, you run the risk of damaging something sensitive and expensive. It's wise to spend the extra 30 seconds to turn the power off before fooling with any cable connections.

Battery Backup

A battery backup unit consists of a battery and special circuitry that allows it to connect to and work with a computer. The size of the unit varies from that of a book to that of a two drawer file cabinet. Size is based on the amount of power supplied and the length of time that power is available. Some small backup units can fit inside your PC and support the unit for only a few minutes. Larger units may support several PCs, monitors, and printers for several minutes or close to an hour. The battery power is intended only to help you quickly wrap up whatever you are working on and save your work to the hard disk drive before shutting down. It's not intended to sustain a long operation.

The main function of a battery backup is to support the continued operation of the computer in case of a brief or long power outage. The computer is very sensitive to instantaneous power fluctuations. When the power to your PC is interrupted, all information on the RAM memory is wiped clean, including everything you have changed or added since the last time you saved data to your hard disk drive. The function of the backup unit is to be on standby and provide instantaneous power, when necessary.

Backup units primarily supply the power for a few minutes while you shut down properly and save your work. Other, more sophisticated units, which are frequently hooked up to computer networks, can automatically shut down the main unit unattended. These units need a special connection to the main PC and special circuitry to work properly with the network software.

For organizations that have a computer network, battery backup is an absolute necessity. Other organizations may have to evaluate their needs based on the frequency of power problems in their area and the value of the backup.

There are three different technologies for power backup: off-line (standby), on-line (UPS: Uninterruptible Power Supply), and internal.

● Off-line systems are the most common and the least expensive of the three. They simply wait on standby for a power interruption, then they switch on within milliseconds, and supply battery power to the system. Generally, the very brief time lapse does not wipe data off the system.

● On-line systems (UPS), on the other hand, are continuously supplying power through the battery while the battery is also being charged. In case of power interruption, the computer does not detect any difference. These units often cost 50% to 100% more than their standby counterparts.

● Internal power backup systems are a cross between the two previous technologies. They do not have enough power to operate the monitor; but, they have special software that automatically records on the hard disk the state the system was in at the time of the interruption. After power is restored, the software automatically returns the system to its last state. These units cost about the same as their standby counterparts.

Turning Your PC On and Off

Should you leave your computer on all the time or should you turn it on when you need it and off when you don't? Different people have different opinions. Some are speculation, some are fact, and some are based on the technology of many years ago.

When you turn your computer on, it puts a higher than usual stress on the hard drive. It also starts heating up the components inside your PC and monitor. After a short while, the hard drive reaches and stays at a constant speed. The heat inside the PC and the monitor also reach a constant level. When the computer is left on idly, the concern is the waste of energy and the wear and tear of the hard drive, the fan, and other components. When the computer is turned off, the components that were heated up and had expanded slightly, start to cool off and shrink to their original size. Either way, various components of your PC experience some change.

The solid state electronic components of PCs and monitors have a long life expectancy. You don't have to leave your system on overnight. However, you should not keep turning the system on or off during the day. We recommend that once you turn your PC on in the morning, leave it on until you are completely finished using it for the day.

Keeping Viruses Away

What started out a few years ago as humorous pranks have recently turned to vicious acts by some computer nerds. Computer viruses, like a disease, are designed to penetrate a PC from the outside and play havoc with the hard drive and other components. The damage may be quite extensive. Loss of data on the hard disk is one of the most common results.

A computer virus is usually a very small program that's hidden inside another ordinary program. Like a communicable human disease, if the infected program is passed on from someone else and installed in your system, it sneaks into your hard disk and stays there. Some viruses have a trigger, which can be a date or a word. When that date arrives or that word is used, the virus becomes active and starts whatever destruction its creator had in mind.

I feel a little dizzy today!

There are several ways to avoid viruses. The most important is to be careful about accepting programs from individuals or private bulletin boards. The other is to install virus detection software on your system to examine every program before loading it onto your hard disk. Viruses keep changing, however, and detection programs get outdated quickly.

11.3. Moving Your PC Around

Whether you just bought a new PC, or decided to move your PC across the hall, across town or across the country, there are certain things that need to be done to make sure that nothing gets damaged. If you have just bought or received a new PC, the first thing to do is examine the shipping boxes for exterior damage. If you are shipping your PC, make sure that you use the original boxes and foam supports that came with it. If they are not available, use crumpled newspapers around the PC to protect it from damage.

Moving your computer system should be handled with care and caution. There are several steps you should follow before you move your computer:

- Turn the computer and monitor off before moving.

- Unplug all the cables from the back of the PC so it can be moved freely.

- Insert the cardboard that came in your floppy drive back in and close the drive door.

- Move each piece separately and carefully.

11.4. Being Prepared Just In Case

You won't drive your car without a spare tire, so why would you use your PC without some sort of backup? Your PC is a lot more reliable than your tires, never-the-less, you need to keep some sort of backup of important information. A problem with your PC may not just be due to equipment failure. You may accidentally erase an important piece of information and lose a lot of time trying to recreate it. There are some very simple things that you can do to ensure that no disaster will ever cripple your operation.

Making a Backup Copy of Program Disks

Programs that operate your PC or help you with various applications are sold on floppy disks. These disks are the main part of your purchase and if damaged, are not going to be replaced so easily. Novice computer users (and some veteran users as well!) often accidentally erase information from a program disk. When that happens, the entire program becomes useless. Therefore, it's important that you make a backup copy of your important program disks and use them for installation purposes. Then if anything happens to one of your program copies, you can make another copy from the original.

Among the programs you should make a backup from are the operating system, the operating environment and application software. It only costs a few dollars per program to make backup copies, but it could save you a lot of headaches.

An important safety measure is to write-protect your disks. On 5.25" disks you need to place a small, write-protect tape over the left notch (most disk brands contain a few write-protect tapes in the disk box). On 3.5" disks you need to move the small tab that opens a small write-protect window on the disk. These steps will protect your disks from accidental erasure.

Three different types of DOS commands can be used for copying disks. The COPY command is used for copying one or more files at a time. It's not the most appropriate command for this purpose. The XCOPY command is used for copying one or more files and directories at a time. It's better than the COPY command, but it's still not the best command for duplicating backup disks.

The DISKCOPY command lets you copy the entire contents of one disk to another. DISKCOPY will format the backup disk and then create an identical copy of the original disk. The only limitation of DISKCOPY is that both your target disk and your source disk should be the same size and capacity. If you use DISKCOPY, you don't need to preformat the blank disks.

Backing Up Your Hard Disk

Hard disk drives have been constantly improved over the past few years. They are now significantly more reliable than their predecessors. They have fewer parts, are less expensive, and faster. However, a hard drive is still one of the most vulnerable parts of your PC. Because your hard drive stores important documents and data that you have spent a great deal of time producing, you should make regular backup copies of your data.

There are several ways to make regular backup copies of your data. You can either use the BACKUP command that's included with your DOS, use a disk backup utility program, or use a tape backup drive. The results are often the same; only the costs and the effort involved are different.

DOS has BACKUP and RESTORE commands that allows you to make a copy of a single file, multiple files, directories, or the entire hard disk on floppy disks. These DOS commands often take longer than the other two alternatives and have fewer features than those two. If you only have a few critical files to backup, DOS may be adequate for you.

Hard disk backup utility programs are specifically designed to produce fast and easy backup of your important files on disk. They are often easier to learn and faster than the DOS commands. Each program has its own set of operating rules.

A tape backup drive is the most convenient method for making backup copies, but it's also the most expensive alternative. If you use your computer full time every day, you might use one tape for each day of the week and one tape for the entire week. Make a complete copy of all your important files on the weekly tape. Then set up the tape software to copy only the changes you make every day on the daily tapes. This way, you minimize your copying efforts and have a full backup if necessary.

Depending on the importance of your data, there are three methods you can use to backup your hard disk with a tape drive. The "Son" method (use one tape to make a complete backup every day), the "Father/Son" method (use 6 rotational tapes, 2 to make a complete backup on Fridays and 4 to backup only the files changed daily from Monday through Thursday), and the "Grandfather/ Father/Son" method (use 10 rotational tapes, 3 to store complete monthly backups, 3 to store complete weekly backups on Fridays, and 4 to make a backup only of files changed daily from Monday through Thursday). Each method gives you a higher degree of security in case something goes wrong with your system or hard drive.

Creating a Boot Disk

Store the most critical information about your PC on a disk that will operate in your drive A:. This will be your emergency disk. To create this disk put a blank disk in drive A: and type FORMAT A:/S and press ENTER. This will format the disk and copy the bootable part of DOS onto it. Next, copy AUTOEXEC.BAT and CONFIG.SYS files onto the emergency disk. At C:> type COPY AUTOEXEC.BAT A: and press ENTER. Again, at C:> type COPY CONFIG.SYS A: and press ENTER. Now copy protect the disk, write emergency disk on the label, and store it in a safe place.

Creating an Uninstall Disk

MS-DOS versions 4,5 and 6 create an "Uninstall Disk" when they are setup on your PC as an upgrade. During setup you are given the option to create the uninstall disk. This disk will hold everything you need to reconstruct your PC to it's old version in case of a problem with the upgrade.

If you install the DOS upgrade yourself, you will be given the option to create an uninstall disk. However, if you buy your PC with DOS preinstalled, there won't be an uninstall disk.

Recording Your Initial Settings

You should make a copy of your initial settings for backup purposes. These settings contain important information about your floppy drives, hard disk type, video, etc. Some of the most important information you need to record and keep in a safe place are:

- System setup information (stored in your CMOS)

- DOS version

- Copies of your AUTOEXEC.BAT and CONFIG.SYS files.

11.5. Giving your Hard Disk a Little TLC

Your hard disk drive is one of the most sensitive and expensive parts of your PC. It's also one of the few moving parts in your computer. It spins at a very high speed, and the read/write heads are located extremely close to the surface of the magnetic disks. Under these conditions, the hard disk is very vulnerable to shock and other physical disturbances. While your computer is turned on, your hard drive spins rapidly, and any sudden movement of the base unit may damage it. Often a damaged hard disk may result in the loss of your data. When your PC is turned on, make sure it does not get hit or moved.

If you take good care of your hard disk and follow the suggestions here, you'll be able to enjoy more of the benefits that it's designed to give you.

Working from Your Hard Disk

Your hard disk is a fast and high capacity storage device that can fetch your information or store it away in a snap. Floppy disks on the other hand are designed for transferring information between machines. They are not as fast as hard disk drives. Therefore, whenever possible, make sure that you copy all your programs and data onto your hard disk before you start to use it. The difference is night and day!

Quitting Programs

When you are done using a program, you need to get out of that program and to a DOS prompt C:\> before you can turn off your PC. Otherwise, if you turn off your computer in the middle of a program, the hard disk may not store everything properly and your data may be scattered all over the place.

Optimizing your Hard Disk

The hard disk is one of the most important components of your computer system. After buying your PC, the hard disk is the only part that you can actually influence and improve. Think of your hard disk as a library with thousands of books or a filing cabinet with several drawers and many folders in each drawer. The way a library organizes and arranges the books directly affects how well it can service its customers. The way you organize the files and directories on your hard disk can have a similar effect on the performance of your hard disk.

When you copy a file onto your hard disk for the first time, the computer tries to find a blank area to store it. As time goes on and you add more to that file, your PC stores it in other available areas but keeps track of where all the various pieces are stored. Although these files are fragmented on the hard disk, as far as you are concerned, it's totally transparent.

When you delete a file from your hard disk, the computer doesn't immediately wipe the area clear; instead it simply deletes the name from your directory and makes the area available for future use. The area made available may not be used immediately, but eventually, the computer will copy a new file over it.

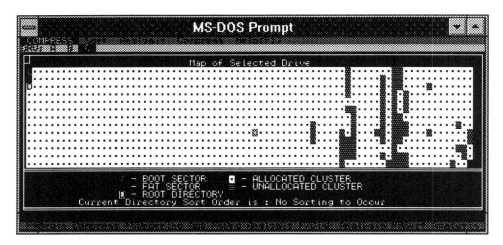

The computer divides a hard disk into sectors. Each sector is 512 bytes long. When you store information on your hard disk, the computer allocates as many adjacent sectors to those files as possible. Almost invariably, the tail end of the last sectors will remain blank. When you end up with several hundred files, obviously a great deal of space is wasted. In both cases cited above, information gradually begins to become scattered on your hard disk. Eventually, having blank spaces and files scattered on your hard disk takes its toll on the performance of the drive. Your drive capacity will diminish faster and it'll take longer to read or write to the disk.

There are special programs for unfragmenting and compacting your hard disk. They are known as disk optimization programs. MS-DOS 6 includes DEFRAG which was described in Chapter 6. You can also buy this type of program by itself or as part of a utility package. When selecting and using these programs, be very careful that it doesn't create a conflict with other things on your PC.

11.6. Storing Your Floppy Disks

Floppy disks store data magnetically. They are vulnerable to dirt, magnets, finger prints, cracks, cuts, and other abuses. It's important that you take proper care of your floppy disks. The following is a list of suggestions for protecting your disks:

- Don't touch the magnetic surface of disks.

- Keep 5-1/4" disks in their protective sleeves.

- Avoid using magnets around disks.

- When not in the PC, the disks should be kept in storage envelopes or boxes.

- Do not expose disks to extreme heat, sunlight, or moisture.

11.7. Using Test, Diagnostic and Utility Programs

These days there is an abundance of programs for doing everything imaginable with your PC. One of the popular categories of software are the testing and diagnostic programs. These programs are capable of analyzing all or specific components of your

PC in order to give you a status report. Some of them can even correct certain problems with your memory management or your hard disk drive. When you purchase a diagnostics program make sure that it specifies your type of computer.

Another popular category of software are called utility programs. These range from simple menu programs that make using your PC easier, to file recovery programs that help recover damaged files or those you may have accidentally erased. MS-DOS versions 5 and 6 include a lot of the functions of these utilities. But there may still be certain things that you may need a utility program. When you decide to shop for a utility package, carefully read the specification sheets or the back of the box. Make sure that the functions offered by the package and the skill level required to use it closely match your situation.

11.8. Registering What You Buy

Most people throw away product registration cards because they don't want to bother. It usually takes less than two minutes to completely fill out one of these cards. Some manufacturers ask a lot of questions and some just need your name and address. These cards serve a very important purpose. They let the manufacturer get in touch with you in case of a product recall or send you information about their other products or upgrades.

With computer software, registering serves an important purpose. The manufacturer can notify you of product upgrades, corrections to problems, or special deals. It's definitely worth the two minutes of your time and the postage stamp.

The registration card at the end of this book helps us get your opinion and feedback, so that we can continue to improve the PC GUIDE series. We will also notify you of specials that may be of interest to you.

11.9. Getting Help When You Are Stuck

What do you do when you get stuck? Well, if you have the PC GUIDE series of books and video tapes on the subject, the first thing you do is look up a solution. If you don't have them, then you have several other choices. For hardware problems during the warranty period, you should always contact the place of purchase or the manufacturer. For software problems you can either contact the software manufacturer or a software support service.

Software companies often provide free telephone support to their registered customers for a certain period of time ranging from 30 to 90 days from the date of purchase. Beyond that period, they charge a usage fee based on the number of minutes you spend on the phone with their technical support staff. Some companies use 1-(900) toll phone services and others simply charge your call to your credit card.

Thousands of programs and their constant upgrades make technical support difficult even for the developers of the software. If you choose to use a technical support service, check with their references and make sure that you fully understand their billing practices before signing on the dotted lines.

11.10. Reading PC Publications

The personal computer field is one of the richest in terms of the vast number of publications that cover every facet of PC products. Most of these publications are available at libraries, computer stores, supermarkets, and book stores. We strongly recommend that you look at a few of them before you buy your PC or upgrade. More importantly, you should make a point of reading at least one of these magazines every month. The informative articles, product reviews, and even advertisements in these publications help you stay abreast of the events in this exciting and constantly advancing field.

A list of some of the most popular PC publications is included in the Appendix. The subscription prices listed are the published rates. You can often subscribe through various organizations for substantially less.

11.11. On-Line Services Bring the World to You

In the mid 1980's, as PC fever spread to millions of homes, various organizations began offering on-line computer services to the public. These services either charge a certain fee per minute of usage, a fixed amount per month, or both. Most people living in cities or metropolitan areas have local phone numbers to call. Others may have to call a toll free 800 number or call long distance. The fees charged by these services vary, depending on the provider and the number of features you use.

The following is an alphabetical list of the most popular services available at the time this guide was prepared. To get additional information, call them at the information numbers provided below. Some services sell a membership starter kit that's available at stores that sell computer hardware and software. Other services advertise a toll free 800 number for you to call with your modem; then, using a credit card or other forms of billing, you can sign up for membership.

America Online

America Online is a service of Quantum Computer Services. It uses a graphical interface with pull down menus. You can access the service through local phone numbers in most cities and metropolitan areas. There is no charge to join; however, there is a monthly membership fee plus usage charges which, like long distance phone charges, are lowest during nights and weekends.

This service offers you news and headlines, access to a searchable encyclopedia, stock market reports and stock price checks, sports and weather, ability to download software from their software library, electronic mail access to other members, plus many other features. You can get free information by calling: (800) 227-6364

Compuserve

One of the oldest on-line services with over 1,000,000 subscribers, Compuserve is primarily a text-based service. Consequently, the flow of information back and forth is faster than in a graphics-based environment. You can access the service through local phone numbers in most cities and metropolitan areas. You must purchase a membership kit to join, but, these kits often contain usage credits that offset the cost of your purchase. You are charged per minute of usage, with the amount varying according to the day of week and the time of day.

The service offers you news and headlines, electronic mail, Fax service, bulletin boards, shopping on-line, stock market data and discount stock trading, sports and weather, airline flight schedules and on-line ticketing, plus many other features. You can get free information by calling: (800) 848-8199

Delphi

This service offers a combination of features, among them thousands of shareware programs that can be down-loaded to your computer. Usage charges are per hour and depend on the time of day and day of the week. You can get free information by calling: (800) 544-4005

Dow Jones News/Retrieval

This service offers financial news and statistics. Usage fees are somewhat complex and depend on the time of day and other criteria. The service can also be accessed through some of the other on-line services. You can get free information by calling: (800) 522-3567

GEnie

This is a service provided by General Electric Information Services. It's a text based service that offers a variety of features. You can get news and weather reports, use an on-line encyclopedia, send and receive electronic mail, check current stock closings, shop on-line, use bulletin boards, check flight schedules and book tickets, play various games on-line, etc. There are no membership fees to join but there are several pay-as-you-use services within GEnie. You can get free information by calling: (800) 638-9636

National Videotex

This service is based on the AT&T digital network. There is a basic service as well as other pay-as-you-use interactive and transactional services once you dial into National Videotex. You can get free information by calling: (800) 348-0069

PC MagNet

PC Magazine's online service is offered 24 hours a day. It provides utility programs offered by the magazine, an index of computer products reviewed, an exchange of opinions with the magazine editors, and access to the magazine's Computer Library and Consumer Reference Library. It can be accessed directly or through CompuServe. There are no sign up or monthly charges; you pay per minute of usage.

To join, you can go through CompuServe, if you are already a member, by entering GO PCMAG at the CompuServe "!" prompt, or you can call one of the following numbers directly: (800) 635-6225, Voice, or (800) 346-3247, Modem connection.

Prodigy

This service was started in 1988 as a joint development venture between IBM and Sears. It has over 2,000,000 subscribers nationwide. Prodigy uses a graphical user interface with various pop up windows. You can access the service through local phone numbers in most cities and large metropolitan areas. There is no charge to join; but there is a flat monthly rate for unlimited use. The service is primarily supported by the advertising fees charged to various suppliers of products and services. At the bottom of every prodigy screen is a one inch wide strip of advertising.

The service offers you news and headlines, special interest clubs and bulletin boards, access to a searchable encyclopedia, stock market reports and stock price checks, on-line stock trading, sports and weather, on-line airline reservations and ticketing, on-line banking and bill paying, on-line shopping for various goods and services including groceries, electronic messaging with other members of the service, plus many other features. Starter kits with some free offers inside can be purchased from computer and software stores. You can get free information by calling: (800) 776-3552

11.12. Bulletin Boards Let You Chat Away

What started in the early days of the PC as a way for computer enthusiasts to exchange information has spawned tens of thousands of systems made available as bulletin boards. In the PC world, a bulletin board system (BBS) is a computer with one or more phone lines and one or more modems made available to the public. The majority of BBS's are available free of charge. The owners generally have certain interests that they would like to share with others. To offset equipment and telephone charges, some BBS's charge a nominal membership fee for the specific information they offer their members.

You can often find the name and number of local BBS's at your local computer dealers and computer stores. Some local computer periodicals print lists of the BBS's in their cities. You can call and connect with a BBS by using your modem. Once connected, the BBS will automatically inform you of the terms and conditions of using it. Then you can decide to proceed or stop and disconnect from the service.

Often you don't know the communications protocol required for proper connection to the BBS. Therefore, set your modem software for the most commonly used parameters and if necessary change them after you are connected. The parameters are: 2400 BPS speed, 8 bits, No parity, one data bit (2400, N, 8, 1).

While using a private BBS, you should exercise some caution when copying some files or programs to your computer. Most private BBS's serve as an exchange medium where users can copy to and from the BBS. The danger when copying from a private BBS is that the file may be infected with a computer virus. Once copied to your hard disk, the virus may harm your files and programs.

Thousands of user groups operate their own BBS, a list of some of them in major cities is included in the Appendix. For more information about bulletin boards in your area you can contact:

> BBS Press Service, Inc.
> 8125 SW 21 Street
> Topeka, Kansas 66615
> 913/478-3157

11.13. Try Shareware Software With Low Money Down!

In the late 1970's and early 1980's, a unique breed of individuals was clicking away at the keyboards of their PCs. They were mostly young, idealistic pioneers in a field that was destined to change the course of civilization in a very short time. As they began to develop small programs for their PCs, they started to share those programs with other PC users. A very special culture began to develop throughout the country and, particularly, around Silicon Valley, California.

Pioneering PC users, including some of today's financial moguls, believed that software was an intellectual property that could be shared among all users and continuously enhanced through feedback from other users. They believed that software should be available at very little cost for people to evaluate. If they felt that the software was useful to them they could mail a check (usually between $5 to $50) to the developer to cover his/her costs. Otherwise, they could simply stop using the program based on the honor system. This was the birth of what has become known as "Shareware" or "Public Domain Software."

Thousands of programs are available as Shareware. These programs are often very powerful and almost as full of features as their commercial counterparts. Their operations manuals and tutorials, are often included on the program disk. You can either view the instructions on your screen or print them out on your printer. Authors of these programs may have different motivations for going through the Shareware channel. Some may believe in the original idea of sharing their intellectual property with others, and some may introduce and enhance their programs through this channel before going commercial. These programs are available through several outlets such as office supply stores, discount stores, mail order ads, etc. Although these programs are often advertised for as little as $2 apiece, if you like the program and start using it, the honor code requires that you compensate the developer properly.

11.14. Games and Entertainment Help Justify Your PC!

Your PC is the key that opens the door to literally thousands of games and entertainment programs. Games cover a very broad spectrum. Some are text based and demand very little from your system. A great majority of new games take advantage of the more powerful microprocessors and video standards available in recent years. For these games you need at least an 80286 or 80386-SX processor with color VGA graphics. These games produce arcade-quality features for hours of challenge and enjoyment for you and others in your home.

Most computer games usually cost less than $50. It's important to get some feedback about a game before you buy it. Sometimes the information on the outside of the package may not be enough to tell you whether or not you'll enjoy that game. Some software suppliers offer demonstrations, see if you can try a game before buying it. Entertainment and special interest programs are abundant, but you have to look into a variety of sources for them. Stores carrying software may have a limited number of the best-selling programs in some categories on hand, but they, as well as mail order sources, may be able to get you other programs.

11.15. The Right Training Can Make You A Pro!

A PC, like an automobile, bicycle, or even a VCR, can be used right out of the box with little training. However, to get the most out of your investment, you should spend the time and the effort to be better trained in using your system and software. You have several options available to you. Obviously, the least expensive option is the material that comes with your PC and software. If you need more focused training, other options are available.

Train Yourself Using Manuals and Program Tutorials

Virtually every computer system is sold with an operations manual. The system manual should be your first source of information about your PC. The key factor to remember is that the manual is written to familiarize you with the overall operation of your PC, as well as to provide more advanced information for expert users, and to serve as a trouble-shooting guide. If you read the manual from start to finish without recognizing the broad spectrum it covers, you are bound to be overwhelmed and discouraged. We recommend that when you read the manual, review only the chapters that familiarize you with the system, without going into complicated technical areas.

Almost all software programs that you buy are supplied with a manual specifically written for the version of software you are using. The style and understandability of these manuals vary from one manufacturer to another, and from one program to another. Therefore, you should use the same approach to reading your software manuals as you do with the system manual. If you find your software manual too confusing (as some really are), you can look at third-party books written for that version of your program.

Many programs include a tutorial that can be operated right on your computer. The tutorials are often a combination of information written in the manual and a series of question-and-answer sessions called interactive training. You can read about the program, and then work on exercises that reinforce the material you read. Some tutorials are actually more effective than the manual. We strongly suggest that after installing your programs, you look at the tutorials before going over the manuals.

Shareware programs are not provided with a paper manual but many often include a manual on the disk. These manuals may be viewed on the screen or printed on your printer. Often the developer of the software offers a more complete manual after you send in a registration fee.

Computer-Based Training

Several companies offer training programs that can be viewed on your computer screen. They usually offer more features than the tutorials included in most programs. These programs are interactive; they try to give you the feeling of being in a classroom environment. The tutorial offers information about the program, then asks relevant questions and evaluates your answers. Some of these programs are text based and others are video-based, making great use of animation and graphics.

Next to the manuals and tutorials that are included with programs, computer-based training packages are often the least expensive alternatives available. Their advantage is that they give you a closer contact with the real program than any other alternatives.

Audio or Video Training

Audio or video training programs are offered by several companies. These programs have been available for several years. Audio tape training programs are designed to be used in a cassette recorder next to your computer. The idea is to listen to the tape while exploring the program.

Training programs on video tape have remained popular among PC users over the years. Their basic advantage is that they can visually illustrate the use and the features of the program. These programs often run from 30 minutes to an hour. They normally highlight the program and its features.

Classroom Training

One of the most familiar training grounds for a lot of people is the classroom. Some people feel that they can learn more in a classroom environment than they can by reading manuals, reviewing tutorials, or watching video tapes. For these people, most cities offer several choices. Some training organizations specialize in classroom-based computer training. Some dealers also offer training classes. Additionally, many colleges and universities have begun offering similar programs. Usually, local schools are less expensive than other classroom training providers. The only exception may be dealers who offer free training classes to customers who purchase computers and software from them.

When evaluating classroom training programs, you should make sure that they offer the full use of a PC per student. That way, you can follow everything the instructor does on your screen, and you can work on the exercises more efficiently

11.16. Make Someone Else Happy, Don't Junk Your Old PC

At some point in time you will outgrow your PC at home or at work. You will buy a newer, more powerful PC and your old computer will sit idle. When that happens remember that a PC is a terrible thing to waste. You can share the joys and benefits of your PC by donating it for a good cause. A needy student or organization will be forever grateful to your generosity. If you donate your business PC, you may be able to take a tax write-off. Contact the National Cristina Foundation, a non-profit organization, at 42 Hillcrest Drive, Pelham Manor, NY 10803, (800) 274-7846.

Chapter 12. Taking Care of Your PC

Your PC is a major investment on your part or the part of your employer. Just like your color TV, if you don't abuse your PC, it will reliably serve you for many years. Taking care of your PC is easy and very inexpensive.

12.1. Regular Maintenance You Can do Yourself

Your computer system requires very little routine maintenance and, if you treat it with

normal care, you'll have to do very little to ensure that your PC will last for many useful and enjoyable years. In fact, the less you tinker with your system, the fewer problems you'll have. The only useful tool you'll need is a small can of compressed air, available at most computer and office supply stores, to remove dust from your computer. You also need a soft cloth to wipe it clean every once in a while.

PC

Once a year, you should take the cover off of your PC and use the compressed air to blow out the dust. If you don't have access to a can of compressed air, simply use a cloth to gently wipe off the dust.

Monitor

Once a month, use a soft cloth to wipe the screen clean. You can use the same cloth to wipe the dust off the air vents on the sides or the top of the monitor.

Printer

Routine maintenance depends on the type of printer you have. If you have a dot matrix printer, you can use the compressed air to blow out the dust and paper shavings once a year. If you have a laser printer, you should use the cleaning tools that come with the printer to clean the inside elements every time you replace a cartridge.

Two of the most frequently occurring problems with dot matrix printers are caused by user negligence. Never pull on the paper as the printer is printing. It may bend one or more of the pins as it strikes the paper. Also, never turn the platten knob when the printer is on. It will damage the plastic gears inside. There are buttons on most printers for moving the paper back and forth automatically.

Peripherals

Most peripherals require little or no maintenance. If you have a mouse, you may take out the roller ball and clean it with a soft cloth once a year.

12.2. What Happens When Your PC Goes on the Blink

Solid state electronic products have been around for more than twenty years. In the past ten years, their quality standards have reached a point where some experts claim that if a product doesn't fail during the first few months, it will probably last for many years. PCs, in general, have proved to be quite durable. Many original IBM and compatible systems are still working. In fact, the main reason for retiring older PCs has been technological obsolescence, rather than product failure. The concern you are most likely to have five years from now is whether your 1993 PC can do what others can do in 1998!

Equipment failure happens to a very small percentage of the millions of PCs sold every year. Most of those failures happen during the first year. Almost all systems have one or more years of parts and labor warranty; so you'll probably be covered for most equipment problems. After the warranty expires, there are several ways to have the problem corrected or the equipment repaired.

Depending on where you plan to use your PC and for what purpose, your priorities and the urgency for repairs may vary greatly. If you use your PC at home for casual applications and it fails, you probably won't be greatly inconvenienced if it takes one or two weeks for repairs. On the other hand, if you use the PC to perform important business functions like accounting, you may not be able to afford more than one day of downtime. Therefore, the level of service and repair you may need will vary according to your degree of dependence on the computer. This factor should have been one of the criteria in your selection process.

As a rule of thumb, if you are buying your computer for business and will be heavily dependent on it for critical daily activities, you should consider buying a service contract. The contract should cover both parts and labor; and it's annual cost should not exceed 10% or, at most, 15% of the purchase price of the hardware. The response time should be no more than a few hours, and a loaner should be provided if your system will be unavailable more than one or two days. On the other hand, if you are buying the PC for home use and can be without it for a few days in case of a breakdown, a reasonably priced service contract may also be a good investment. The contract should cover both parts and labor, its annual cost should not exceed 5% of the purchase price, and your computer should not be unavailable to you longer than a specified number of days. In either case, make sure that the service contract is offered by a well established and financially solid provider.

Thank God its Under Warranty

All computer systems are sold with at least a one year parts and labor warranty. The standard warranty usually requires that you take or ship the defective unit to the place of purchase for repair or replacement. Some manufacturers sweeten their package by offering additional benefits, like providing service at your site, or extending the warranty beyond the one year period.

If you encounter a hardware problem that can't be corrected by following some of the suggestions outlined in "Troubleshooting Guide", then you should call your supplier for assistance. Some manufacturers have specific rules about opening up your PC during the warranty period, so read your warranty document before you get into anything. If your supplier is not local, make sure you use their toll free 800 phone number (if they have one). Frequently, the technical support staff can help resolve your problem over the phone.

When you prepare your computer for shipment to the supplier for service, it's best to use the original packing materials and boxes. If you don't have the original materials, use foam or crumpled newspapers to surround the unit. Make sure that you attach a label with your name, address and phone number to every item. Almost all suppliers require a photocopy of your purchase invoice. Don't send the original. Most suppliers give you an RMA "Return Authorization Number" when you call and decide to send the unit back. The number should be written on the outside of the box as well as on the item(s) you send back.

Whether you take or ship your system back for service, always make it a point to call back after a few days to check that it was received and ask when it's going to be looked at. Call back again a few days later to ask about the unit's status, and the date it'll be shipped back to you. After you receive the unit, hook it up as soon as possible and check it out carefully. Make sure that the problem has been corrected, and make sure that you have gotten everything back (even internal components). Sometimes technicians may take the system apart and forget to put everything back in. If anything is missing or not working properly, call the supplier back as soon as possible.

Out of Warranty, Out of Luck!

Once your warranty period is over, you have many choices about how and where you can get your system serviced. They are primarily divided into three groups: the place where you purchased your system, organizations that only provide service and repair, and last but not least, yourself. The important point to keep in mind is that your entire system is basically made up of plug-in components. Usually, if a component fails, it's less expensive to pull it out and replace it than to repair it. Another important point is that, unlike everything else, over time the prices of computer components go down, and the replacement costs are often less than the original purchase price of an item.

Fix it Where You Bought it

After the warranty period is over, your ties to the original supplier depend on the mutual relationship that may have developed between you. There are some advantages to dealing with the original supplier, especially if it's a local dealer. In many small communities and towns, computer dealers tend to be privately held and relatively stable. They tend to become familiar with your needs and provide you with personal service. However, to be fair to that group of suppliers, you should be aware that smaller, more personal operations will cost you more than large volume organizations.

Many mail order computer companies have set up sophisticated systems to keep in touch with their customers. Because most of them value your continued business and satisfaction, they will provide you with service on the systems they have sold you.

In spite of the advantages of going to the original supplier for service, you should not restrict yourself to that supplier alone. As mentioned earlier, computer service and repair has, in most cases, boiled down to diagnosing the problem and exchanging the malfunctioning component. You should shop around for the best price. Most local computer suppliers and service providers perform a diagnostic check for approximately $50 or less. Afterwards, you have the option of having the PC serviced by them or by another service provider.

Have Someone Else Fix it

With the proliferation of personal computers in the past few years, thousands of service and repair organizations have sprung up throughout the country. The majority are privately owned and operated. There are also several nationwide organizations with branch offices in most cities and metropolitan areas. Some of the nationwide organizations are used by mail order computer companies to provide local or on-site service to their customers.

Third-party service organizations provide you with another choice for service and repairs. Their rates are often consistent with those of computer sales organizations. However, as indicated earlier, you should shop around among service providers as you did to choose your original PC supplier. Appendix D has a list of companies that provide on-site service nationwide.

Service It Yourself and Save a Bundle

The modular design of PC components and the availability of diagnostic programs and publications have simplified the work of do-it-yourself PC owners. If you are handy with a screwdriver and can carefully read and follow directions, then you can be the best and the least expensive service provider for

your PC. As you may recall from Chapter 2, there aren't that many components in your system. If a hardware problem occurs, you can get the necessary tools to diagnose the problem and purchase the part(s) to replace the malfunctioning component(s) yourself. Your savings could be substantial, compared to having someone else perform the service. In most cases, you'd save the service charges as well as the mark-up on the part(s).

You don't have to be a computer technician to service your PC, but if you are not sure of your abilities, it's safer to have someone with more expertise perform the work.

12.3. Opening up your PC Safely

It's very easy to look under the hood and see the inside of your PC. Someday, you may be so comfortable opening up your PC that if it ever fails, you'll be able to save a bundle by fixing it yourself.

Your PC is one of the technological marvels of the twentieth century, yet it's very simple to understand its basic operating principles. The modular design of the IBM and compatible PCs makes them easy to repair and upgrade. Even if you are not technically oriented, you should take a little time to understand the basics of your PC. Knowing how to open up your PC will save you time and money when repairing and upgrading it.

There are some precautions to take and some steps to follow whenever you decide to open up your PC. Just remember that it takes only a few minutes longer to follow correct procedures than it would to carelessly jump in and possibly damage something.

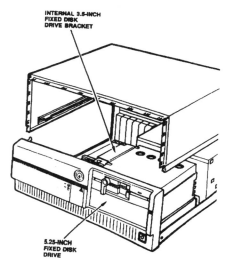

INTERNAL 3.5-INCH
FIXED DISK
DRIVE BRACKET

5.25-INCH
FIXED DISK
DRIVE

• Before opening your PC, turn off the power and disconnect all the cables from the base unit. Sort the cables properly so that you can reconnect them easily.

• Make sure there is enough room on a flat (preferably desk) surface to work on. Don't place the computer on the rug or carpet.

• Using the proper type of screwdriver (flat blade or Phillips), take out the screws attaching the cover to the base unit.

• Carefully and slowly pull up or pull out the cover. Some covers have a small latch inside which may catch a cable as it's pulled out.

• Before you touch anything inside the computer, locate the power supply that's usually a shining steel box in the back. Touch the power supply to discharge any static electricity that may be on you.

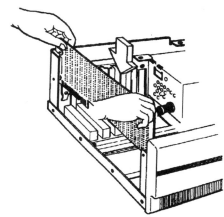

• If you remove any adapter boards or drives, be sure to disconnect any cable attachments necessary and then carefully remove them and place them on a flat surface without touching each other. If necessary, write down the orientation of the cable attachments (most have a unique shape or a color strip on one side). Arrange the items you take out in such a manner that you can easily put them back.

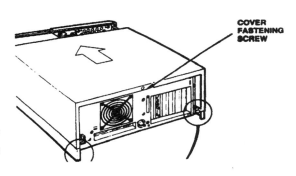

- If you have to remove the motherboard, note the orientation of the power cables and the way the board is attached to the base unit.

- When you start putting the system back together, simply reverse the previous steps.

12.4. Upgrading and Expanding Your PC

Finding someone with the budget and the ability to buy a computer that can satisfy both their current and future needs is rare. Moreover, every time more powerful hardware is introduced, more interesting and fascinating software is rapidly developed to utilize it. Few people can avoid the temptation to upgrade their PCs to take advantage of the newer software. That's why PCs are designed with memory sockets, expansion slots, available drive bays, and extra ports. Because of the foresight of the original designers of the IBM PC who built expandability into their computer, expanding most IBM and compatible computers is very straightforward.

From 1981 to 1987, the standards were based on exactly the same criteria as the IBM PC, XT, and AT systems. Since then, several different memory, interface bus, and drive standards have been introduced. Upgrading your PC is still very straightforward. If you are handy with a screw-driver and have the nerve to open up the PC, you may be able to invigorate your system every couple of years. You just have to make sure that you get the correct parts for your PC.

Before you invest in faster, larger, or more powerful components for your PC, you have to evaluate the viability of buying a new computer. The primary factor is economy, followed by performance.

Before you take the plunge to upgrade or replace your PC, you have to set some limits as to how far you are willing to go. Spending over $1,000 to upgrade a PC now worth less than $500 may not be a wise move. The following sections describe the process of upgrading various components:

The Microprocessor

Every year, more powerful and more user friendly software make it easier to get the most from your PC. At the heart of all this lies the ability of your CPU to comfortably handle your requirements. If you have already been using your PC for several months, you are probably wishing that your computer was just a little faster! Most PC users start demanding more power from their system soon after they master the use of their machine. The CPU is the main source of processing power for your PC.

Replacing the Motherboard

If you are going to replace the motherboard in your PC, there are several items you should check before buying the new board:

- Check to see whether your expansion slots have 8, 16, or 32 bit buses.

- Are your existing buses ISA, EISA, or Micro Channel?

- What type of memory chips do you currently have? DRAM, SIMM, SIPP?

- How many interface boards do you currently have? How many slots do you need?

- Do you currently have memory cache on the motherboard?

When you start looking for a new motherboard, you should make sure that all, or most of, your existing components can be used with or on the new board. Also make sure that the following conditions are met:

- The size of the new motherboard should fit your case.

- All your existing interface boards should be compatible with the new motherboard.

- If you had memory cache before, you definitely want cache on the new board.

- If your existing memory chips are the correct type and speed, you should use them.

- Can you trade in your existing motherboard?

- Does the motherboard come with a warranty? Can you install it yourself?

- How much does the supplier charge to install the board and test everything?

After you buy the motherboard, if you are installing it yourself, you should follow the steps outlined below:

- Carefully read the installation manual that comes with the motherboard.

- Backup important data from your hard disk drive.

- Record the system setup information from your existing motherboard.

- Follow the instructions for "Opening up your PC" in this chapter.

- Take all the interface boards out and place them on non-static surfaces.

- Unscrew and remove the existing motherboard.

- Take advantage of the opportunity to clean the inside of your PC.

• Set up the jumpers and switches on the new motherboard to closely match the settings of the old motherboard.

• Install the new motherboard and reverse the previous steps to put the PC back together.

• Place the cover back on, plug everything back into the base unit, and turn the power on.

• Perform system setup to configure your new motherboard with your peripherals.

Memory

If you have done a good job of selecting the right type of computer for your needs, then adding memory may be one of the most common upgrades you may have to do. For most PCs manufactured in the last couple of years, adding more memory is simply a matter of purchasing the chips or chip modules and installing them. Since 1989, most manufacturers have designed their motherboards with enough capacity to hold at least 4 MB, and sometimes 8, 16, or as much as 32 MB of memory. For most home and business applications, 4 MB is more than adequate. However, some applications require or simply work faster with more than 4 MB of memory.

Before you purchase any additional memory, you should answer several questions, either by checking your PC manual, calling your supplier, or looking inside your system:

• Exactly how much RAM do you currently have?

• Are the memory chips or modules on the motherboard or on a memory board?

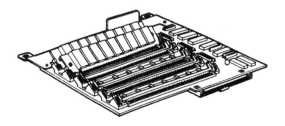

- What type of memory do the sockets on the board accept? DRAM, SIMM, SIPP?

- What's the size and speed of the memory chips you currently have?

- How many more and what type of memory chips can you add?

After you determine the answers to the above questions you can proceed with the following steps:

- Contact your supplier and determine the cost of the additional memory.

- Contact a few other sources to get comparative prices for the additional memory.

- If your existing memory has to be taken out, ask for a trade-in allowance.

- Check your new memory chips before installing them.

- Follow the instructions for "Opening up your PC" in this Chapter.

- Add the memory to the PC and adjust any necessary switches. If you are adding DRAM chips, make sure that the new chips are inserted with the same orientation of the notch as the existing chips. If you are adding SIMM or SIPP modules, make sure that they have the same orientation as the existing modules.

- Put the computer back together and modify the system configuration, if necessary.

Floppy Drive

There are two primary reasons for upgrading a floppy drive: you are either replacing an existing drive with a higher capacity one, or adding a drive of a different type. In either case, several questions need to be answered:

- What type, size, and capacity drive(s) do you currently have?

- How many and what capacity drives can your controller operate?

- How many drives can fit into the base unit?

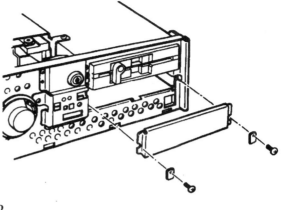

- Do you have any more power cables for the new floppy drive?

- If the new drive is different from those described in Chapter 2, can your BIOS support it?

To answer these questions you need to refer to your PC operating manual, consult with your supplier, or open the PC to look inside. Once you have answered these questions, you can check prices with your supplier, as well as other resources. If you are replacing an existing drive, ask about trade-in allowances, as well as the cost of installation and testing. If you are somewhat handy with a screwdriver and can be careful inside a PC, you may install the drive yourself. It's not very complicated and the following steps should guide you through:

- Open your PC as outlined earlier in this chapter.

- Find an empty drive bay inside the case.

- Take out the face plate in front of that empty drive bay.

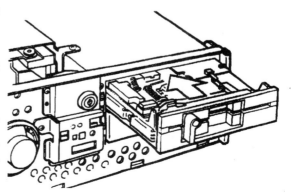

- Insert the drive into the bay and tighten the screws that hold the drive in the case. Don't use screws longer than 1/4".

- Connect a power cable from the power supply to the floppy drive.

- Connect the data cable to the drive.

- Put the case back together and power up the computer.

- Most system configurations automatically recognize the new drive; if yours does not, modify it manually.

- Test the new drive by formatting a disk and reading from a disk.

Hard Disk Drive

Software keeps getting more powerful and demanding more hard disk space. Even if you thought that you bought a large drive, after a year or two you may decide to increase your storage capacity by adding a new drive. Next to memory, adding a hard drive is one of the more common upgrades most people make to their PCs. The increasing popularity of graphics-based software, like those that work in the Microsoft Windows 3.X or OS/2 environments, is the leading cause of the high demand for storage capacity.

Instead of upgrading the hard drive, you can also use programs that can more than double the capacity of a hard disk. These programs are generally available for under $100. MS-DOS 6 and DR-DOS 6 (by Digital Research) include a disk doubling program. But if you are going to add a hard drive, follow these steps:

- Check your manuals to determine the name and specifications of your hard disk drive.

- Check the number of drive bays still available in your base unit. If one is available, you can simply add a second hard drive. If none is available, you must replace your existing hard drive or add a hard card.

- Note the make, model, type, size, and speed of your existing drive. Also note whether your hard drive cable has a built-in connector for a second hard drive.

- Based on the size of your existing hard drive, the speed with which you filled it up, and your future storage needs, determine the size of the new drive.

- Contact your primary supplier to determine the price and availability of drives in the capacity range you are looking for. Also check prices with other sources. Besides price, capacity, speed, and warranty, if you are going to install the drive yourself, you should ask what type of installation guide will be included with the drive. Drives are often sold without instructions.

After you buy your new drive, if you are installing it yourself, follow these steps to make sure the new drive is prepared and installed properly:

- Check for any installation guides, test sheets, or video guides that may be packed with the drive. Review the material carefully. Note the drive parameters, such as the number of heads, cylinders, sectors, etc.

- If you are replacing your existing hard drive, you need to make a backup copy of all important files you don't al-
ready have on floppy disk or backup tape. If you are using the DOS BACKUP command to create your backup copies, make sure that you have a copy of the same version of DOS to prepare the new drive. DOS versions prior to 6, will not allow backing up with one version and restoring with another. Also write down the existing system configuration of your PC.

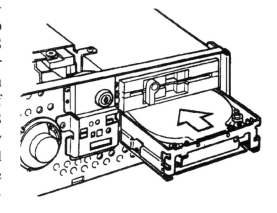

- Follow the instructions in "Opening up your PC" in this chapter.

- Carefully unwrap the new drive and insert it into the available drive bay. Do not drop or shake the drive. Hold the drive in position and attach it to the case with four screws. Don't use screws longer than 1/4", and don't tighten them excessively.

- Connect the power cable and the data cable to the back of the drive (correct orientation).

- Put the case back together and plug the cables into the PC.

- Power up your PC and go through the hard disk preparation steps outlined in your PC manual. Different systems have their own methods for preparing a hard disk for use. After the initial preparation (some PCs call it setup), you may need to perform low level format to partition the drive, and then format it to prepare it for DOS.

Monitor and Graphics Adapter

If you decide that you need a better monitor or graphics adapter, you should find the following information:

- Find out exactly what type of monitor you have (monochrome, CGA, EGA, VGA, etc.).

- Find out what type of video adapter you have (monochrome, CGA, EGA, VGA, SVGA, etc.).

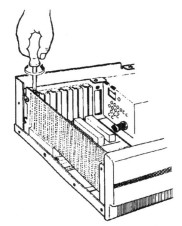

- If you plan to run any type of special purpose software, find out what type of monitor it requires.

Current consumer-oriented technology peaks at Enhanced Super VGA (8514/A) with 1,024x768 resolution. In this range, the monitor has 0.28 mm dot pitch and the video card has 1 MB of RAM. If your present level is well below this, then it's very easy to justify the cost of the upgrade. If, on the other hand, you have a good color VGA monitor and VGA card, you might wait a little longer and upgrade to the level above Enhanced Super VGA (8514/A).

To upgrade from a monochrome VGA monitor to color VGA, all you have to do is buy a color VGA monitor. To upgrade from an older video standard like Monochrome, CGA, or EGA, you need to purchase a color VGA monitor as well as a VGA card. In this case, if you can afford to buy the Enhanced Super VGA, you will be able to take advantage of newer features and the latest technology.

12.5. Upgrading Software

If someone gave you unlimited funds and the freedom to buy everything you wanted, you'd probably want to have the fastest PC with the largest hard disk, tons of memory and the latest collection of popular software. As life goes, you're probably not that lucky! So, you have to settle for whatever fits within your budget. You have a PC and some software, but now you read about all these great programs and their wonderful features. You are probably wondering what you should buy and how often should you give in and buy upgrades of software you currently own. If you have used PC GUIDE Introduction to Computers, you probably know the answer to both questions. Otherwise, you need to take a close look at your needs and determine what you need the software to do for you. After you purchase a program and send in your registration card, the software company will inform you of their upgrades. You need to evaluate the benefits of the upgrades versus your needs to see if you should buy the new version.

Like PC hardware, software programs are periodically enhanced and updated. As PCs become faster and the cost of RAM memory and hard disk capacity decrease, software manufacturers tend to take advantage of these features to make their programs more powerful and more user friendly. They add more features, more bells and whistles, and more intuitive abilities. These features are offered in upgrades about once a year.

Since the late 1980's, PC programs have become so powerful and full of features that recent upgrades are not as revolutionary as they used to be. They are a great source of revenue for the software companies. Millions of registered users are encouraged to upgrade every time a new version is released.

You have to be careful not to be easily persuaded to buy a new version every year.

Carefully evaluate your needs versus the capabilities of your current software version and then decide if you need the upgrade. Some upgrades offer significant improvements and can be cost justified. The wealth of features in recent PC software is so immense that they are like an iceberg. You only use a small number of the basic features, while most of the bells and whistles will often go unused.

Your PC is a wonderful tool and you should use it to its fullest potential. As you discover ways to enjoy your PC, remember that your imagination is your only limitation.

Operating System

DOS plays such an important role in the day to day operation of your PC that whenever possible, you should seriously consider upgrading from an older DOS version. Fortunately, MS-DOS is upgraded every couple of years and the upgrade cost is less than $50.

The MS-DOS 6 upgrade offers a number of significant benefits such as: doubling the capacity of your hard disk, automatically optimizing your memory, easy backup program, virus detection and removal, diagnostic of your PC's configuration, and defragmenting your hard disk, etc.

User Environment

If you use a user environment like Windows, you are already aware of the impact of graphics on the speed of your PC. Every upgrade to Windows offers better speed and other features that help you justify the upgrade cost. Windows 3.0 was introduced in 1990 and version 3.1 was introduced in 1992. The upgrade cost is less than $50.

Personal Applications Software

You probably have some programs that you use for your personal things like personal finance, tax preparation, personal health, genealogy, geography, etc. Some of these programs may suit your needs for many years, just as they are.

Others, such as tax preparation software need to be updated every year. When you are faced with the option to upgrade your personal applications software, you need to cut through the promotional ads and the razzle-dazzle of new product descriptions to determine if you need the improvements and new features. Remember that just having software on your shelf or loaded onto your PC, doesn't make you any smarter. On the other hand, major improvements to software that you use often may save you a lot of time and make you more productive.

Business Applications Software

Software that you use at work is designed to make you more productive. Most often these are accounting, order processing, word processing and data analysis programs. Certain of these programs can benefit you and your organization by offering you greater efficiencies and ease-of-use. Most accounting, payroll, order processing and inventory programs need to be updated every one or two years. Other programs should be upgraded only if you plan to take advantage of the improvements.

APPENDIX

A. Directory of Manufacturers

3-D Visions
412 S. Pacific Coast Hwy.
Redondo Beach, CA 90277
800/729-4723 213/540-8818
Products: software

ADI Systems, Inc.
2121 Ringwood Ave.
San Jose, CA 95131
800/228-0530
Products: monitors

AOC International
10991 NW Airworld Dr.
Kansas City, MO 64154
800/343-5777
Products: monitors

ASG
4000 Bridgeway #309
Sausalito, CA 94965
415/332-2123
Products: software

AST Research
16215 Alton Pkwy
Irvine, CA 92713
714/727-4141
Products: PCs, monitors

AT&T Computer Systems
1776 On The Green
Morristown, NJ 07962
800/247-1212
Products: PCs

Atech Software
5964 La Place Ct., #100
Carlsbad, CA 92008
619/438-6883
Products: software

Abacus Software
5370 52 Street.
Grand Rapids, MI 49512
800/451-4319 616/698-0330
Products: software, books

Abaton Inc.
48431 Milmont Dr.
Fremont, CA 94538
800/444-5321 415/683-2226
Products: scanners

A Bit Better
1551 Broadway, #300
Tacoma, WA 98402
206/627-6111
Products: software

Abtech, Inc.
1431 Potrero Ave. #B
S. El Monte, CA 91733
818/575-0007
Products: PCs

Acco USA
770 S. Acco Plaza
Wheeling, IL 60090
708/541-9500
Products: accessories

Accton Technology Corp.
46750 Fremont Blvd. #104
Fremont, CA 94538
800/926-9288 415/226-9800
Products: modems

Ace Software Corp.
1740 Technology Dr., #680
San Jose, CA 95110
408/451-0100
Products: software

Acer America
401 Charcot Ave.
San Jose, CA 95131
408/922-0333
Products: PCs, monitors

Acme Electric Corp.
20 Water St.
Cuba, NY 14727
716/968-2400
Products: battery backup

Action Plus Software
11485 S. High Mountain Dr
Sandy, UT 84092
801/572-3304
Products: software

Ad Lib Multimedia, Inc.
220 Grande Allee E., #850
Quebec City, QUE G1R2J1
418/529-9676
Products: boards

Adobe Systems, Inc.
1098 Alta Ave.
Mountain View, CA 94039
800/833-6687 415/961-4400
Products: software

Adstor, Inc.
1040 Marsh Rd.
Menlo Park, CA 94025
415/688-0470
Products: software

Adtech Inc.
2701 Lasiter Lane
Turlock, CA 95380
800/326-6548
Products: PCs, mail order

Advanced Graphics Softw
333 W. Maude Ave. #105
Sunnyvale, CA 94086
408/749-8620
Products: software

Advanced Gravis Com Tec
7400 MacPherson Ave., #111
Burnaby, BC V5J5B6
604/431-5020
Products: boards, joy sticks

Advanced Logic Research
9401 Jeronimo
Irvine, CA 92718
800/444-4ALR
Products: PCs

Advanced Vision Resear.
2201 Qume Dr.
San Jose, CA 95131
800/544-6243 408/434-1115
Products: scanners

Advantech Computer Cor
3420 Oakcliff Road, #109
Atlanta, Ga 30340
404/458-7700
Products: PCs

Aitech International Corp
830 Hillview Ct., #145
Milpitas, CA 95035
408/946-3291
Products: multimedia

Aldus Corp.
411 First Ave. S, #200
Seattle, WA 98104
206/343-3277
Products: software

Alpha Software Corp.
One North Ave.
Burlington, MA 01803
617/229-2924
Products: software

Altima Systems, Inc.
1390 Willow Pass Rd. #105
Concord, CA 94520
800/356-9990 415/356-5600
Products: PCs

Altos Computer Systems
2641 Orchard Pkwy.
San Jose, CA 95134
800/ALTOS-US
Products: PCs, monitors

Amax Engineering Corp.
47315 Mission Falls Ct.
Fremont, CA 94539
800/888-2629 415/651-8886
Products: PCs, mail order

Amdek
3471 N. First Street.
San Jose, CA 95134
800/GET-WYSE
Products: monitors

American Covers, Inc.
9192 S 300 W, Bldg. 4
Sandy, UT 84070
801/566-3100
Products: accessories

American Digicom Corp.
1233 Midas Way
Sunnyvale, CA 94086
408/245-1580
Products: PCs

American Megatrends Inc
6145-F Northbelt Pkwy
Norcross, GA 30071
404/263-8181
Products: boards, software

American Mitac Corp.
410 E. Plumeria Dr.
San Jose, CA 95134
408/432-1160 800/648-2287
Products: PCs, monitors

American Power Convers
132 Fairgrounds Rd
West Kingston, RI 02892
800/800-4APC
Products: battery backup

American Small Business
One American Way
Pryor, OK 74361
918/825-4844
Products: software

Amkly Systems
60 Technology Dr.
Irvine, CA 92718
714/727-0788
Products: PCs

Analog Tech. Corp.
1859 Business Center Dr.
Duarte, CA 91010
818/357-0098
Products: printers

Anchor Automation Inc.
20675 Bahama Street.
Chatsworth, CA 91311
818/998-6100
Products: modems

Apple Computer, Inc
20525 Mariani Ave.
Cupertino, CA 95014
408/996-1010
Products: computers

Application Techniques
10 Lomar Park Dr.
Pepperell, MA 01463
800/433-5201
Products: software

Approach Software Corp
311 Penobscot Dr.
Redwood City, CA 94063
415/306-7890
Products: software

Aptech Systems
26250 196 Pl.
South East Kent, WA 98042
206/631-6679
Products: software

Arabesque Software, Inc
10608-B NE 37th Cir
Kirkland, WA 98033
206/822-8172
Products: software

Archive Corp.
1650 Sunflower Ave.
Costa Mesa, CA 92626
714/641-1230
Products: tape drives

ARK Multimedia Pub
1318 Jamestown Rd.
Williamsburg, VA 23185
804/220-4722
Products: software

Artisoft, Inc.
691 E. River Road
Tucson, AZ 85704
602/293-4000 602/293-6363
Products: software, networks

Ashlar Inc.
1290 Oakmead Pkwy.
Sunnyvale, CA 94086
408/746-1800
Products: software

Asymetrix Corp.
110 110th Ave. #717
Bellevue, WA 98004
800/624-8999
Products: software

Atari Corp.
1196 Borregas Ave.
Sunnyvale, CA 94089
408/745-2000
Products: computers

ATI Technologies, Inc
3761 Victoria Park Ave.
Scarborough, ONT M1W3S2
416/756-0718
Products: boards

Attitash Software Inc.
20 Trafalgar Square
Nashua, NH 03063
800/736-4198
Products: software

Austin Computer Systems
10300 Metric Blvd.
Austin, TX 78758
800/752-1577
Products: PCs, mail order

Autodesk Inc.
2320 Marinship Way
Sausalito, CA 94965
415/332-2344 800/445-5415
Products: software

Automated Computer Tec
10849 Kinghurst
Houston, TX 77099
800/521-9237
Products: PCs

Aztech Labs, Inc.
46707 Fremont Blvd.
Fremont, CA 94538
510/623-8988
Products: sound boards

Banner Band
830-3 Seton Ct.
Wheeling, IL 60090
800/333-0549
Products: paper

Bantam Electronic Pub.
666 Fifth Ave., 23rd Floor
New York, NY 10103
212/765-6500
Products: books

BLOC Publishing
800 SW 37 Ave. #765
Coral Gables, FL 33134
305/445-5010
Products: software

BOSS Technology
6050 McDonough Dr.
Norcross, GA 30093
800/628-1787
Products: PCs, mail order

Berkeley Systems, Inc.
2095 Rose St.
Berkeley, CA 94709
510/540-5535
Products: software

Best Data Products, Inc.
9304 Deering Ave.
Chatsworth, CA 91311
818/773-9600
Products: modems

Bit Software, Inc.
47987 Fremont Blvd.
Fremont, CA 94538
510/490-2928
Products: software

Boca Research, Inc.
6413 Congress Ave.
Boca Raton, FL 33487
407/997-6227
Products: modems, boards

Borland International
1800 Green Hills Rd.
Scotts Valley, CA 95066
800/331-0877 408/438-5300
Products: software

Brooks Power Systems
1400 Adams Rd, #E
Bensalem, PA 19020
800/523-1551
Products: battery backup

Brother International
200 Cottontail Lane
Somerset, NJ 08875
908/356-8880
Products: printers

Brown-Wagh
160 Knowles Dr.
Los Gatos, CA 95030
408/378-3838
Products: software

Bureau of Electronic Pub.
141 New Rd.
Parsippany, NJ 07054
201/808-2700
Products: CDs

Business Sense, Inc.
318 Sapphire St.
Kemmerer, WY 83101
801/963-1384
Products: software

CADworks Inc.
222 Third Street. #1320
Cambridge, MA 02142
617/868-6003 800/866-4223
Products: software

CAF Technologies
600 S. Date Ave.
Alhambra, CA 91803
800/289-8299
Products: PCs

CMS Enhancements, Inc.
2722 Michelson Dr.
Irvine, CA 92715
714/222-6000
Products: drives

CPT Corporation
8100 Mitchell Rd.
Eden Prairie, MN 55344
800/447-1189 612/937-8000
Products: printers

CTX Display Solutions
6090 Northbelt Pkwy. #F
Norcross, GA 30071
404/729-8909
Products: monitors

Cadkey Inc.
440 Oakland Street.
Manchester, CT 06040
203/647-0220 800/654-3413
Products: software

Caere Corp.
100 Cooper Ct.
Los Gatos, CA 95030
408/395-7000
Products: scanners, software

CalComp Inc.
2411 W. La Palma Ave.
Anaheim, CA 92803
800/225-2667
Products: printers, plotters

Calera Recognition Syst.
2500 Augustine Dr.
Santa Clara, CA 95054
800/544-7051
Products: software

Canon USA
One Canon Plaza
Lake Success, NY 11042
516/488-6700 800/652-2666
Products: printers, scanners

Cardinal Technologies
1827 Freedom Rd.
Lancaster, PA 17601
800/233-0187 717/293-3000
Products: PCs, modems

Central Point Software
15220 NW Greenbriar Pkwy.
Beaverton, OR 97006
503/690-8090 800/445-4076
Products: software

Chaplet Systems USA
252 N. Wolfe Road
Sunnyvale, CA 94086
408/732-7950
Products: PCs

Chinon America, Inc.
660 Maple Avenue
Torrance, CA 90503
213/533-0274
Products: drives

ChipSoft Inc.
6330 Nancy Ridge Dr. #103
San Diego, CA 92121
800/487-8297 619/453-8722
Products: software

Chronologic Corp.
5151 N. Oracle #210
Tucson, AZ 85704
800/848-4970
Products: software

Citizen America
2450 Broadway #600
Santa Monica, CA 90411
213/453-0614
Products: printers

Clarion Software
150 E. Sample Rd.
Pompano Beach, FL 33064
800/354-5444
Products: software

Claris
5201 Patrick Henry Dr.
Santa Clara, CA 95054
408/987-7000
Products: software

Colorado Memory System
800 S. Taft Ave.
Loveland, CO 80537
800/432-5858 303/669-8000
Products: drives

Commax Technologies
2031 Concourse Dr.
San Jose, CA 95131
800/526-6629 408/435-5005
Products: PCs, mail order

Commodore Bus. Mach
1200 Wilson Dr.
West Chester, PA 19380
215/431-9100
Products: Amiga computers

Compaq Computer Corp
20555 State Hwy. 249
Houston, TX 77070
800/231-0900
Products: PCs,monitor,Print

Complete PC
1983 Concourse Dr.
San Jose, CA 95131
408/434-0145
Products: scanners, modems

CompuAdd Corp.
12303 Technology Blvd.
Austin, TX 78727
800/627-1967 800/999-9901
Products: PCs, mail order

Compudyne Direct
15151A Surveyor
Addison, TX 75244
800/932-COMP 214/702-0055
Products: PCs, mail order

Computer Associates
711 Stewart Ave.
Garden City, NY 11530
800/645-3003 408/432-1764
Products: software

Computer Expressions
4200 Mitchell St.
Philadelphia, PA 19128
800/443-8278
Products: software

Computer Friends, Inc.
14250 NW Science Park Dr.
Portland, OR 97229
800/547-3303 505/626-2291
Products: modems, multimed

Computer Peripherals Inc
667 Rancho Conejo Blvd.
Newbury Park, CA 91320
800/854-7600
Products: modems

Conner Peripherals
3081 Zanker Rd.
San Jose, CA 05134
408/456-3167
Products: drives

Contact Software
1840 Hutton Dr.
Carrollton, TX 75006
800/365-0606
Products: software

Corel Systems Corp.
1600 Carling Ave.
Ottawa, Ontario K1Z8R7
613/728-8200 Canada
Products: drives, software

Cougar Mountain Softwar
2609 Kootenai
Boise, ID 83707
800/388-3038
Products: software

Creative Labs, Inc.
1901 McCarthy Blvd.
Milpitas, CA 95035
408/428-6600
Products: multimedia

Creative Multimedia Corp
514 NW 11th Ave., #203
Portalnd, OR 97209
503/241-4351
Products: meltimedia

Cumulus Corp.
23500 Mercantile Rd.
Cleveland, OH 44122
216/464-2211
Products: drives, PCs

Cyma Systems
1400 E. Southern Ave.
Tempe, AZ 85282
800/292-2962
Products: software

DAC Easy, Inc.
17950 Preston Rd. #800
Dallas, TX 75252
214/248-0205
Products: software

DCA, Inc.
1000 Alderman Dr.
Alpharetta, GA 30202
800/348-3221 404/442-4000
Products: modems, software

DCS Fortis Corp.
1820 W. 220 Street. #220
Torrance, CA 90501
800/736-4847 213/782-6090
Products: printers

DFI
2544 Port Street.
W. Sacramento, CA 95691
916/373-1234
Products: PCs

DMA Inc.
1776 E. Jericho Turnpike
Huntington, NY 11743
516/462-0440
Products: software

DTK Computer
17700 Castleton Street. #300
City of Industry, CA 91748
818/810-8880
Products: PCs

Dariana Technol. Group
6945 Hermosa Circle
Buena Park, CA 90620
714/994-7400
Products: software

Data General
4400 Computer Drive
Westboro, MA 01580
800/328-2436 508/366-8911
Products: PCs, printers

Data One Inc.
5420 Southern Ave. #106
Indianapolis, IN 46241
317/244-2999
Products: software

DataProducts Corp.
6200 Canoga Ave.
Woodland Hills, CA 91367
818/887-8000
Products: printers

Datanalysis
P O Box 45818
Seattle, WA 98145
206/682-1772
Products: software

Datastorm Technologies
P O B 1471
Columbia, MO 65205
800/333-4559 314/443-3282
Products: software

Dauphin Technology Inc.
1125 E. Street. Charles Rd.
Lombard, IL 60148
708/627-4004
Products: PCs, mail order

DCA
1000 Alderman Dr.
Alpharetta, GA 30202
404/442-4000
Products: software

DeScribe Inc.
4047 N. Freeway Blvd.
Sacramento, CA 95834
916/646-1111
Products: software

Dell Computer
9505 Arboretum Blvd.
Austin, TX 78759
800/289-3355
Products: PCs, monitors,

DeLorme Mapping
Lower Main St.
Freeport, ME 04032
207/865-1234
Products: software

Delrina Technology, Inc.
15495 Los Gatos Blvd. #8
Los Gatos, CA 95032
800/268-6082 408/363-2345
Products: software

Delta Products Corp.
3225 Laurelview Ct.
Fremont, CA 94538
510/770-0660
Products: monitors

Dest Corp.
1015 E. Brokaw Rd.
San Jose, CA 95131
408/436-2700
Products: scanners

DiagSoft
5615 Scotts Valley Dr. #1
Scotts Valley, CA 95066
408/438-8247
Products: software

Digicom Systems, Inc.
188 Topaz Street.
Milpitas, CA 95035
800/833-8900
Products: modems

Digital Equipment Corp.
146 Main Street.
Maynard, MA 01754
800/344-4825 508/493-5111
Products: PCs, printers

Digiview
300 McGaw Dr.
Edison, NJ 08837
908/255-8899
Products: monitors

Dolch Computer Systems
2029 O'Toole Ave.
San Jose, CA 95131
408/435-1881
Products: PCs

Eastman Kodak Co.
343 State Street.
Rochester, NY 14650
800/242-2424 716/724-4000
Products: printers

Elan Software Corp
4917 Gerald Ave.
Encino, CA 91436
818/999-9872
Products: software

Emerson Compute Power
9650 Jeronimo Rd.
Irvine, CA 92718
714/457-3600
Products: battery backup

Enable Software
313 Ushers Rd.
Park Ballston L, NY 12019
518/877-8236 800/766-7079
Products: software

Epson America
20770 Madrona Ave.
Torrance, CA 90509
213/782-0770
Products: PCs, printers

Everex Systems
48431 Milmont Dr.
Fremont, CA 94538
800/992-3839
Products: PCs, drives

Evolution Computing
437 S. 48 Street
Tempe, AZ 85281
602/967-8633 800/874-4028
Products: software

Exide Electronics
8521 Six Forks Rd.
Raleigh, NC 27615
919/870-3285
Products: battery backup

Feldstar Software
P O Box 871564
Dallas, TX 75287
214/407-1006
Products: software

Fifth Generation Systems
10049 N. Reiger Rd.
Baton Rouge, LA 70809
504/291-7221
Products: software

First Computer Systems
6000 Live Oak Pkwy. #107
Norcross, GA 30093
800/325-1911 404/447-8324
Products: PCs

Fora International
3081 N. First Street.
San Jose, CA 95134
800/FOR-FORA408/944-0393
Products: PCs, monitors

Foresight Resources Corp
10725 Ambassador Dr.
Kansas City, MO 64153
816/891-1040 800/231-8574
Products: software

FormWorx Corp.
1601 Trapelo Rd.
Waltham, MA 02154
800/992-0085 617/890-4499
Products: software

FormalSoft
P O Box 1913
Sandy, UT 84091
801/565-0971
Products: software

Fox Software
134 W. South Boundary
Perrysburg, OH 43551
800/837-FOX2 419/874-0162
Products: software

Franklin Quest Co.
2550 S. Decker Lake Blvd.
Salt Lake City, UT 84119
801/975-9992
Products: software

Fujikama USA
865 N. Ellsworth Ave.
Villa Park, IL 60181
800/883-8830
Products: monitors

Fujitsu America
3055 Orchard Dr.
San Jose, CA 95134
408/432-1300 800/626-4686
Products: printers, drives

Funk Software, Inc.
222 Third Street.
Cambridge, MA 02142
800/822-3865 617/497-6339
Products: software

Future Trends Software
1508 Osprey Dr., #103
Desoto, TX 75115
214/224-3288
Products: software

GCC Technologies Inc.
580 Winder Street.
Waltham, MA 02154
800/422-7777 617/890-0880
Products: printers

GFA Software Tech.
27 Congress Street.
Salem, MA 01970
508/744-0201
Products: software

GVC Technologies Inc.
99 Demarest Rd.
Sparta, NJ 07871
800/289-4821 201/579-3630
Products: modems

Galaxy Networks, Inc.
8921 DeSoto Ave. #205
Canoga Park, CA 91304
818/998-7851
Products: modems

Gateway 2000
610 Gateway Dr.
N. Sioux City, SD 57049
800/523-2000
Products: PCs, mail order

Gazelle Systems, Inc.
305 N. 500 W.
Provo, UT 84601
801/377-1288
Products: software

Generic Software Inc.
11911 North Creek Pkwy. S
Bothell, WA 98011
206/487-CADD 800/228-3601
Products: software

Genicom Corp.
One Genicom Dr.
Waynesboro, VA 22980
800/443-6426 703/949-1000
Products: printers

GeoWorks International
2150 Shattuck Ave.
Berkeley, CA 94704
510/644-0883
Products: software

Gimeor Inc.
185 Berry #4604
San Francisco, CA 94107
415/546-1874 800/676-0176
Products: software

GoldStar Technology, Inc.
3003 N. First Street.
San Jose, CA 95134
800/777-1192 408/432-1331
Products: PCs, monitors

Golden Image Tech. Corp.
3578 E. Enterprise Dr.
Anaheim, CA 92807
714/630-7765
Products: monitors, mice

Golden Software, Inc.
809 14th Street.
Golden, CO 80401
800/972-1021 303/279-1021
Products: software

Granville Software
10960 Wilshire Blvd. #826
Los Angeles, CA 90024
800/873-7789
Products: software

Great American Software
615 Amherst Street.
Nashua, NH 03063
800/388-8000
Products: software

Grid Systems Corp.
47211 Lakeview Blvd.
Fremont, CA 94537
415/656-4700
Products: PCs, monitors

HDC Computer Corp.
6742 185 Ave.
Redmond, WA 98052
800/321-4606
Products: software

HSC Software
1661 Lincoln Blvd. #101
Santa Monica, CA 90404
213/392-8441
Products: software

Hayes MicroComp Prod.
5835 Peachtree Corners East
Norcross, GA 30092
800/635-1225 404/441-1617
Products: modems, software

HealthDesk
1801 Fifth St.
Berkeley, CA 94710
510/843-8110
Products: software

Helix Software Co.
83-65 Daniels Street.
Briarwood, NY 11435
800/451-0551 718/262-8787
Products: software

Hewlett-Packard
P O Box 10301
Palo Alto, CA 94303
800/752-0900
Products: PCs, printers, scan

Hilgraeve
111 Conant Ave. #A
Monroe, MI 48161
800/826-2760
Products: software

Hitachi Electronics
50 Prospect Ave.
Tarrytown, NY 10591
914/332-5800
Products: monitors, drives

Home Automation Lab
5500 Highlands Pky, #450
Smyrna, GA 30082
404/319-6000
Products: software/Hardware

Hooper International
P O Box 50200
Colorado Spring, CO 80949
800/245-7789
Products: software

HumanCad Inc.
1800 Walt Whitman Rd.
Melville, NY 11747
516/752-3568
Products: software

Hyperdyne Inc.
4004 Woodland Rd.
Annadale, VA 22003
703/354-7054
Products: software

Hyundai Electronics
166 Baypointe Pkwy.
San Jose, CA 95134
800/727-6972
Products: PCs, monitors, Prt

IBM
1133 Westchester Ave.
White Plains, NY 10604
800/426-9292
Products: PCs,printrs,montrs

IMSI
1938 Fourth Street.
San Rafael, CA 94901
415/454-7101 800/833-4674
Products: software

Iiyama North America
650 Louis Dr. #120
Warminster, PA 18974
215/957-6543
Products: monitors

Image Systems Corp.
11543 K-Tel Drive
Hopkins, MN 55343
800/IMAGES-O 612/935-1171
Products: monitors

Incomm Data Systems
652 S. Wheeling Rd.
Wheeling, IL 60090
800/346-2660 708/459-8881
Products: modems

Individual Software, Inc.
5870 Stoneridge Dr.
Pleasanton, CA 94588
510/734-6767
Products: software

Integrated Comp Graphic
1120 Hope Road #100
Atlanta, GA 30350
404/552-8800
Products: software

Intel Corp.
3065 Bowers Ave.
Santa Clara, CA 95052
800/538-3373
Products: CPUs, PCs,modms

Intergraph Corp.
1 Industrial Park
Huntsville, AL 35894
205/730-2000 800/345-4856
Products: software

Intuit
P O Box 3014
Menlo Park, CA 94026
800/624-8742
Products: software

Iocomm USA
12700 Yukon Ave.
Hawthorne, CA 90250
213/644-6100
Products: monitors

Iomega Corp.
1821 W. 4000 South
Roy, UT 84067
801/778-1000
Products: drives

Irwin Corp.
2101 Commonwealth Blvd.
Ann Arbor, MI 48105
313/930-9000 800/421-1879
Products: drives

Isicad Inc.
1920 W. Corporate Way
Anaheim, CA 92803
714/533-8910
Products: software

Jandel Scientific
65 Coach Rd.
Corte Madera, CA 94925
800/874-1888 415/924-8640
Products: software

Jensen-Jones, Inc.
328 Newman Springs Rd.
Red Bank, NJ 07701
908/530-4666
Products: software

JetForm Corp.
163 Pioneer Dr.
Leominster, MA 01453
800/267-9976
Products: software

Jian
127 Second St.
Los Altos, CA 94022
415/941-9191
Products: software

Kalok
1289 Anvilwood Ave.
Sunnyvale, CA 94089
408/747-1315
Products: drives

Ketiv Technologies, Inc.
6601 NE 78 Ct. #A8
Portland, OR 97218
503/252-3230
Products: software

Kingston Technology Cor
17600 Newhope St.
Fountain Valley, CA 92708
714/435-2600
Products: memory boards

Kraft Systems, Inc.
450 W. California Ave.
Vista, CA 92083
619/724-7146
Products: mice, joysticks

Kye International Corp.
2605 E. Cedar Street.
Ontario, CA 91761
800/456-7593 714/923-3510
Products: mice, scanners

Kyocera Unison Inc.
1321 Harbor Bay Pkwy.
Alameda, CA 94501
800/367-7437 510/748-6680
Products: printers

Labtec Enterprises, Inc
11010 NE 37th Cir, #110
Vancouver, WA 98682
206/896-2000
Products: speakers

Laser Digital Inc.
1030-H E. Duane Ave.
Sunnyvale, CA 94086
408/737-2666
Products: multimedia

LaserMaster Corp.
6900 Shady Oak Rd.
Eden Prairie, MN 55344
800/365-4646 612/944-9331
Products: Printers

LaserSmith Inc.
430 Martin Ave.
Santa Clara, CA 95050
408/727-7700
Products: printers

Leading Edge Products
117 Flanders Rd.
Westborough, MA 01581
800/874-3340
Products: PCs

Leading Technology, Inc.
10430 Fifth Street.
Beaverton, OR 97005
800/999-4888
Products: PCs, monitors

Liant Software Corp.
675 Mass. Ave.
Cambridge, MA 02139
800/233-3733
Products: software

Logitech Inc.
6505 Kaiser Dr.
Fremont, CA 94555
415/795-8500
Products: mice, scanners

Longshine Technology
2013 N. Capitol Ave.
San Jose, CA 95132
408/942-1746
Products: modems

Lotus Development Corp.
55 Cambridge Pkwy.
Cambridge, MA 02142
617/577-8500
Products: software

Lucky Computer Co.
1701 Greenvile Ave. #602
Richardson, TX 75081
800/966-5825
Products: PCs, mail order

M-USA Business Systems
15806 Midway Rd.
Dallas, TX 75244
800/345-4243
Products: software

MECA Software Inc.
55 Walls Dr.
Fairfield, CT 06430
800/288-6322
Products: software

Macola Software
333 E. Center Street.
Marion, OH 43302
800/468-0834
Products: software

Mag Innovision
4392 Corporate Center Dr.
Los Alamitos, CA 90720
800/827-3998 714/827-3998
Products: monitors

Magnavox
1 Philips Dr.
Knoxville, TN 37914
615/521-4366
Products: PCs, monitors

Mannesmann Tally Corp.
8301 S. 180 Street.
Kent, WA 98032
206/251-5500
Products: printers

MapInfo Corp.
200 Broadway
Troy, NY 12180
518/274-6000
Products: software

Mass Memory Systems
1414 Gay Dr.
Winter Park, FL 32789
800/347-5722
Products: drives

Mass Microsystems, Inc.
810 W. Maude Ave.
Sunnyvale, CA 94086
408/522-1220
Products: drives

Matesys Corp.
900 Larkspur Landing Cir.
Larkspur, CA 94939
800/777-0545 415/925-2900
Products: software

MathSoft, Inc.
201 Broadway
Cambridge, MA 01239
800/MATHCAD
Products: software

Maxa Corp.
116 N. Maryland St, #100
Glendale, CA 91206
818/543-1300
Products: software

Maxtor Corp.
211 River Oaks Pkwy.
San Jose, CA 95134
800/284-4629 408/432-1700
Products: drives

Maynard Electronics
36 Skyline Dr.
Lake Mary, FL 32746
800/821-8782
Products: drives

Media Vision
3185 Laurelview Ct.
Fremont, CA 94538
510/770-8600
Products: multimedia

MegaCADD
65 Marion Street. #301
Seattle, WA 98104
206/623-6245 800/223-3175
Products: software

Megahertz Corp.
4505 S. Wasatch Blvd.
Salt Lake City, UT 84124
801/272-6000
Products: modems

Merasoft
384E E. 720 S. #204
Orem, UT 85048
800/368-0362
Products: software

Metheus Corp.
600 NW Compton Dr.
Beaverton, OR 97006
800/638-4387
Products: modems

Micro Integrated Comm.
3255-3 Scott Blvd. #102
Santa Clara, CA 95054
408/980-9565
Products: modems

Microsoft Corp.
One Microsoft Way
Redmond, WA 98052
800/426-9400 206/882-8080
Products: mice, software

Microcom Inc.
500 River Ridge Dr.
Norwood, MA 02062
800/822-8224 617/551-1000
Products: modems

Micrografx Inc.
1303 Arapaho
Richardson, TX 75081
800/755-5940 214/234-1769
Products: software

Microlytics
2 Tobey Village Office Pa
Pittsford, NY 14534
800/828-6293 716/248-9150
Products: software

Micropolis Corp.
21211 Nordhoff Street.
Chatsworth, CA 91311
818/718-7771
Products: drives

Microrim
15395 SE 30 Pl.
Bellevue, WA 98007
800/628-6990 206/649-9500
Products: software

Microscience Int'l Corp.
90 Headquarters Dr.
San Jose, CA 95134
408/433-9898
Products: drives

Microtek Labs
680 Knox Street.
Torrance, CA 90502
213/321-2121
Products: scanners

Microvitec, Inc.
1943 Providence Ct.
College Park, GA 30307
404/991-2246
Products: monitors

Migraph Inc.
200 S. 333 Street.
Federal Way, WA 98003
206/838-4677
Products: scanners

Minuteman UPS
P. O. Box 815188
Dallas, TX 75381
800/238-7272
Products: battery backup

Mitsubishi USA
5665 Plaza Drive
Cypress, CA 90630
800/344-6352 714/220-2550
Products: monitors

Mitsumi Electronics Corp.
6230 Beltline Rd.
Irvine, TX 75063
214/550-7300
Products: drives

Modgraph, Inc.
83 Second Ave.
Burlington, MA 01803
800/327-9962
Products: monitors

Moniterm
5740 Green Circle Dr.
Minnetonka, MN 55343
612/935-4151
Products: monitors

Moon Valley Software
21608 N. 20th Ave.
Phoenix, AZ 85027
602/375-9502
Products: software

Mouse Systems Corp.
47505 Seabridge Dr.
Fremont, CA 94538
415/656-1117
Products: mice, scanners

MultiTech Systems
2205 Woodale Dr.
Mounds View, MN 55112
800/328-9717 612/785-3500
Products: modems

Multisoft Corp.
15100 S.W. Koll Pkwy.
Beaverton, OR 97006
503/644-5644
Products: software

Mustang Software, Inc.
P O B 2264
Bakersfield, CA 93303
800/999-9619 805/395-0223
Products: software

Mustek Inc.
15225 Alton Pkwy.
Irvine, CA 92718
800/366-4620
Products: scanners

NCL America
1753 S. Main Street.
Milpitas, CA 95035
408/956-1040
Products: scanners

NCR
1601 S. Main Street.
Dayton, OH 45479
513/445-5000
Products: PCs

NEC Technologies
1414 Mass. Ave.
Boxborough, MA 01719
800/632-4636
Products: PCs,prtrs,monitrs

Nanao USA
23535 Teld Ave.
Torrance, CA 90505
800/800-5202 213/325-5202
Products: monitors

National Micro Systems
2979-B Pacific Drive
Norcross, GA 30071
800/642-7649 404/446-0520
Products: PCs, mail order

NewGen Systems Corp.
17580 Newhope Street.
Fountain Valley, CA 92708
714/641-8600
Products: printers

Nisca Inc.
1919 Old Denton Rd. #104
Carrollton, TX 75006
214/242-9696
Products: scanners

Northlake Software
160 Gibson Dr., #14
Markham, ONT L3R3K1
416/513-9684
Products: software

Norton-Lambert
P O Box 4085
Santa Barbara, CA 93140
805/964-6767
Products: software

Novell Inc.
122 E. 1700 South
Provo, UT 84606
800/346-7177 801/429-5900
Products: software

ObjectSoft Corp.
50 E. Palisade, #411
Englewood, NJ 07631
201/816-8900
Products: software

OCR Systems, Inc.
1800 Byberry Rd. #1405
Huntingdon Vall, PA 19006
215/938-7460
Products: software

Ocean Isle Software
80 Royal Palm Blvd.
Vero Beach, FL 32960
407/770-4777
Products: software

Ocean Microsystems, Inc.
246 E. Hacienda Ave.
Campbell, CA 95008
800/262-3261
Products: drives

Office Automation System
9940 Barnes Canyon Road
San Diego, CA 92121
619/452-9400
Products: printers

Okidata Corp.
532 Fellowship Rd.
Mount Laurel, NJ 08054
800/654-3232 609/235-2600
Products: printers

Olivetti Office USA
P O Box 6945
Bridgewater, NJ 08807
800/527-2960 908/526-8200
Products: PCs, printers

OnTrack Computer Syst.
6321 Bury Dr.
Eden Prairie, MN 55346
800/752-1333 612/937-1107
Products: software

Open Systems, Inc.
7626 Golden Triangle Dr.
Eden Prairie, MN 55344
800/328-2276 612/829-0011
Products: software

Optiquest Inc.
9830 Alburtis Ave.
Sante Fe Spring, CA 90670
800/THE-OPTI 213/948-1185
Products: monitors

Output Technology Corp.
E. 9922 Montgomery Dr.
Spokane, WA 99206
509/926-3855
Products: printers

PC Accountant
P O B 2278
Kirkland, WA 98083
800/827-1303
Products: software

PC Brand
877 Supreme Dr.
Bensenville, IL 60106
800/722-7263 800/662-7378
Products: PCs, mail order

PC Globe, Inc.
4700 S. McClintock Dr.
Tempe, AZ 85282
602/730-9000 800/255-2789
Products: software

PKWare Inc.
9025 N. Deerwood Dr.
Brown Deer, WI 53223
414/354-8699
Products: software

Packard Bell
9425 Canoga Ave.
Chatsworth, CA 91311
800/733-4411
Products: PCs, monitors

Panamax
150 Mitchell Blvd.
San Rafael, CA 94903
415/499-3900
Products: battery backup

Panasonic Systems
333 Meadowlands Pkwy.
Secaucus, NJ 07094
201/348-7000 800/742-8086
Products: PCs,prtrs,monitrs

Paradigm Systems
959 Fairway Dr.
Walnut, CA 91789
714/594-9961
Products: mice

Parsons Technology
One Parsons Dr.
Hiawatha, IA 52233
800/223-6925
Products: software

PC Voice, Inc.
11205 Alpharetta Hwy., #C-4
Roswell, GA 30076
404/343-8201
Products: voice board

Peachtree Software
1505 Pavilion Pl.
Norcross, GA 30093
800/247-3224
Products: software

Perma Power Electronics
5601 W. Howard St.
Niles, IL 60714
708/647-9414
Products: battery backup

Personal Computer Prod.
10865 Rancho Bernardo Rd.
San Diego, CA 92127
800/225-4098 619/485-8411
Products: printers

Philips Consumer Electro
One Philips Dr.
Knoxville, TN 37914
615/521-4438
Products: drives

Platinum Desktop Softwa
15615 Alton Pkwy. #300
Irvine, CA 92718
714/727-3775
Products: software

Point Line Graphics Inc.
8383 Greenway Blvd.
Middleton, WI 53562
608/831-0077 800/447-6468
Products: software

Polaris Software
17150 Via Del Campo, #307
San Diego, CA 92127
619/674-6500
Products: software

Power Up Software Corp.
2929 Campus Dr.
San Mateo, CA 94403
800/851-2917
Products: software

Practical Peripherals
31245 La Baya Dr.
Westlake Village, CA 91362
800/442-4774 818/706-0333
Products: modems

Presenta Corp.
21311 Hawthorne Blvd. #23
Torrance, CA 90503
213/543-5326
Products: monitors

Priam Systems Corp.
1140 Ringwood Ct.
San Jose, CA 95131
408/954-8680
Products: drives

Primavera Systems, Inc.
2 Bala Plaza
Bala Cynwyd, PA 19004
800/423-0245 215/667-8600
Products: software

Princeton Graphics
1125 Northmeadow Pkwy. #1
Roswell, GA 30076
800/221-1490 404/664-1010
Products: monitors

Procom Technology, Inc.
200 McCormick Ave.
Costa Mesa, CA 92626
800/800-8600 714/549-9449
Products: drives

Prolab Technology Co.
3140 De La Cruz Blvd.
Santa Clara, CA 95054
408/748-0125
Products: scanners

Prometheus Products
7225 S.W. Bonita Rd.
Tigard, OR 97224
800/477-3473 503/624-0571
Products: modems

Prophet Software Corp.
571 Rochester Ave, #G101
Coquitlam, BC V3K2V3
604/939-6995
Products: software

Puretek Industrial Corp.
4607 Enterprise Common
Fremont, CA 94538
510/656-8083
Products: monitors

QMS Inc.
1 Magnum Pass
Mobile, AL 36618
800/631-2692 205/633-4300
Products: printers

Qualitas Inc.
7101 Wisconsin Ave. #1386
Bethesda, MD 20814
800/676-0386
Products: software

Quantum Corp.
500 McCarthy Blvd.
Milpitas, CA 95035
408/894-4000
Products: drives

Quarterdeck Office Syst.
150 Pico Blvd.
Santa Monica, CA 90405
213/392-9851
Products: software

Qume Corp.
500 Yosemite Dr.
Milpitas, CA 95035
800/457-4447 408/942-4000
Products: monitors

QVS, Inc.
9844 Harrison
Romulus, MI 48174
800/622-9606
Products: accessories

Reference Software Int'l
330 Townsend Street. #123
San Francisco, CA 94107
415/541-0222
Products: software

Relisys Inc.
320 S. Milpitas Blvd.
Milpitas, CA 95035
408/945-9000
Products: monitors

Ricoh Corp.
5 Dedrick Pl.
W. Caldwell, NJ 07006
800/327-8349 201/882-2000
Products: printers

RoseSoft Inc.
P O B 70337
Bellevue, WA 98007
206/562-0225
Products: software

Roykore Inc.
2215 Filbert Street.
San Francisco, CA 94123
800/227-0847 415/563-9175
Products: software

SBT Corp.
One Harbor Dr.
Sausalito, CA 94965
800/227-7193
Products: software

STSC Inc.
2115 E. Jefferson Street.
Rockville, MD 20852
800/592-0050 301/984-5123
Products: software

Sampo America
5550 Peachtree Ind. Blvd.
Norcross, GA 30071
404/449-6220
Products: monitors

Samsung Info Systems
3655 N. First Street.
San Jose, CA 95134
408/434-4000 800/446-0262
Products: PCs, monitors

Samtron
14251 E. Firestone Blvd.
La Mirada, CA 90638
213/802-8425
Products: monitors

Santron Computers
1185 Chess Dr. #1
Foster City, CA 94404
800/748-6355 800/748-6324
Products: PCs, monitors

Scitor Corp.
393 Vintage Park Dr. #140
Foster City, CA 94404
415/570-7700
Products: software

Seagate Technology, Inc.
920 Disc Dr.
Scotts Valley, CA 95066
408/438-6550
Products: drives

Seiko Instruments USA
1130 Ringwood Ct.
San Jose, CA 95131
408/922-5800 800/888-0817
Products: monitors, printers

Seikosha America
10 Industrial Ave.
Mahwah, NJ 07430
201/327-7227 800/338-2609
Products: printers

Serif, Inc.
78 Northeastern Blvd.
Nashua, NH 03062
603/889-8650
Products: software

Shapeware Corp.
1601 Fifth Ave.
Seattle, WA 98101
206/467-6723
Products: software

Sharp Electronics Corp.
Sharp Plaza
Mahwah, NJ 07430
201/529-9594 800/237-4277
Products: PCs, printers

Shiva Corp.
One Cambridge Center
Cambridge, MA 02142
617/252-6300
Products: modems

Sigma Designs, Inc.
1 Van de Graff Dr.
Burlington, MA 01803
617/270-1000 800/356-4568
Products: software

Simon & Schuster Softw.
15 Columbus Circle
NY, NY 10023
800/825-7638
Products: software

SoftLogic Solutions
One Perimeter Rd.
Manchester, NH 03103
800/272-9900 603/627-9900
Products: software

Software Link
3577 Parkway Lane
Norcross, GA 30092
800/766-LINK 404/448-5465
Products: software

Software Products Int'l
9920 Pacific Heights Blvd
San Diego, CA 92121
800/937-4774
Products: software

Software Publishing Corp
1901 Landings Dr.
Mountain View, CA 94039
800/336-8360
Products: software

Sony Corp.
655 River Oaks Pkwy.
San Jose, CA 95134
408/432-0190
Products: monitors, drives

Social Software, Inc.
311 W. 43rd St.
New York, NY 10036
212/956-2707
Products: software

Sola Electric
1717 Busse Rd.
Elk Grove Village, IL 60007
708/439-2800
Products: battery backup

Spectrum Holobyte
2061 Challenger Dr.
Alameda, CA 94501
800/695-GAME 415/522-1164
Products: software

Spinnaker Software Corp.
201 Broadway
Cambridge, MA 02139
800/826-0706 617/494-1200
Products: software

Spiral Software
6 Perry Street. #2
Brookline, MA 02146
800/833-1511 617/739-1511
Products: software

Stac Electronics
5993 Avenida Encinas
Carlsbad, CA 92008
619/431-7474
Products: software

Stairway Software Inc.
700 Harris Street. #204
Charlottesville, VA 22901
800/782-4792 804/977-7770
Products: software

Star Micronics
420 Lexington Ave. #2702
NY, NY 10170
800/447-4700 212/986-6770
Products: printers

Star Software Systems
363 Van Ness Way
Torrance, CA 90501
800/242-7827 213/533-1190
Products: software

StatSoft
2325 E. 13 Street.
Tulsa, OK 74104
918/583-4149
Products: software

Sun Microsystems Inc.
2550 Garcia Ave.
Mountain View, CA 94043
800/821-4643 415/960-1300
Products: computers,printers

SuperCom Industries
4710 S. Eastern Ave.
Los Angeles, CA 90040
213/721-6699
Products: monitors

Supra Corp.
1133 Commercial Way
Albany, OR 97321
800/727-8772 503/967-9075
Products: modems

SyQuest Technology
47071 Bayside Pkwy.
Fremont, CA 94538
510/226-4122
Products: drives

Symantec Corp.
10201 Torre Ave.
Cupertino, CA 95014
800/441-7234 408/253-9600
Products: software

T-Maker Software
1390 Villa Street.
Mountain View, CA 94041
800/395-0195
Products: software

TEAC America
7733 Telegraph Rd.
Montebello, CA 90640
213/726-0303
Products: drives

TEC America Electronics
2710 Lakeview Ct.
Fremont, CA 94538
510/651-5333
Products: printers

TVM Corp.
1109 W. Ninth Street.
Upland, CA 91786
714/985-4788
Products: monitors

TW Casper Corp.
47430 Seabridge Dr. #A
Fremont, CA 94538
415/770-8500
Products: monitors

Tandem Computers Inc.
19333 Vallco Pkwy. #4-40
Cupertino, CA 95014
800/538-3107 408/725-6000
Products: PCs, printers

Tandon Corp.
405 Science Dr.
Moorpark, CA 93021
800/800-8850
Products: PCs

Tandy Corp.
1800 One Tandy Center
Fort Worth, TX 76102
817/390-3011
Products: PCs, monitors

Tatung USA
2850 El Presidio Street.
Long Beach, CA 90810
800/827-2850
Products: monitors

Taxan America
161 Nortech Pkwy.
San Jose, CA 95134
408/263-4900
Products: monitors

Tecmar Inc.
6225 Cochran Blvd.
Solon, OH 44139
800/624-8560
Products: drives

Tektronix, Inc.
P O B 1000
Wilsonville, OR 97070
503/682-3411 800/835-6100
Products: printers

TeleVideo Systems, Inc.
550 E. Brokaw Rd.
San Jose, CA 95161
408/954-8333
Products: PCs

Telebit Corp.
1315 Chesapeake Terr.
Sunnyvale, CA 94089
800/835-3248 408/734-4333
Products: modems

Texas Instruments, Inc.
P O Box 202230
Austin, TX 78720
800/527-3500
Products: PCs, printers

Texim Inc.
833 Portland Ave.
St.Paul, MN 55104
612/290-9627
Products: software

Timeworks
444 Lake Cook Rd.
Deerfield, IL 60015
708/948-9200
Products: software

Top Ten Software
40308 Greenwood Way
Oakhurst, CA 93644
209/683-7577
Products: software

Toshiba America
9740 Irvine Blvd.
Irvine, CA 92718
714/583-3000
Products: PCs, printers

Touchstone Software
2130 Main St. #250
Huntington Bch, CA 92648
800/531-0450 714/969-7746
Products: software

Tripp-Lite Manufacturing
500 N. Orleans
Chicago, IL 60610
312/329-1777
Products: battery backup

Tune 1000
7710 Boul. Hamel W
St. Foy, QUE G2G2J5
800/263-0094
Products: sound board

UDS Motorola
5000 Bradford Dr.
Huntsville, AL 35806
800/451-2369 205/430-8000
Products: modems

UMAX Technologies, Inc.
2352 Walsh Ave.
Santa Clara, CA 95051
800/562-0311 408/982-0771
Products: scanners

US Robotics
8100 N. McCormick Blvd.
Skokie, IL 60076
800/342-5877 708/982-5001
Products: modems

Unisys Corp.
P O Box 500
Blue Bell, PA 19424
215/986-4011
Products: PCs, printers

Vector Automation, Inc.
Village of Cross Keys #25
Baltimore, MD 21210
301/433-4200 800/431-4347
Products: software

Ven-Tel Corp.
2121 Zanker Rd.
San Jose, CA 95131
408/436-7400
Products: modems

Ventura Software Inc.
15175 Innovation Dr.
San Diego, CA 92128
800/822-8221 619/673-0172
Products: software

Viewsonic
12130 Mora Drive
Santa Fe Spring, CA 90670
800/888-8583 213/946-0711
Products: monitors

Wang Labs
1 Industrial Ave.
Lowell, MA 01851
800/835-9264
Products: PCs, printers

Wangtek
41 Moreland Rd.
Simi Valley, CA 93065
805/583-5255
Products: drives

Western Digital
8105 Irvine Center Dr.
Irvine, CA 92718
708/882-8731
Products: drives

Within Technologies, Inc.
8000 Midlantic Dr. #201-S
Mount Laurel, NJ 08054
609/273-9880
Products: software

WordPerfect Corp.
1555 N. Technology Way
Orem, UT 84057
800/321-3248 801/226-2690
Products: software

WordStar Int'l
201 Alameda Del Prado
Novato, CA 94949
415/382-8000
Products: software

Wyse Technology
3471 N. First St.
San Jose, CA 95134
800/800-9973
Products: monitors

Xerox Imaging Systems
185 Albany St.
Cambridge, MA 02139
800/777-3520 617/864-4700
Products: scanners

ZSoft Corp.
450 Franklin Rd. #100
Marietta, GA 30067
404/428-0008
Products: software

Zenith Data Systems
2150 East Lake Cook Rd.
Buffalo Grove, IL 60089
800/553-0331
Products: PCs, monitors

Zoom Telephonics Inc.
207 South St.
Boston, MA 02111
800/666-6191 617/423-1072
Products: modems

B. User Groups

Alabama
Birmingham IBM PC Users
Birmingham
205/871-1939

Huntsville IBM PC Users
Huntsville
205/539-5940

Alaska
Polar PC Users Group
Fairbanks
907/452-2500

Ankor-Guide Group
Anchorage
907/349-2459

Arizona
Phoenix PC Users
Phoenix
602/943-7907

Tuscon Computer Society
Tucson
602/577-3261

The Homeport
Scottsdale
602/451-5340

Arkansas
Arkansas PC Users Group
Fort Smith
501/784-8400

Central Ark. PC Users
Little Rock
501/225-9304

Twin Lakes Computer Users
Mountain Home
501/425-9061

NW Ark. Microcomp Users
Springdale
501/361-2963

Data Point
Fayetteville
501/442-8777

California
Berkeley PC Comp Users
Berkeley
415/526-4033

Valley Computer Club
Burbank
818/842-3707

Fog Int'l Computer Users
Daly City
415/755-2000

IBM Humboldt Users
Eureka
707/442-4621

Microlink PCUG
Hacienda Height
818/917-6470

Antelope Valley Micro Users
Lancaster
805/948-5166

San Luis Obispo PC Users
Los Osos
805/528-0121

Monterey Bay Users
Monterey
408/373-6245

Napa Valley PC Users
Napa
707/255-9241

Channel Islands PC Users
Oxnard
805/983-4741

Pasadena IBM Users Group
Pasadena
818/795-2300

Riverside IBM Comp. Club
Riverside
714/685-5407

Sacramento PC Users
Sacramento
916/386-9865

Inland Empire Computer
San Bernardino
714/864-3093

San Diego Computer Society
San Diego
619/549-3787

San Francisco Comp Society
San Francisco
415/929-0252

San Francisco PC Users
San Francisco
415/221-9166

Santa Barbara PC Users
Santa Barbara
805/969-9961

Silicon Valley Comp. Society
Santa Clara
408/286-1271

North Bay Users
Vallejo
707/644-9327

Colorado
Metro Area Comp. Enthus.
Aurora
303/830-9143

Colorado Springs PC Users
Colorado Spring
719/596-6938

Mile Hi Comp. Resource Org.
Denver
303/286-7455

Windows on Rockies Users
Denver
303/733-1277

Front Range PC Users
Fort Collins
303/233-8654

Conneticut
Central CT PC Group
Coventry
203/742-6083

Bus/Pro Micro Users Group
West Hartford
203/242-6587

Delaware
PC Professional Users
Wilmington
302/656-8200

District of Columbia
IDI
Washington, DC
202/408-1163

Florida
SW Fla. PC Users Group
Ft. Meyers
813/997-0910

HogTown Hackers
Gainesville
904/392-3151

Miami PC User Group
Hollywood
305/962-8889

Jax PC Users Group
Jacksonville
904/737-6327

PB Bug
Naples
813/261-8208

Suncoast Users Group
St. Pete
813/343-2668

Sarasota IBM PC Users
Sarasota
813/924-4480

USF PC Users
Tampa
813/974-3190

Palm Beach PC Users
West Palm Beach
407/689-8841

Georgia
Atlanta PC Users
Atlanta
404/255-0258

CSRA Computer Society
Augusta
404/790-5241

Idaho
Idaho PC Users Group
Boise
208/939-9120

Illinois
N. Illinois Computer Society
Arlington Height
708/824-2650

Chicago Computer Society
Chicago
312/794-7737

Fox Valley Comp. Users
N. Aurora
708/879-6462

Peoria Computer Club
Peoria
309/685-8289

N. Illinois Computer Owners
Winfield
708/653-3416

Indiana
Anderson Computer Users
Anderson
317/646-3316

Indianapolis Comp Society
Indianapolis
317/251-2003

Iowa
Quad-Cities Computer
Society
Davenport
319/386-3484

Hawkeye PC Users
Iowa City
319/351-7462

NE Iowa PC Users
Waterloo
319/234-0654

Kansas
Topeka PC Users Club
Topeka
913/266-4505

Kentucky
Central Ky. Computer
Society
Lexington
606/266-7446

Kentucky-Indiana PC Users
Louisville
502/560-2562

Heartland Users
Paducah
502/898-2489

Louisiana
Baton Rouge Serious IBM
Users
Baton Rouge
504/924-8066

Acadiana Micro Users
Lafayette
318/235-6701

NW Louisiana PC Users
Shreveport
318/868-5950

Maine
Portland Maine IBM Users
Old Orchard Beach
207/934-5521

Maryland
Capital PC Users
Rockville
301/762-6775

Chesapeake PC Users
Annapolis
301/647-7139

Massachusetts
Boston Computer Society
Cambridge
617/252-0600

Michigan
Flint Area Comp. Enthusi-
asts
Flint
313/667-3183

SW Michigan PC User Group
Kalamazoo
616/349-5381

Minnesota
Twin Cities PC Users
Edina
612/888-0557

Missouri
Kansas City PC User Group
Kansas City
816/444-8709

Microcomputer Users
Kansas City
816/587-8820

St. Louis Users Group
St. Louis
314/458-9604

Nevada
Las Vegas PC Users
Las Vegas
702/431-4333

New Hampshire
Pemi-Baker Computer
Group
Plymouth
603/536-3880

New Jersey
PC Club of South Jersey
Cherry Hill
609/428-8759

New Jersey PC Users
Paramus
201/447-7111

Amateur Comp. Group of NJ
Scotch Plains
908/574-1282

New York
Buffalo IBM PC Users
Buffalo
716/695-2593

Hudson Valley PC Club
Kingston
914/657-6354

Creative Computing
New York City
212/888-3953

NY Amateur Computer Club
New York City
212/505-6021

NY Personal Computer
Group
New York City
212/686-6972

FROG Computer Society
Rochester
716/244-4038

Syracuse Microcomputer
Club
Syracuse
315/492-6437

Westchester PC Users
White Plains
914/923-1337

North Carolina
Asheville IBM PC Users
Asheville
704/274-5331

Foothills PC Users
Hickory
704/256-6924

North Dakota
Magic City IBM PC Users
Minot
701/839-6008

Ohio
Cincinnati PC Users
Cincinnati
513/745-9356

Cleveland Computer Society
Cleveland
216/781-4132

Dayton Microcomp
Associates.
Dayton
513/252-1230

Toledo PC Users
Toledo
419/471-9444

Western Res. IBM PC Assoc
Warren
216/373-2745

Oklahoma
OKC PC Users Group
Oklahoma City
405/791-0894

Tulsa Computer Society
Tulsa
918/622-3417

Oregon
Eugene PC Users
Eugene
503/484-3306

Portland PC Users
Portland
503/226-4143

Pennsylvania
Computer Users of Erie
Erie
814/454-1658

Harrisburg PC Users
Harrisburg
717/652-9097

Phil. Area Computer Society
Philadelphia
215/951-1255

Greene County PC Users
Waynesburg
412/852-1494

Rhode Island
South County Comp Users
Wakefield
401/539-6034

South Carolina
Charleston Computer Club
Charlest803/722-7445

Palmetto PC Club
Columbia
803/754-7525

Tennessee
Music City IBM PC Users
Nashville
615/662-0322

East Tenn. PC Users Group
Oak Ridge
615/435-3311

Texas
Brazos Valley PC
College Station
409/779-5050

North Texas PC Users
Dallas
214/746-4699

Ft. Worth IBM PC Users
Ft. Worth
817/656-0446

Bay Area PC Organization
Houston
713/483-4807

Dallas-Fort Worth Users
Irving
214/986-9228

Alamo PC Organization
San Antonio
512/655-1058

Utah
Utah Blue Chips
Salt Lake City
801/521-7830

Virginia
The Virginia Connection
Reston
703/648-1841

Washington
Pacific NW IBM PC Users
Bellevue
206/646-6570

Borderline PC Users
Bellingham
206/671-9113

West Virginia
Huntington PC Users
Huntington
304/529-2391

Wisconsin
Madison IBM PC Users
Madison
608/255-1205

Milwaukee Area IBM PC
Users
Milwaukee
414/679-9075

C. PC Publications

Byte
P. O. Box 552
Hightstown, NJ 08520
(12 issues/year, $29.950

Compute
P. O. Box 3245
Harlan, IA 51537-3041
(800) 727-6937
(12 issues/year, $19.94)

Computer Buyer's Guide
P. O. Box 318
Mt. Morris, IL 61054-9942
(800) 877-5487
(12 issues/year, $36.00)

Computer Buying World
P. O. Box 3020
Northbrook, IL 60065-9847
(617) 246-3800
(12 issues/year, $72)

Computer Shopper
P. O. Box 52568
Boulder, CO 80321
(800) 274-6384
(12 issues/year, $29.97)

Corporate Computing
One Park Avenue
New York, NY 10016
(609) 461-2100
(12 issues/year, $50 or free to
qualified applicants)

InfoWorld
P. O. Box 3014
Northbrook, IL 60065
(708) 564-0694
(52 issues/year, $110 or free
to qualified applicants)

New Media
901 Mariner's Island Blvd.
San Mateo, CA 94404
(415) 573-5170
(12 issues/year, $48 or free to
qualified applicants)

PC Computing
P. O. Box 58229
Boulder, CO 80322-8229
(800) 365-2770
(12 issues/year, $24.97)

PC Magazine
P. O. Box 54093
Boulder, CO 80322-4093
(800) 289-0429
(22 issues/year, $44.97)

PC Sources
P. O. Box 53298
Boulder, CO 80322-3298
(800) 827-2078
(12 issues/year, $29.90)

PC Week
P. O. Box 1770
Riverton, NJ 08077-7370
(609) 461-2100
(52 issues/year, $160 or free
to qualified applicants)

PC World
P. O. Box 55029
Boulder, CO 80322-5029
(800) 234-3498
(12 issues/year, $16.97)

Windows
P. O. Box 386
Carpinteria, CA 93014
(805) 566-1282
(12 issues/year, $35.95)

D. National Service Providers

AT&T Computer Systems
One Speedwell Avenue
Morristown, NJ 07960
(800) 247-1212

Bell Atlantic Business Sys
50 East Swedesford Road
Frazer, PA 19355
(800) 767-2876

Compu-Gard, Inc.
36 Maple Ave.
Seekonk, MA 02771
(800) 333-6810

Intelogic Trace, Inc.
Turtle Creek Tower 1
San Antonio, TX 78229
(800) 531-7186

Memorex Telex
6929 North Lakewood
Tulsa, OK 74117
(800) 331-7410

Texas Instruments
P. O. Box 202230
Austin, TX 78720
(800) 527-3500

TRW Customer Service
15 Law Drive
Fairfield, NJ 07004
(800) 922-0897

Warrantech
300 Atlantic Street
Stamford, CT 06901
(203) 975-1100

Glossary of Terms

Following is a list of the most commonly used PC-related terms. You don't need to read this section to simply increase your knowledge. Refer to it only if you need to look up the meaning of something real quick.

286: is the abbreviated name for a family of PC microprocessors using the 80286 chip. This PC family is also called AT, which stands for Advanced Technology. PCs using the 286 chip are now considered old, outdated and slow.

386: is the abbreviated name for the 80386 family of microsprocessor chips and PCs using that chip. Slightly scaled down version of these chips are called 386 SX.

486: is the abbreviated name for the 80486 family of microprocessor chips and PCs using that chip. Slightly scaled down versions of these chips are called 486 SX.

80X86: Intel Corporation, the inventor of the microprocessor chip began a numbering scheme using 80X86 where the X varied depending on the chip generation. The chip used in the original IBM PC in 1981, was an 8088. It was followed by 80286, 80386 and 80486. In 1993, Intel discountinued using the generic numbers for newer chips in favor of a name they could trademark. The latest generation Intel chip is called "Pentium" which would have been called 80586 under the old scheme.

Access Time: is expressed in milliseconds (one thousandth of a second) and is the length of time it takes a drive to get a certain piece of information from a disk.

Address: is a specific location in a computer's memory or on a disk.

Analog: is a method of data flow that is continuous, as opposed to digital, which is based on the two digits zero and one. For example, if you used a paint brush to paint a wall it would be similar to analog, and if you used a pen to place thousands of tiny dots on that wall, it would be similar to digital.

ANSI: American National Standards Institute has established a 256 character set that the computer uses to translate your keystrokes into the symbols that you see on the screen or on printed documents. The ANSI character set includes the upper and lower case letters of the alphabet, numbers, and other related characters and symbols.

Applications Software: This is a general term refering to programs written to perform particular activities such as word processing, database management, accounting, computational analysis, etc.

ASCII: American Standard Code for Information Interchange is the code that establishes how various characters including numbers and letters of the alphabet are represented by binary numbers. Binary numbers are represented by the digits zero and one. Computers process data in ASCII format. Various programs translate your input into ASCII for the computer to understand and then translate the computer's output from ASCII to English so you can understand.

Asynchronous: is the most common form of communication between serial devices. It controls the flow of information between two devices by sending start and stop codes at the beginning and at the end of each byte of data being transmitted.

AUTOEXEC.BAT: is a set of instructions for the computer to execute when it is first powered up or reset. It is activated automatically.

Backspace key: is the key often located on the top right hand corner of your keyboard. Every time it is pressed, it moves the cursor on your screen back one space to the left. It also deletes the character or space in that location.

Background: in more powerful computers that can perform several tasks simultaneously, background refers to the program or programs that do not have the highest priority. Therefore, they may be running in the background and out of sight while the program with the highest priority is running in foreground on the screen.

Backslash: "\" is the opposite of slash "/", and it's function is entirely different from slash. It is used to identify a directory, or to move you from one directory to another. For example, \LETTERS identifies a directory called LETTERS. The backslash key is often on the top right corner of your keyboard.

Basic: Beginner's Algebraic Symbolic Instruction Code is one of the oldest and most widely used PC programming languages. Basic commands are closely related to simple English. Therefore it is one of the easiest programming languages available. But as far as you are concerned, don't worry about programming.

Batch file: is a series of DOS commands that are executed sequentially one after another when the batch file is called upon, e.g. AUTOEXEC.BAT which is activated when you power up your PC.

BAUD: Baud rate is the unit of measure indicating the number of changes in data signal per second. In modems it is used to measure the speed with which a communication link can transfer data. The higher the Baud rate the faster the modem. Baud rate is no longer used as an indicator of speed for modems. It's replaced by Bits Per Second (BPS).

Beeps: are the intermittent sounds emitted by your computer under different circumstances. The computer uses the beeps to communicate with you. Certain number of beeps when the computer is turned on or when certain events take place can tell you if the computer has a problem or is stuck. For example, if your monitor or keyboard accidentally get disconnected, the computer will emit a number of beeps which is different from the single beep that it sounds when everything is all right.

Benchmark: is a special program designed to measure the performance of certain components of your PC and compare them to others in the same category. Different benchmark programs may produce different comparative results.

Binary: is a mathematical method for representing numbers based on 2 digits instead of the 10 digits that we are used to. In our daily use of numbers we have ten digits from 0 to 9 and we use these digits to count up from 10, 11, 12, and so on. In the binary method there are only two digits 0 and 1 and the numbers following those are represented by a combination of those two digits. Computers use the binary method as electronic "on" and "off" switches to express numbers, letters of the alphabet and other characters.

BIOS: Basic Input/Output System is a software program that is stored in a microchip installed by the manufacturer on your computer's motherboard. It contains the basic instructions that tell your PC how to operate.

Bit: A bit is the smallest unit of measure in computer terminology. It represents the "on" or "off" status of a microprocessor switch.

Boot: is the act of starting the computer. There are two types of boots: cold boot and warm boot. They are both described later in this section.

BPS: Bits Per Second is a unit of measure indicating the number of bits a modem is capable of transferring in a communication link. BPS is a more accurate measure of data transmission than Baud rate. Newer modems are capable of transmitting more than one bit per data signal, therefore BPS is now the standard measure of modem transmission rate rather Baud.

Buffer: is a certain amount of memory between the microprocessor and another device. It temporarily holds data and feeds it to that device at a speed the device can process. Buffer can be part of the computer memory, a hard disk or an external device with built-in memory. Buffers are often built into printers, so that the printer can accept a certain number of pages, free up the PC and regulate the printing speed.

Bug: is an error or problem in computer hardware or software. It causes the PC or the software to do some strange things like freeze or mess up your data.

Bus: is a connector through which the microprocessor communicates with other devices attached to the motherboard. It is often called an expansion slot. It is an opening about 4 inches or longer, with a row of gold plated connectors on each side of the opening. Adapter boards that serve as interfaces between the motherboard and other devices have a protrusion on their bottom side that is inserted into the bus opening. A PC may have one or more expansion slots. The more unused expansion slots a PC has, the more room it has to expand.

Byte: is a unit of measure for storage of characters or numbers in the computer. Each Byte is 8 Bits. Because there are 8 positions of "on" or "off" in a Byte, there are 256 different values that can be represented by a single Byte. Size of the computer memory as well as the capacity of floppy, hard disk, tape backup and CD drives are measured by Bytes. One simple rule of thumb to relate Bytes to storage device capacity is that the average typed page contains about 2,000 Bytes. Therefore, a 40 Mega Byte (40,000,000 Bytes) hard drive can store the equivalent of 20,000 (40,000,000 divided by 2,000) pages of information.

Caps Lock: is a key usually located on the left hand side of the keyboard. When pressed, it locks the keyboard into upper case letters. Most keyboards have a small light which turns on when the Caps Lock Key is depressed. If the Caps Lock Key is pressed again, the keyboard goes into lower case letters and the light goes out.

CD-ROM: is a new and popular way of storing and using a huge amount of information. Compact Disk-Read Only Memory means that the disk can only give you the information that was stored on it at the facory. It can not let you store information on the compact disk. CDs are capable of storing complete sets of encyclopedias, or the entire phone directories of the United States. During the 1990's, CD-ROMs will become a necessity in every PC.

CGA: Color Graphics Adapter is an old video technology which was used in the earlier generation of PCs. It has poor resolution and limited colors. If you have an old PC with CGA, donate it to charity and get yourself a faster PC with VGA so that you can really enjoy using your computer.

Character: is a single digit, a letter of the alphabet, or a symbol.

Chip: is brief for microchip, which is a small integrated circuit. The chip is built on a silicon crystal wafer. The tiny silicon unit is enclosed in a small plastic or ceramic case with short metallic legs. It is inserted into various printed circuit boards. Different chips are designed to perform specific functions.

Click: is the sound of the little buttons on your mouse. When you read or hear someone say click the left button, it means that you move your mouse until the little pointer goes over your target, then you press the left button and release it.

Clock: is a special crystal that is mounted on the motherboard of your PC. The clock crystal produces a regular pulse or signal which like the human heartbeat, regulates the functions of the PC and all its components. The clock pulse is measured in Mega Hertz or millions of pulses per second.

CMOS: is a special type of memory inside your PC. It keeps track of the important components that are connected to your PC. It knows your configuration, date, time, hard disk drive, floppy drives, etc. This information is maintained by a small battery that usually lasts about five years.

Cold Boot: is the process of starting the computer by turning its switch on. Because the computer was started from an off position, the computer memory starts out blank.

Command: is a special set of instructions for the computer.

CONFIG.SYS: is a configuration batch file that executes various configuration commands as the computer is turned on. CONFIG.SYS is executed when the computer is turned on with a cold boot or is reset. It is stored on the hard disk or bootup floppy disk. It clears out of memory after the computer is turned off.

Control key: is a special key usually located on the bottom left side of the keyboard. DOS and other software programs use it to perform specific tasks.

Conventional Memory: is the first 640 K of memory (RAM). It's used by DOS and other programs as the main area of interaction between you, the user, the programs, and various devices attached to the PC.

CPS: Characters Per Second is the unit of measure for printing speed. Its often established by the printer manufacturer and is usually based on somewhat ideal conditions. CPS is expressed in draft as well as enhanced or letter quality modes. Draft speed is faster than letter quality.

CPI: Characters Per Inch is a unit of measure that determines the number of characters printed per inch by a printer. Most regular correspondence is printed in 10 characters per inch. All printers except daisywheel, are capable of printing a wide range of characters per inch. Some headings may be 1 CPI, and some fine prints may be 17 CPI.

CPU: Central Processing Unit is the microprocessor chip that is the brains of your computer. It performs all data processing, interpretation, and command executions.

CRT: Cathode Ray Tube is the picture tube inside your monitor and has a conical shape. Rays of light are generated in the back of the tube and travel to the front which is the screen of the monitor. Conventional monitors that look like a TV set, use CRT's. Other types of screens used on portable computers, are flat and use a different technology called LCD (Liquid Crystal Display), similar to calculators and digital watches.

Cursor: is a blinking indicator that appears on the screen of your monitor. It shows where you are currently located. In DOS programs it's a blinking "-" dash. In Windows it looks like a pointer and is easily moved around by a mouse.

Cylinder: a hard disk drive is made up of several magnetic platters (plates) stacked up vertically. Each platter has concentric circles called tracks, on both sides. A cylinder is the set of tracks that are located vertically in the same position. For example, the first 5 tracks on both sides of every platter may be the first cylinder.

Daisy Wheel: is a round wheel that contains letters, digits and other symbols. It's used in electronic typewriters or daisy wheel printers. The wheel resembles the shape of a daisy, and when a character (petal) is hit against the ribbon the shape of that character is printed on paper.

Data: is any type of information, symbols, letters, numbers, etc. that is processed by a computer.

Database Management: is a popular type of software that can store and retrieve information quickly and easily.

Decimal: is the numbering system we use in our daily life. It is based on the ten digits 0 to 9.

Default: is a set of predetermined numbers or rules that establish what you want your PC to do in most cases until you decide to change the rules. For example, in word processing, if you want all the lines in your letters be single spaced, make single space a default. You will no longer have to tell your PC that you want single spaced every time you type a letter.

Density: is the capacity for the amount of data that can be stored in a certain amount of space. It is primarily used for measuring the storage capacity of floppy disks. Common terms are double density or high density. Almost all newer PCs are sold with high density floppy disk drives.

Device: is a component or instrument inside or outside the PC that performs a certain function.

Digital: is the standard for expressing information in digits. In the computer world all values are expressed by the digits 0 and 1.

Directory: is a designation or container on a floppy disk or hard disk. It may contain programs, files and other pieces of information that you would like to group together. If you think of a floppy disk or hard disk as a filing cabinet, a directory is like a drawer in that cabinet. It helps you organize various information by category or function. For example all your personal letters can be stored in a directory called: C:\Personal\Letters\

Disk: brief for diskette is the magnetic data storage media that comes in two sizes of 5.25 or 3.5 inches.

Display: refers to the screen of your PC monitor.

DOS Prompt: is the familiar C:\>- which means that your PC is ready to do whatever you tell it to do in drive C:. If your prompt shows A:\>- then it is ready to work in drive A:.

Dot Matrix: is the printing technology that creates letters, numbers, symbols and graphics by forming the shape of the characters using small dots.

DPI: Dots Per Inch is a unit of measure of how many horizontal and vertical dots can be printed per inch. The higher the two numbers, the smaller the dots, and therefore the better and crisper the printed results. For example, standard laser printers produce 300 DPI in horizontal and vertical. Their output look sharp and crisp. Dot matrix printers are usually capable of 150 to 300 DPI horizontal and 150 to 240 DPI vertical.

Dot Pitch: Computer monitors display information by forming characters made up of thousands of small dots. Dot Pitch is the distance between the display dots on a monitor. It is expressed in millimeters. The smaller the dot pitch the better the crispness of characters and the higher the price. Dot pitch ranges from 0.20 to 0.50 millimeters. A regular VGA monitor has a .42 mm dot pitch, while a Super VGA monitor is usually .28 mm.

Double Sided/Double Density: DS/DD is the description of a type of diskette. All diskettes currently in use are at least DS/DD. Earlier generation diskettes could only store data on one side of the magnetic media. They also stored data relatively sparsely on each track. As the densities increased and both sides were utilized, the DS/DD diskettes became the standard. DS/DD disk drives were used in early generation PCs and XT's that were based on the 8088 processor. The DS/DD capacity of 5.25" disks is 360 K, and for the 3.5" disks is 720 K.

Double Sided/High Density: DS/HD is the description of a type of diskette. DS/HD disks usually contain twice or four times the capacity of DS/DD disks. DS/HD disk drives are used in 80286 and higher generation PCs. The DS/HD capacity of 5.25" disks is 1.2 MB, and for the 3.5" disks is 1.4 MB.

Drag: is the process of pointing at something on the screen with your mouse, holding down the button and moving the item your mouse is holding to a different location.

DRAM: Dynamic Random Access Memory is a type of memory that holds information as long as power is supplied to the computer. Also see RAM.

DR-DOS: is the Disk Operating System developed by Digital Research Corporation. Operationally it is compatible with MS-DOS developed by Microsoft Corporation. However, it offers features that are different from MS-DOS. The latest version, DR-DOS 6.0 was released September 1991.

Driver: is a specific program or set of commands which make a particular type of software work with a PC. Most commercially available software already incorporate drivers into their software to work with various devices. For example, most word processing programs include built in drivers for a wide variety of monitor and printer types. In case a program does not have a built-in driver for something you have on your PC, the driver may be obtained separately from the software company or the equipment manufacturer.

Duplex: is a communication standard between two devices. Full duplex allows two devices to communicate with each other simultaneously. Half duplex only allows one device to send information at a time.

EGA: Enhanced Graphics Adapter was introduced in the mid-1980's as a better means of displaying information on your PC. It was later abandoned in favor of VGA which produces better colors and sharper characters.

EISA: Extended Industry Standard Architecture was introduced in 1989. It was designed to increase the power and throughput rate of IBM compatible PC's. Motherboards with EISA expansion slots can transfer data 32 bits at a time instead of 16 bits for ISA boards, and 8 bits for XT and PC type boards. An EISA motherboard can work with regular 16 and 8 bit controller boards as well as the special EISA controller boards.

EEMS: Enhanced Expanded Memory Specification is an enhanced version of the EMS standard.

EMS: Expanded Memory Specification is a standard developed by Lotus, Intel, and

Microsoft that lets some programs access memory above 640 K.

ENTER: is the process of submitting a certain amount of data to the microprocessor by pressing the "ENTER" (or sometimes marked RETURN) key. Pressing the "ENTER" key after you type a command or a certain amount of data, tells the computer to process that information.

Environment: is the space on your PC screen where you work. If you only use DOS, you are working in a text based environment, because everything is done by typing text into your PC, using your keyboard. If you use DOS Shell or Windows, you are using a graphical environment, because to tell your PC to execute a command you can simply point at a graphic image with your mouse.

Escape Key: is the key that lets you get out of most situations. Some programs tell you to use it if you want to quit, or go back to something else. Other programs let you use it if you get stuck.

ESDI: Enhanced Small Disk Interface is an advanced hard disk interface standard that is capable of reading and writing data to the drive faster than other standards.

Execute: in computer language is the process of running a program or performing a command.

Extension: every file name can have up to 8 characters. After the file name a 3 character extension allows a program or the user further identify a file by type or group. For example, your letters can all have the extension ".ltr", i.e. personal.ltr

Expanded Memory: is memory that uses the EMS or EEMS standard to access up to 32 MB of RAM.

Extended Memory: is memory above 1 MB (1,024 K) in 80286, 80386, and 80486 systems. Certain programs can take advantage of this memory to perform their functions much faster than having to use the hard disk drive. Some programs like Windows 3.X and OS/2 can use extended memory to simulate expanded memory.

External DOS command: is a command that resides in the DOS directory and is not loaded into RAM memory when the computer is powered up. To access an external command, the computer needs to read that command file from the hard disk or floppy disk where it's located.

FAT: File Allocation Table is the main map that the PC maintains on each floppy disk and hard disk to keep track of the location of files and directories. If this table is messed up or damaged, all your data on the hard disk may be lost.

FDC: Floppy Disk Controller is the adapter board that controls the operation of the floppy disk drive(s).

FILE: is a collection of data that may be as little as a few lines of text to as big as a book. A file name is almost like the name on a folder. The folder may contain just one sheet of paper or several hundred.

Fixed Disk: is another name for the hard disk drive. It contains one or more rigid disks called platters. The platter is coated with a special magnetic material that allows it to store electronic signals similar to a cassette tape.

Floppy Disk: is a flexible data storage device used in floppy disk drives. The storage media is a thin, circular item made of paper-thin plastic and coated with special magnetic particles. It's contained in a square protective cover. There are two sizes of floppy disks 5.25 x 5.25 or 3.5 x 3.5 inches.

Foreground: powerful PCs that are capable of running several programs simultaneously, do so in foreground and background. Foreground refers to the program that is currently running on the screen and has the highest priority. Other program(s) with lower priority may run in the background.

FORMAT: is used for preparing a floppy disk or a hard disk for use for the first time. It is also used to completely erase everything from the disk and start as if new. Disks use magnetics to store information. The surface of the disk is specially treated and has microscopic grooves. Due to imperfections that may exist on the magnetic surface of the disk, manufacturers provide more capacity than is ultimately produced on the disk after formatting. For example a 1.4 MB floppy disk may actually have a 2.0 MB manufactured capacity, or a 40 MB hard disk may have a 45 MB manufactured capacity. The FORMAT command of DOS, analyzes the disk surface for imperfections and then marks-off all defective or suspicious areas. DOS then writes a very precise and detailed map of the areas to avoid at the beginning of the disk. Thus the controller will avoid writing any data in those areas. For consistency, DOS trims down all disks with similar manufactured capacities to a standard formatted capacity. For example, all different brands of 2.0 MB floppy disks are formatted down to 1.4 MB, regardless of the amount of defects found by formatting.

Function: is an activity performed or a role played by a command or program in order to accomplish a specific objective.

Gigabytes: is one billion bytes. Some very high capacity hard disk drives used by large organizations have gigabyte capacities. One gigabyte stores the equivalent of 500,000 typed pages of information.

Graphical User Interface: is also called GUI (pronounced Goo-ey). It means that instead of typing commands like DOS, you use picutres and graphics to communicate with your PC. To use GUI comfortably, you need to have a mouse.

Hand Shake: is a communication process between two devices through which they acknowledge the connection and determine each other's settings and operating criteria. For example when two modems are connected, the first thing they do is to exchange each other's settings so that each knows how to send and receive data.

Hard Disk: which is also called fixed disk, is a storage device that contains one or more rigid disks called platters. The platter is coated with a special magnetic material that allows it to store electronic signals similar to a cassette tape.

Hardware: refers to all the physical components of a computer.

Head: is a component inside a floppy or hard disk drive that moves back and forth and reads or writes the magnetic codes on the disk. Floppy drives have two heads attached to an arm that moves them simultaneously back and forth on both sides of the floppy diskette. Hard disk drives also have a similar design, except that they may have more than one disk platter, a drive with 4 platters will have 8 heads.

Hex: or Hexadecimal is a numbering system based on the number 16.

Hidden files: are files that may reside on a floppy or hard disk drive but their names or characteristics are hidden from view. A hard disk drive, or a floppy disk that has DOS for booting up the computer, contains two hidden files created by DOS and necessary for the boot up. They are shown as a single dot and two dots. You can hide some of your own files for security reasons.

High Level Format: is a process performed on the hard disk drive after low level format. It writes essential information for DOS on the hard disk. It is performed by the FORMAT command in DOS.

IC: Integrated Circuit is a small microchip built on a silicon crystal wafer. The small silicon unit is enclosed in a small plastic or ceramic case with short metallic legs. It's inserted into various printed circuit boards. Different IC's or chips are designed to perform specific functions.

Initialize: refers to the initial process of preparing a floppy disk or hard disk drive for use the first time. It encompasses activities such as formatting the disk.

Input: is the data that you give to the computer. It can be entered into the computer by several means such as through the keyboard, a mouse, digitizer, scanner, or modem.

I/O: Input and Output is the process of giving data to or getting data from the PC. An I/O board refers to an interface card that contains a parallel port, one or two serial ports, and a game port.

Ins key: the Insert Key is usually located on the upper right hand side of the keyboard. It's used by most programs to insert something that could be as small as a character or as large as a whole document into the position of the blinking cursor.

Interactive System: gives you immediate results and allows an interchange of information between you and the computer. It differs from the old batch system where you had to wait for packs of information to go back and forth to the main computer.

Interleave: is the number of hard disk sectors that the hard disk drive controller skips while storing data. It's expressed as 4:1 (4 to 1), 3:1, 2:1, or 1:1. The smaller the number, the faster the data transfer rate. In the early days of hard disk drives for PCs, the controllers could not keep up with the high speed spin of the hard disk. Therefore, the controller would store data on one sector and then wait for one or more sectors to go by before storing the next batch of data. This process is similar to people trying to get into compartments of a moving Ferris Wheel at an amusement park. Because the Ferris Wheel is moving, they may not be able to get into every single compartment, so they skip every other. More recent, and more advanced hard disk drives and controllers use a 1:1 interleave, which means there are no skipped sectors. Data is stored in adjacent, available sectors.

Internal DOS Command: is a command that is loaded into the RAM memory of the PC when it is first powered up. The internal commands are readily available to use instantly. They don't need to be read from a DOS floppy disk or hard disk drive.

Interface: is the interaction between two devices, like a PC and a printer.

Interpreter: is a program that acts as a translator between computer readable codes and human readable codes in a program. Since a computer is based on the binary system, the information that goes into and out of the machine is binary. However, interpreter programs translate our English commands to binary and vice versa.

ISA: Industry Standard Architecture refers to the type of expansion slots (data transfer bus) located on the motherboard of a PC. When the IBM PC was introduced in 1981, it had 8 expansion slots on the motherboard. Those slots were used for adding adapter boards to the computer in order to operate the monitor, drives, printers, etc. The original slots could only move data 8 bits at a time. When the IBM AT was introduced in 1984, it had a faster 80286 processor and slightly longer expansion slots that could move data 16 bits at a time. That 16 bit bus has become known as the Industry Standard Architecture.

KB: Kilo Bytes is a thousand bytes. That's approximately equivalent to the information on half of a typed page.

Kermit: Named after Kermit the Frog, is a popular file transfer protocol for modems. It establishes a communication link between two computers and ensures that data flows error free.

Keyboard: is the device that looks like the keys on a typewriter and is attached to the PC.

Language: is a set of communication characters, symbols and rules that allow interaction between a program and the computer. Some of the better known languages are Basic, FORTRAN, Assembly, C, Pascal, COBOL, etc.

Load: is the process of transferring data from a floppy disk or hard disk into RAM memory so that the PC can readily access that information. Data that is in memory can be accessed much faster than on a disk.

Low Level Format: is the initial hard disk drive preparation performed by the disk controller. It defines the number of sectors per track and the interleave factor. Most hard drives that have the controller built into the drive (IDE and SCSI) are low level formatted by the drive manufacturer. IDE and SCSI drives do not need to and should not be low level formatted.

Macro: is the process of assigning a series of frequently used steps or commands to one or two keystrokes. It simplifies working with a particular program or file. For example, if in your letters you always put your name and address at a specific location, you may create a Macro for that purpose. By pressing the one or two keys for that Macro, the computer automatically types your name and address at a predesignated area.

Mainframe: refers to a large computer, often costing millions of dollars and requiring a large amount of space.

Math Coprocessor: is a microprocessor that only performs mathematical calculations. The math coprocessor used with 80286 and 80386 family of microprocessors is a separate chip. In 80486 chips the math coprocessor function is built into the microprocessor.

Media: is the data storage material in floppy disks, hard disks, and tapes.

Megabytes (MB): is a million bytes. It's the equivalent of approximately 500 pages of typed information. The memory in your PC as well as the storage capacity of your hard disk and floppy disks are measured in MB.

Memory: is a part of the PC which stores data while your computer is powered up. It is sometimes called RAM (Random Access Memory). Information coming in and going out of your PC is handled in memory. Data from the memory is fed to the microprocessor and output from the microprocessor is handled through memory to the screen, disk, or other devices.

Memory Resident: describes a program or programs that need to reside in your PC memory in order to operate. These programs are often relatively small and need to be within easy access. An example is a virus detection software that's in your memory actively checking for viruses.

Menu: is like a convenient collection of commands or program names arranged in an easy-to-use manner for you to simply choose and execute. Just like the menu at a restaurant, you simply choose a meal and don't need to specify all the ingredients that go into it.

MFM: Modified Frequency Modulation was the most popular hard disk drive encoding method in the 1980's. It has since been replaced by more powerful methods.

MHZ: Megahertz is a measure of computer processor speed. It's one million beats per second. That's how fast a small clock on the motherboard of the computer regulates electronic signals. The original IBM PC introduced in 1981, ran at 4.77 MHZ. Top speed of some current 80486 computers reach 66 MHZ. For comparison purposes, MHZ should be used within the same microprocessor family. For example a 33 MHZ 80386 is faster than a 25 MHZ 80386. However, the same microprocessor is not as fast as a 25 MHZ 80486.

Microchannel: Microchannel Architecture was introduced in 1987 by IBM in certain models of PS/2 computers. Microchannel is a proprietary 32 bit architecture designed to increase power and throughput rate. Motherboards with the microchannel expansion slots transfer data 32 bits at a time and only work with controller boards built with the same microchannel design.

Microprocessor: is the integrated circuit chip that is the brains of your PC. It's designed with thousands of small, electronic switches that process data and interpret various commands. The original IBM PC used the 8088 microprocessor running at 4.77 MHZ, which had 29,000 switches. A more recent microprocessor chip like the 80486-50 MHZ has 1,200,000 switches.

MIPS: Million Instructions Per Second is a measure of data throughput rate in a PC.

MNP: Microcom Networking Protocol is used for error correction in high speed modems. MNP is built into the modem hardware. It compresses data and checks for error correction at both ends. There are several levels of MNP. The higher the level, the more powerful the capabilities.

Modem: Modulate/Demodulate is a communication device that uses the telephone lines to allow two computers exchange data back and forth..

Monitor: is a data display device that is used to view the information being given to the computer and the response from the computer. Most monitors look like a TV screen.

MS-DOS: Microsoft - Disk Operating System is the program developed by Microsoft Corporation. Some major computer companies purchase DOS from Microsoft and slightly modify or enhance it for their own brand of PCs. MS-DOS version 6.0, released in April of 1993, is the latest version of MS-DOS.

Motherboard: is the printed circuit board that often contains the microprocessor, memory, expansion slots and other key components of the PC.

Multi-tasking: is the capability of a PC to run more than one program at a time.

Multi-user: is an environment or program that can be used by more than one user at the same time. All programs are available as single user and some of them may be available as multi-user. To be multi-user, a program needs to have some built-in safeguards so that users do not alter the same information simultaneously and therefore create errors or confusion.

ns: nano-second is one billionth of a second. It measures the speed of memory chips.

Numeric: is a number based character or key on the keyboard.

Num Lock Key: is usually located on the top right hand side of the keyboard. When it's pressed, a small light on the keyboard signals that it's active. It makes the numeric group of keys that are located to the right of the keyboard function strictly like the keys on a calculator. This key was necessary for the earlier generation of keyboards that had other commands on the numeric keys, therefore each key served a dual function.

Object Oriented Environment: is an operating environment whereby various commands are displayed as small, often pictorial objects. For example, the Delete command may be shown as a trash can, or a file may be displayed as a folder.

Operating System: is a program that contains various commands that control the operation of your computer. The operating system also governs how various programs interact with the PC and vice versa.

Output: is the data produced by the computer. It can be displayed on the monitor, sent to a printer, stored on a disk or tape, or sent to another computer through a modem.

Parallel: is a predefined communication standard between two devices. It's primarily used by the majority of printers. A parallel printer needs to be connected to the parallel output of a PC by a parallel cable. The cable has 8 wires and data travels 8 bits at a time over the cable. This is significantly faster than the serial port which transfers data one bit at a time.

Parity: is a form of checking for errors in serial data communication like a modem. The transmitting device sends an extra digit with every eight bits of data. The extra digit is dependent on the number of 0's or 1's in the eight bits. The receiving device compares the extra digit with the eight bits received. If an error is detected in any eight bit packet of data, the transmitting device is ordered to retransmit it.

Partition: is the process of dividing a single, physical hard disk drive into several smaller, logical (fake) drives. The earlier versions of DOS only recognized up to 32 MB (mega bytes) of capacity in a hard disk drive. Therefore, by partitioning a larger hard drive into several logical drives, each one smaller than 32 MB, the DOS limitation could be circumvented and the entire drive could be used. Another use of partitioning a drive into several smaller drives was the ability to create separate storage areas. Newer versions of DOS, 4.01 and higher have resolved the 32 MB limitation.

Peripheral: is a term that encompasses a lot of devices that are internal or external to the PC and attach to it to perform specific functions. When the IBM PC was first introduced, it only contained the case, power supply, motherboard, memory, floppy drive, and keyboard. Hard disk drive, monitor, mouse, modem, tape backup, printer, etc. were added by the dealer and were called peripherals. Today's PCs often come with built-in hard disk drives, and the monitor is considered so vital that it's no longer a peripheral. Therefore, the latest reference to peripherals often encompasses printer, mouse, modem, tape backup, etc.

Pixel: computer monitors form characters on the screen by generating thousands of small dots. A pixel is derived from "Picture Element" and refers to one of those dots.

Port: is a point of interface or connection between your PC and external devices attached to it. A video port is the connection often at the back of the PC that the monitor cable attaches to. A printer port is the parallel port which is found at the back of most PCs and the printer cable plugs into it.

Postscript: is a page description programming language for printers. It simplifies the task of transferring characters and graphics from the computer to the printer. It's primarily used as a hardware or software option with laser printers. Laser printers with postscript can print a variety of characters of different shapes, sizes and shades. Postscript laser printers cost more than comparable standard laser printers.

Power Supply: is a part of the PC that is often enclosed in a chrome plated steel box and is located at the back of the system unit. It includes a transformer that converts the 110 volt AC power into 5 and 12 volts DC power for the computer components. It also includes a small cooling fan that pulls the air in from the front and sides of the PC and blows it out the back.

Print Screen: is a key often located at the top right hand side of your keyboard. Under most circumstances, if you press this key, it will print everything that appears on your screen. However, if you are in certain programs, the PC may not respond to the command.

Processor: is another term for CPU (Central Processing Unit).

Program: is a collection of commands and instructions; written in computer language; which tell your computer how to perform certain tasks. Programs also act as interpreters between you and your PC. You interact with the program in English, and it converts that to machine language in order to communicate with your PC.

PROMPT: is the familiar C:\>- which is also called DOS Prompt. It identifies the drive which is ready to perform what ever you tell it to do. If you have A:\>- then it's ready in floppy drive A:.

Queue: is a series of commands or tasks waiting to be processed by a device. A queue may exist for the CPU, for the printer, or other devices.

RAM: Random Access Memory is the main computer memory that becomes active when your PC is powered up. The memory is capable of storing information and passing it back and forth between the processor and other components of the PC. When power is turned off, all information in RAM is wiped clean. The role of this type of memory is very similar to the countertop of a fast food restaurant or library where items are handed back and forth on the surface of the counter.

Reboot: is the process of resetting your computer after it has been powered up. Reboot also clears the RAM as if the computer was physically turned off and then back on. If you get stuck, rebooting your PC is better than turning it off and on.

RGB: stands for Red-Green-Blue which is the way the tube inside a monitor shoots colors on the screen. This is an old term from the eralier days of PCs and refers to a color monitor.

RLL: Run Length Limited is a hard disk encoding method developed as an enhancement over the MFM method of recording data. It was popular in the mid 1980's.

ROM: Read Only Memory is a type of memory chip that permanently stores certain information placed in it at the factory. Unlike RAM, if the power is turned off, the ROM chip retains the data stored in it.

Root: refers to the main part of a floppy or hard disk. The disk is like a tree with a root, trunk, and branches. In computer terminology the root is actually like the trunk of the tree with branches coming off of it. Directories which you or the software you use create on the disk, help compartmentalize special sets of information together. Those directories are like branches on the tree. For example, if you create several directories, one for DOS, one for Word Processing, Database, etc., your root directory only contains the names DOS, Word Processing, Database, etc. If you then go into the word processing directory, you may create sub-directories called Letters, Reports, etc. Sub-directories are like smaller branches off of larger ones.

RS-232: is a communication interface between the computer and other devices. It's one of the oldest standards for PCs and other computers. RS-232 is commonly called serial port or COM port and connects a modem, mouse, serial printer, etc. to the computer. There are several components within the serial port that must be defined to match the characteristics of data flowing back and forth between the PC and the serial device. In serial communication, individual bits of data are sent one at a time, sequentially and on a single wire. Other wires in the cable are used for setting up specific characteristics of the sending and receiving devices.

Run: means to start or execute a program.

Scroll: is the process of having several pages of information flow upwards on your screen.

SCSI: Small Computer System Interface (called "scuzzy"), is a general purpose interface that allows up to seven SCSI compatible devices like hard disk drives, CD drives, printers, etc., be connected together and to the PC.

Sector: is a basic unit of storage on floppy and hard disks. It's made up of 512 Bytes. The way sectors are organized varies from one manufacturer and one drive to another.

Serial: see RS-232.

Shell: is a special utility program which shows other programs in an overview format. For example a DOS shell shows various important DOS commands in an organized manner that's easier to use.

SIMM: Single In-line Memory Module is a small circuit board that holds several DIPP memory chips. The bottom of the board looks somewhat similar to an adapter board with gold plated fingers. The SIMM board is inserted into a SIMM socket on the motherboard or memory board. SIMM boards come in 256 K, 1 MB, or 4 MB sizes. Chip speeds often range between 60 to 80 nanoseconds.

SIPP: Single In-line Pin Package is a small circuit board very similar to a SIMM, except that the bottom of the board has a series of pins. The pins of the SIPP board are inserted into a SIPP socket with a series of corresponding pin-holes. SIPP boards come in 256 K, 1 MB, or 4 MB sizes. Chip speeds often range between 60 to 80 nanoseconds. SIPP modules are less popular than SIMM.

Source Code: is the English form of the machine language part of a program. With the source code for a specific program, a knowledgeable person can modify that program without having to know the machine language used by programmer specialists who developed that program.

Spool: is a buffering function that acts as interface between your PC and devices like printers, and modems. If the printer or modem cannot process data at the same speed as the PC, data is temporarily stored in memory or on hard disk and fed to the device at the speed the device can process. This frees up the PC to perform other functions.

SRAM: Static Random Access Memory is a type of memory chip that is faster (25 nanoseconds), and costs more than DRAM. It's primarily used as hard disk cache memory which needs the higher speed and can justify the cost.

ST 412 / ST 506: was the first hard disk controller standard used with IBM and compatible PCs. It's no longer produced and can only be found in first generation PCs and XTs.

String: is a series of numbers, letters, or symbols that are treated as characters.

Sub-directory: is a directory within another directory, like the branches coming off of bigger branches on a tree. For example in your word processing directory, you may create subdirectories called letters, memos, legal forms, etc.

Synchronous: is a form of data communication between two devices whereby the flow of data is based on a timing signal emitted between the two devices.

Tab: is the key that is often located on the middle left hand side of your keyboard. It's a special key that moves the cursor a certain number of spaces to the right every time it's depressed. Pressing Shift and Tab together moves the cursor back to the left.

Tape Drive: is a special drive which uses a cassette tape for data storage. It's often used to make backup copies of important data on a hard disk.

Telecommunication: is the process of transmitting data back and forth over the telephone lines via modem.

Telecommuting: is a term used for people who work at home and use their PC and telephone to communicate with the computer at their office.

Terminal: is an input and output device hooked up to another computer. A terminal primarily consists of a monitor and a keyboard. A "Dumb Terminal" is the most basic system with no processing capability or memory. Every bit of data flows directly back and forth from the terminal to the host computer. An "Intelligent Terminal" contains a microprocessor and some memory so that it does not have to move every single bit of information back and forth to the host computer. Terminals were and still are frequently used for hook up to mainframe and mini-computers. Sometimes a PC that is hooked up to a host computer in a network environment is erroneously called a terminal.

Text: is the written part of a program or something you have typed into the computer. Text is different from graphics which is an image drawn by means other than the keyboard.

Track: The surface of a floppy disk or a hard disk magnetic media is made up of concentric circles, somewhat similar to grooves on a music record. Each concentric circle is a track. Each track is divided into a certain number of sectors, which vary by disk type, capacity and manufacturer.

Terminate and Stay Resident (TSR): refers to small programs that stay resident in your memory while you are doing other things with your PC.

Utility: is a program that facilitates or enhances the use of another program or device.

V.29: is the most widely used data transfer standard for Fax communications.

V.32: is the most widely used communication standard for high speed 9600 BPS modems. It allows the computers at both ends of the line to send and receive data simultaneously and rapidly on the same frequencies.

V.42: is the latest high speed communication standard that incorporates sophisticated data compression techniques.

Vdisk: is short for "Virtual Disk" which converts a designated amount of computer memory (RAM) to act like a disk. Data stored in the Vdisk can be accessed instantly. However, as soon as the computer is turned off all data in Vdisk will be wiped clean.

VGA: Video Graphics Array is a video standard made popular by IBM during the late 1980's. It offers high resolution and a wide assortment of colors on your screen. Practically all monitors sold since 1991 are based on the VGA standard. A higher resolution version of VGA is called Super VGA or SVGA.

Virtual Memory: is a technique that uses part of a hard disk capacity to simulate additional memory.

Warm Boot: is the process of resetting or restarting your computer by pressing the "Control-Alt-Delete" keys at the same time. It clears everything from RAM and reads the DOS commands from the boot disk in order to start over again. In case your PC locks up and no other alternatives are available, instead of turning the PC off, a warm boot restarts the computer. Warm boot causes no strain on the PC and is the recommended method of getting out of a lock-up situation.

Write Protect: is a helpful feature that makes sure you don't accidentally write over an existing set of information on a disk. Floppy disks can be easily write protected. On 3.5 inch floppy disks there is a small, sliding tab on the top right hand side of the disk. If you move the tab so that a little window opens, then you can't write or delete anything on that disk.

XMODEM: is one of the earliest file transfer protocols (originally developed in the 1970's) for larger computers and later adapted for PCs. It's still incorporated in some communication software programs.

ZMODEM: is a more advanced file transfer protocol than XMODEM, offering greater speed and accuracy.

Index

Thank you

for buying PC GUIDE.
Please tell your friends and associates
about this easy learning series.
Check with your favorite store or
call us about other

PC GUIDE

Special Value Packs

PC GUIDE for **DOS**

ISBN 1-881979-03-2
$19.95 for book/video

PC GUIDE for **Windows**

ISBN 1-881979-06-7
$19.95 for book/video

PC GUIDE Introduction To **Computers**

ISBN 1-881979-09-1
$19.95 for book/video

(800) 653-7363   (404) 446-2650

PC GUIDE for DOS - Registration Card

Thank you for buying PC GUIDE for DOS.

You have joined thousands of PC GUIDE readers in the United States and throughout the world. Your feedback and comments will help us make the PC GUIDE series better and more useful.

Please fill out and return this card, so that we can send you periodic bulletins with new information you can use.

Name: _____ Title: _____

Business Name: _____

Mailing Address: _____

City: _____ State: _____ Zip: _____

What do you think about this book? _____
_____

Why did you buy this book? _____
_____

Where did you buy this book? _____
Computer/Software Store____ Bookstore____ Discount Store____ Warehouse Club____
Office Supply Store____ Electronics Store____ Other: _____
What made you choose this book? Saw it in store____ Friend recommended____
Advertisement____ Other: _____
What parts of this book are most helpful to you? _____
_____

What parts of this book are least helpful to you? _____
_____

How would you rate this book? Excellent____ Very good____ Good____ Average____
Below Average____
Did you also buy the PC GUIDE video? Yes____ No____
What other PC GUIDE products do you have? _____
What do think we can add or change, to make PC GUIDE more useful to you? _____
_____

Other comments: _____
_____

Would you like us to use your name and quote your comments in various PC GUIDE products? If you agree, please put your initials here: _____

Fold Here

Place
First
Class
Stamp
Here

Attn: PC GUIDE Registration
Inter Trade Corporation
ITC Publishing Group
6767-B Peachtree Industrial Blvd.
Norcross, GA 30092

Tape Here